THE MODERN CITY
Readings in urban economics

David W. Rasmussen
Charles T. Haworth
Florida State University

Harper & Row, Publishers
New York, Evanston, San Francisco, London

To Milton

CONTRIBUTORS

William J. Baumol, Princeton University
John Dyckman, University of California, Berkeley
Marc Fried, Boston College
Herbert J. Gans, Columbia University
Peggy Gleicher, Boston College
Michael A. Goldberg, University of British Columbia
Niles M. Hansen, University of Texas
Joan G. Haworth, Florida State University
Walter W. Heller, University of Minnesota
Edgar M. Hoover, University of Pittsburgh
Carolyn Jackson, Social Security Administration
Edward D. Kalachek, Washington University
Norton E. Long, University of Missouri, St. Louis
John R. Meyer, Yale University
Edgar O. Olsen, University of Virginia
Jerome P. Pickard, Consultant, Appalachian Regional Commission
David W. Rasmussen, Florida State University
Roger Sherman, University of Virginia
George Sternlieb, Rutgers University
James L. Sundquist, The Brookings Institution
Terri Velten, Social Security Administration
William S. Vickrey, Columbia University
Burton A. Weisbrod, University of Wisconsin
James Q. Wilson, Harvard University

THE MODERN CITY:
Readings in urban economics

CONTENTS

PREFACE *viii*

v

PART 7   POPULATION DISTRIBUTION

PREFACE

I view great cities as a pestilential to the morals, the health and the liberties of man. True, they nourish some of the elegant arts, but the useful ones can thrive elsewhere, and less perfection of the others, with more health, virtue and freedom, would be my choice.

Thomas Jefferson

Thomas Jefferson's attitude is not unlike many modern observers who see the American city in a state of crisis. The poverty, slums, and crime that appear to characterize our large cities seem to testify to the wisdom of Jefferson. The problem of the city, the so-called "urban crisis," is likely to remain a major issue throughout the present decade. This text presents a collection of papers that discuss the nature of major urban problems and suggest some guidelines for public policy designed to remedy these problems.

The volume is divided into seven parts. Part 1 is an overview of urbanization, describing it as an unrelenting process that has been going on in the United States for over two centuries. Parts 2 through 7 focus on major aspects of the urban crisis.

Part 2 discusses the distribution of income. Much of the urban crisis can be linked to the poverty in our relatively affluent metropolitan areas. The poor cannot pay for adequate housing; thus their neighborhoods are often characterized by blight and crime. As a result, the middle class moves to the suburbs in search of newer homes and more desirable neighbors, while at the same time they reduce their tax support of the poor population left behind in the central city. The flight to the low density suburban areas causes an increased dependence on the au-

viii

tomobile with its accompanying costs of congestion and pollution. Although this interpretation may neglect many aspects of the urban crisis, it does underscore the prevailing influence of poverty on the urban scene.

The spread of economic activity from the central city to the suburban ring has been a principal force behind the decline of the central city. The core of most metropolitan areas still has not declined as an employment center in absolute terms although relative to the suburban ring, it has. In fifteen metropolitan areas that have a high density urban core, however, this decline has been absolute. The decline of these cities, that were to a large extent developed before the widespread use of automobile and truck transportation, is not surprising since their multistory manufacturing lofts are not attuned to the use of production line techniques or truck transportation. The changing location of economic activity, analyzed in Part 3, is a product of changing production and transportation technology. Many government actions contribute to the decline of the urban core and in the process may lower the welfare of a large proportion of the population.

The distribution of high quality housing in metropolitan areas plays an important role in the urban crisis. The flight of middle-class residents from the central city is in part due to their demand for modern housing. Part 4 analyzes the nature of housing services and presents a framework for analyzing various policies designed to improve the quality of housing in metropolitan areas. Shortcomings in present efforts at urban renewal are outlined, and the strategies for reclaiming the central city are suggested.

A basic advantage of urban life is that it overcomes the costs imposed by distance between people and places of employment. However, the transportation system within many metropolitan areas is often choked by a crush of automobiles and trucks that greatly increases the costs of movement within the city, thereby frustrating one of the basic purposes of city living. Part 5 of this volume presents two interpretations of the urban transportation problem. Both suggest that it is related to inadequate pricing of automobiles and public transportation. Thus many of the problems plaguing urban transportation may be solved with changes in pricing policies. Of course, although the automobile plays an important role in modern life, it seems clear that changes in the relative importance of public and private transportation will not solve some of the more basic issues in urban areas.

The modern city is a complex web of interactions among people and institutions. The interdependence of economic units in a modern industrial society increases the number of externalities or third-party effects that cannot be controlled by the private market mechanism. It is not surprising that the role of government gets larger as a society becomes more industrialized and more urbanized. Part 6 discusses the role of the government in urban areas and analyzes some of the reasons for the financial crisis in which most cities find themselves. Methods of increasing the tax base of cities are explored, although increased resources can only help the city if there is also a serious commitment to work for their renewal.

Social scientists have often stressed the advantages of urban agglomeration when discussing city size. Larger cities have generally been assumed to offer residents more efficient production of commodities and greater consumer choice, but the costs associated with residence in larger cities have until recently been ignored. Perhaps more importantly consumer preferences for size of urban place have been totally ignored in most policy discussions concerning the distribution of population by city size. Part 7 discusses the problems associated with the current distribution of the population and potential methods of correcting any shortcomings.

DAVID W. RASMUSSEN
CHARLES T. HAWORTH

part 1 THE URBANIZATION PROCESS

The process of urbanization and the analysis of trends in urbanization are presented in this part. The first four chapters provide the historical background and setting of urbanization in the United States. The changes that will take place in the role and the function of the modern city are analyzed.

The selection by Jerome P. Pickard is largely self-explanatory. He describes the process of urbanization in the United States from colonial times to the present, a period during which the United States changed from a rural agrarian nation to an urban industrial society. He shows that the problems of the city, to a large extent, coincide with the problems of the nation. Pickard's selection also includes projections of population to the year 2000. His projection envisions a highly urban population with a large share of the residents living in a few megalopolises. The projections underscore the importance of our understanding the nature and role of the metropolitan areas in which most Americans will reside.

1

The second selection by James Q. Wilson helps clarify much of the loose thinking and sloppy terminology that characterize discussions of the "urban crisis." He describes three separate phenomena that have been grouped together as "the urban problem" and demonstrates that different problems require different policies.

In Chapter 3, Joan G. Haworth's short essay on externalities in the city describes why the private market mechanism fails to correct many of the problems that affect the modern city. In the last selection, John Dyckman presents a far-ranging analysis of the functions and role of the city in the past and present. His analysis is extended to a stimulating and imaginative vision of the future role of the city.

Before these selections are presented, a technical note on the term "metropolitan area" will be useful. City boundaries are often the result of past circumstances. Although city areas may be small by present standards, the original city boundaries usually enclosed a dominant share of the population and economic activity of the urban area. Changes in transportation and population growth in urban areas have created, in many cases, a ring of communities around the original city.

These suburban communities are independent politically but are integrated socially and economically with the original city. To look at the city and not the surrounding satellite towns would yield an erroneous picture of such characteristics as employment, population growth, and per capita income.

In order to improve the collection and meaning of statistics concerning the multitude of political units in urban areas, the government began, in 1949, to designate these areas as Standard Metropolitan Statistical Areas (SMSAs). There are now 243 SMSAs in the United States. Each metropolitan area is an integrated economic and social unit with a large population nucleus. Each SMSA contains at least one central city with 50,000 inhabitants or more, or two cities having contiguous boundaries and constituting, for general economic and social purposes, a single community with a combined population of at least 50,000, the smaller of which must have a population of at least 15,000.

The SMSA includes the county in which the central city is located and adjacent counties that are economically and socially integrated with a county of the central city. An SMSA may contain more than one city of 50,000 inhabitants. The largest city is always included in the title of the SMSA, and it sometimes includes the name of one or two additional cities. An SMSA may include counties in more than one state.

The Sacramento (California) SMSA is an example of a multiple county SMSA. The city of Sacramento had a 1970 population of 254,000. However, around Sacramento are three counties which are socially and economically integrated with the city for employment, shopping, and services. Thus statistics on the Sacramento SMSA include data from Placer County, Sacramento County, and Yolo County. The population of the SMSA is 801,000. The Washington, D.C. SMSA is made up of the nine counties in Virginia and Maryland that surround the District of Columbia. In this case, the .75 million people living in the District of Columbia are only 26 percent of the 2.8 million people living in the SMSA.

Two other terms which are important in dealing with SMSAs are "central city" and "the suburban ring." In census terminology, the central city is always the largest city in the SMSA. However, in some literature the term "central city" is used as an euphemism for the ethnic ghettos of the city. Since most central cities still have a majority of white residents, this usage can give erroneous impressions. The suburban ring is simply all of the SMSA that is not part of the central city.

4

1
GROWTH OF URBANIZED POPULATION IN THE UNITED STATES: Past, Present, and Future
Jerome P. Pickard

INTRODUCTION: SEVERAL MEASURES OF URBANIZATION

Urbanization is a multidimensional phenomenon—therefore it needs to be discussed in a much broader frame of reference than simply population numbers or the spectacular growth of urban areas in their population and land coverage. We shall discuss urbanization in four-dimensional aspects:

(a) population and land; regionalization of urbanization
(b) technology and stages of economic development
(c) socioeconomic aspects of urbanization
(d) urbanization of the Nation: impacts and adjustments.

In the United States, urbanization has accompanied the Nation's growth. In terms of people and land, urbanization has meant a continuous expansion in four dimensions: (1) a continuous *increase in the number* of urban places, by whatever size measured; (2) a continuous *increase in the individual population size* of the larger urban places (also reflected in a continuous progression of the urban population as a percentage of the United States total); (3) a continuing *spread of urbanization* from its original core on the Atlantic Seaboard to the entire Nation; and (4) continuing *decongestion* of the cities, with new development spreading out in the urban fringes at a fraction of the densities in the old city core areas.

This paper was originally presented at the Conference on the National Archives and Urban Research, Washington, D.C., June 18, 1970.

In less than 200 years the technological stage of transportation and communication has progressed from water transport, horse-drawn wagons and "pony express" couriers to the modern age of high-speed air travel and instant communication by radio and television. Borchert[1] recognizes four stages but I have added a fifth representing the period since 1960. These stages are:

(1) Sail—Wagon Epoch (1790–1830)
(2) Iron Horse Epoch (1830–1870)[2]
(3) Steel Rail Epoch (1870–1920)[3]
(4) Automotive Age (1920–1960)[4]
(5) High-Speed Communication-Travel-Amenity (1960–2000 ±)

Economic development has progressed from a dominantly agrarian society to a dominantly industrial–technological-urban society. The urban network has evolved from a series of very small towns and small city seaports in 1790 functioning in an agrarian society where 4/5 of the population were agriculturally employed to the present national urban network which covers the country and has seen employment in agriculture diminish to 5 percent of the labor force.

Socioeconomic aspects of urbanization include progressively rising levels of education, income, access to communication (especially rapid media including newspapers, radio, and television), and a progressive spreading of urban life styles to larger and larger proportions of the American population, whether resident in urban areas or outside of them. The last-named trend is not new; what is ever new is the *degree* to which the American population—and the people in many other nations—have become urbanized. This was expressed by Professor Wirth in 1938:

> The degree to which the contemporary world may be said to be "urban" is not fully or accurately measured by the proportion of the total population living in cities. The influences which cities exert upon the social life of man are greater than the ratio of the urban population would indicate, for the city is not only in ever larger degrees the dwelling-place and the workshop of modern man, but it is the initiating and controlling center of economic, political, and cultural life that has drawn the most remote parts of the world into its orbit and woven diverse areas, peoples, and activities into a cosmos.[5]

[1] Borchert, John R., "American Metropolitan Evolution," *Geographical Review,* LVII, No. 3 (July 1967), pp. 301–332.
[2] The telegraph was invented and became widespread during this epoch.
[3] The telephone was invented and became widespread during this epoch.
[4] During the automotive age, radio, and then television became widespread. In 1960, intercity travel by air reached 50 percent of total United States intercity travel by common carrier and had attained 75 percent of the total by 1969.
[5] Wirth, Louis, "Urbanism as a Way of Life," *American Journal of Sociology,* XLIV, No. 1 (July 1938), p. 2.

American urban populations are heterogeneous in virtually all respects: physically, economically, socially, occupationally, educationally, and culturally. The diffusion of both urban characteristics and urban-oriented population into the "rural" areas of the Nation—especially those areas not far removed from major urban centers—has been very rapid in the last two decades. In a socioeconomic sense, urbanization of the population has less and less to do with the relatively high population density which has (and still is) the basis for measuring "urban" population, and is becoming more a matter of individual life styles and modes of thought, type and levels of education, and daily economic and social activity.

In the evolution toward an urban Nation, massive impacts have occurred in American life. In 1970, 42 percent of the Nation's population resides in 42 large urbanized areas of more than 500,000 population each, and 42 states are estimated to have a majority of their population urban (including small towns and cities of 2500 population and over).

The Supreme Court "one man–one vote" rule for representation has emphasized the urban character of the Nation. As of 1967 (90th Congress), (with 30 states redistricted after 1963) 316, or 73 percent, of the 435 Representative districts had an urban majority;[6] in 209 districts (48 percent of the total), the *proportion* of 1960 urban population exceeded the United States average, ranging upward from 70 to 100 percent. Only 119 House seats represented districts with a rural majority, though these were distributed in 39 states. Undoubtedly the urban population impact will be even greater after 1970 reapportionment.

Indeed, one wonders whether the "urban-rural" dichotomy is any longer decisive or meaningful in the traditional sense. The Nation is urbanized, and "rural" areas are developing clearly complementary roles in serving an urban Nation, providing recreation; water resources and food; minerals and raw materials; and a more open and less intensively occupied environment to counterbalance conditions in the crowded metropolises. With the mechanization of agriculture and extractive industries, "rural" producers now depend heavily upon the industrial products of modern urban society. With high-speed travel and widespread use of motor vehicles, hordes of "urbanites" urbanize parts of the countryside on weekends and in holiday seasons, not to mention the millions of urban people who "live in the country" all or part of the year.

---

[6] Eight additional states (including California and New York) redistricted in 1968; three other states which redistricted in the 1963–1967 period made district changes in 1968.

URBANIZATION OF THE UNITED STATES POPULATION

Definition of urban.   The first reference to urban population, cited by Truesdell,[7] was in the *Compendium of the Seventh Census, 1850:*

The census does not furnish material for separating the urban and rural population.

Curiously, exactly one century later, at the Census of 1950, the Bureau of the Census finally perfected a method of identifying urban population in fringes around incorporated cities and their suburbs by defining "urbanized areas"; as well as including unincorporated places of urban population size (2500 or more population) in the urban population for the first time.

Previous efforts to separate urban and rural population on the basis of population size of places always tended to distort the urban population count by excluding urban fringes and by including some low-density areas.

Philadelphia had a significant urban fringe in 1790, (1st Census); Boston developed one in the early nineteenth century. At the earliest census which defined and separated urban population (1880), the New York metropolis had already grown to a huge complex of 2.2 million population.

The lower limit of urban population size was set in 1880 at 8000, though a tabulation of "semiurban" population down to 4000 was included. In 1906, the lower population limit was dropped to 2500. One could argue for a lower limit of 2000 (as used in Canada) or an overlapping margin in the range between 2000 and 5000, as used in France. One could also include contiguous suburban areas of cities under 50,000 as urban in character.

Population urbanization.   The progress of urbanization in the United States from 1790 to 1940 as defined by 2 lower limits of place size is shown in Table 1. The continuous growth in number of places and aggregate urban population, and its rise from 5 to over 56 percent of total United States population is shown clearly.

Using the 1960 definition, the 1940 urban population of the United States (50-state area) was 78 million, or 59 percent of the Nation's total. This expanded to 64 percent in 1950 and 70 percent in 1960, while total urban population went to 125 million—a growth of 47 million in two decades, for an annual growth rate of 2.4 percent! Nearly 24 million of this growth, or just over one-half, was added to the 37 larger urbanized areas of 1960.

[7] Truesdell, Leon E., "The Development of the Urban-Rural Classification in the United States: 1874 to 1949." Washington: U.S. Bureau of the Census, *Current Population Reports,* Series P–23, No. 1, August, 1949.

TABLE 1. Growth in number of major urbanized areas, by population size group, United States, 1800–2000

Census Year	Number of Major Urbanized Areas by Population Size Group				Total Major Areas	Percentage of United States Population in Urbanized Areas	
	100,000–499,999	500,000–1 million	1 million–5 million	Over 5 million		Over 100,000	1 million
1800	—	—	—	—	0	0%	0%
1820	2	—	—	—	2	2½%	0%
1840	5	—	—	—	5	n.a.	0%
1860	7	1	1	—	9	n.a.	3½%
1880	14	2	1	—	17	n.a.	3½%
1900	30	3	4	—	37	n.a.	12%
1920	55	9	5	1	70	33%	16%
1940	79	9	9	1	98	40%	23%
1960	123	21	13	3	160	51%	29%
1980[b]	136	28	22	6[a]	192	62%	41%
2000[b]	151	29	35	8	223	70%	53%

n.a. Data not available.
[a] Counting Delaware Valley (Philadelphia-Trenton-Wilmington) as one area.
[b] Growth in number of areas after 1960 is slowed down by mergers.
SOURCE: Historical data compiled by author from various sources. Data for period 1920–2000 derived from *Dimensions of Metropolitanism* (Washington, D.C.: Urban Land Institute, 1967).

TABLE 2. Growth in number and population of larger urbanized areas (500,000 population and over), United States, 1850–2000

	Number of Larger Urbanized Areas	Total Population (millions)	Percentage of United States Population
1850	(1)	0.7	3%
1860	(2)	1.6	5%
1880	(3)	3.6	7%
1900	(7)	11.0	15%
1920	(15)	23.9	23%
1940	(19)	36.6	28%
1960[a]	(37)	65.9	37%[a]
1970	(42)	85.0	42%
1980	(56)	114.0	49%
2000	(72)	183.0	60%[b]

[a] Alaska and Hawaii admitted as states in 1959; included in United States totals since then.
[b] Based on a United States population of 304 million.

TABLE 3. Regional location, larger urbanized areas (500,000 population and over), United States, 1850–2000

Census Year	TOTAL	Atlantic Seaboard[a]	Great Lakes[b]	California	North Central[c]	South	West[d]
1850	1	1	—	—	—	—	—
1860	2	2	—	—	—	—	—
1880	3	2	1	—	—	—	—
1900	7	4	2	—	1	—	—
1920	15	4	6	2	3	—	—
1940	19	6	6	2	4	1	—
1960	37	7	6	3	7	10	4
1970[e]	44	9	8	4	7	12	4
1980	56	11	9	5	8	15	8
2000	72	12	13	6	9	21	11

[a] Atlantic Seaboard Region from Maine to Norfolk, Va.; includes Albany-Schenectady-Troy, N.Y.
[b] Great Lakes Region includes areas from Syracuse, N.Y. and Pittsburgh to Green Bay, Wisconsin but *excludes* inland areas in Ohio and Indiana (Columbus, Cincinnati, Indianapolis).
[c] Exclusive of Great Lakes Region centers.
[d] Exclusive of California; from 1960 forward includes Alaska and Hawaii.
[e] New larger urbanized areas added in the 1960s: Sacramento, Oklahoma City, Akron, Hartford-New Britain, and Rochester. In addition, the 1970 census showed that Jacksonville and Springfield-Holyoke had exceeded 500,000.

"Threshold" Urbanized Area: First Area in Each Region to Reach 500,000:

Atlantic Seaboard: New York-Brooklyn	by 1850
Great Lakes: Chicago	by 1880
North Central: Saint Louis	by 1900
California: San Francisco-Oakland	by 1910
South: New Orleans	by 1940
West: Seattle	by 1950

The growth of major and large urbanized areas is shown in Tables 1 through 3. The continuing progression of urbanized areas both in number and in larger sizes is projected (on the basis of existing trends) to 2000—at which time 72 larger urbanized areas will contain a total population equal to that of the Nation in 1960.

The first great metropolis—New York–Brooklyn—passed 1 million population by 1860. One century later, there were 16 such great metropolises, and the New York–Northeastern New Jersey urbanized area exceeded 14 million in population. Three of every 10 Americans live in these great centers; by the end of the century it will be over one-half, unless trends change sharply. In 1970 a total of 24 states are already involved in at least one "great metropolis" and at least 9 more states are projected by 2000 when two-thirds of all states will be involved in at least one "million-population metropolis."

Metropolitan areas. Metropolitan areas, called "metropolitan districts," were first defined in the 13th Census (1910) for 25 cities then over 200,000 population. These had a total land area of 7371 square miles and a population of 22.1 million, or 24 percent of the United States population. They accounted for 36 percent of the Nation's population growth in 1900–1910; thus, the trend toward concentration was strong 6 decades ago.

By 1940, metropolitan districts had increased to 140 in number, with lowering of the "threshold" central city size to 50,000, and their total population was 63 million, or 48 percent of the United States total. The land area of these districts (based on minor civil divisions) was 44,626 square miles—only about one-fourth of this gross area was urbanized.

In 1950 and subsequently, metropolitan area definitions shifted to entire county units (excepting in New England); as of 1970 these areas, with the addition of newly qualified areas, contain about 70 percent of United States population.

Over the half century from 1910 to 1960, the 15 largest metropolitan or urbanized areas form an extraordinarily stable group, though their relative positions have changed. The same 15 largest metropolitan districts of 1910 were the 15 largest urbanized areas in 1920; in 1960 the *same* 15 urbanized areas were included in the 17 largest, only Washington and Houston having been added to the list, and Cincinnati and Buffalo having slipped to 16th and 17th rank. Since Washington ranked 17th in 1910, only Houston represented a "newcomer" to the "top 17" largest metropolises, replacing Providence [see Table 4].

Future projections to 2000 suggest that this stability will be lessened by the addition of 4 more "newcomers" to the 15 largest, of which one,

TABLE 4. Relative rank of leading metropolitan or urbanized areas, by population size, 1910–2000

Urban Area	M.D.	Urbanized Area			
	1910	1920	1940	1960	2000
New York	1	1	1	1	1
Chicago	2	2	2	3	3
Philadelphia	3	3	3	4	6
Boston	4	4	6	7	12
Pittsburgh	5	6	7	10	21
Saint Louis	6	7	9	11	15
San Francisco-Oakland	7	9	8	6	5
Baltimore	8	11	11	12	17
Cleveland	9	8	10	9	9
Cincinnati	10	13	15	16	25
Minneapolis-St. Paul	11	12	12	13	20
Detroit	12	5	5	5	4
Buffalo	13	14	16	17	27
Los Angeles	14	10	4	2	2
Milwaukee	15	15	14	15	23
Providence	16	18	18	27	46
Washington	17	16	13	8	8
Houston	x	48	21	14	11
Miami[a]	x	x	43	21	7[a]
Dallas[a]	x	45	30	18	10[a]
San Diego	x	x	40	23	13
Connecticut City	[b]	[b]	[b]	[b]	14

[a] In 2000, Miami extends to West Palm Beach and Dallas merges with Fort Worth.
[b] Connecticut City does not exist as a total unit until 2000.

Connecticut City, will be a new type of multicentered urban mass of about 3 million population.

Urban regions. In the spread of metropolitanism, the urban region has now evolved. This has been described and defined by numerous authors.[8] The urban region is a region of urban dominance with relatively high population density, composed of a continuous series of urbanized areas and smaller urban places in close proximity, and having a total population of at least 1 million. With improved ground transportation, commuting over distances of 20 to 60 miles is frequent, and in many cases better than shorter trips within congested metropolitan cores.

The urban region is defined as a contiguous grouping of metropolitan

[8] See, among others: Gottmann, Jean. *Megalopolis: The Urbanized Northeastern Seaboard of the United States.* New York, 1961; Pickard, Jerome P. "Urban Regions of the United States," *Urban Land,* XXI, No. 4 (April 1962).

and urban counties, including an "orbital zone" of less urbanized counties which have relatively high rates of in-migration. The archetype, and
largest United States urban region, extends along the Atlantic Seaboard
from Maine to Northern Virginia and has a present population of about
42.5 millions.

A projection of future urban regions, based on recent trends, indicates that over five-sixths of the United States population will concentrate in these regions by 2000; in 1970 these future regions already
contain 77 percent of the United States population!

The many forces and influences which we call "urban" operate with
higher intensity in the urban region. Most urban regions have a dominant regional center; a few have 2 or more.

An urban region around New York emerged by 1900, including Philadelphia and southern New England; by 1920 this region extended from
northeastern Massachusetts to Wilmington, Delaware. With the passage of time, urban regions are becoming larger, but internal communication and access is growing even faster due to advancing technology.

Spreading urbanization—by state.   During the century from 1870 to
1970,[9] the number of states with a majority of urban population has
grown from 2 to 42. Fewer than one-half of the "urban" states have
a majority of population living in *larger* urbanized areas of 500,000 or
more.

By 1900, 6 North Atlantic Seaboard states, plus Illinois and California, had over 50 percent urban population. An increasing proportion
of states, first in the North, then in the West, and finally in the South,
reached a majority of urban population. The same regional progression
marked the spread of the larger urbanized areas [Table 3].

Over the most recent 2 decades (1940–1960), only 3 states in the
North exceeded the United States *average growth rate* for urban population (Plains states: North Dakota, South Dakota, and Kansas). All states
in the West and South exceeded the United States average excepting
Montana, Kentucky and West Virginia.

Urban research implications.   A vast wealth of information about the
United States urban population is available for analysis. Many studies
have been made; however, a great majority of these are specialized
types of inquiry.

A potential exists for the analysis over time of the evolution of urbani-

[9] Urban population counts in New England prior to 1930 did not distinguish towns with nuclei of
urban population size from the rural towns; therefore the historic Census data show both Massachusetts and Rhode Island as 50 percent urban by 1850. A better definition, using only the larger
urban size places, yields a later date.

zation of the population in the United States; the spreading of characteristics and the changes in level of these; differences in urban population character derived from or induced by migration, and the "absorption" of disadvantaged groups into middle- and upper-socioeconomic
levels.

TABLE 5. Population and area of future urban regions of the United States (revised)

Urban Region[a]	1970 Land Area (square miles)	Population (in millions)[a] 1970	Population (in millions)[a] 2000[a]
Metropolitan Belt	180,128	85.9	118.4
Atlantic Seaboard	70,264	45.7	62.0
Lower Great Lakes	109,864	40.2	56.4
California Region	54,986	19.3	37.9
Florida Peninsula	22,195	5.9	13.9
Gulf Coast	29,736	5.8	9.6
E. Cent. Texas-Red River	23,436	4.6	8.1
Southern Piedmont	24,968	4.4	6.0
No. Georgia-S.E. Tenn.	12,135	2.6	4.2
Puget Sound	6333	2.2	3.9
Twin Cities Region	16,219	2.8	3.9
Colorado Piedmont	11,320	1.8	3.5
Saint Louis	5383	2.4	3.2
Metropolitan Arizona	12,677	1.4	3.2
Willamette Valley	9651	1.7	2.8
Cent. Okla-Ark. Valley	14,974	1.8	2.6
Missouri-Kaw Valley	5665	1.6	2.2
North Alabama	13,052	1.8	2.1
Bluegrass	5377	1.4	1.9
Southern Coastal Plain	7814	1.1	1.7
Salt Lake Valley	4721	0.9	1.6
Central Illinois	7682	1.1	1.4
Nashville Region	6692	0.9	1.3
East Tennessee	5869	1.0	1.2
Oahu Island	593	0.6	1.2
Memphis	1839	0.8	1.1
El Paso-Ciudad Juarez[b]	3457	0.4	0.7[b]
Platte Valley	3851	0.8	1.1
Las Vegas	4605	0.3	1.1
East Iowa-Miss. Valley	5447	0.8	1.0
United States Total	500,805	155.9	240.6
Percentage of United States	17%[c]	77%	84%

[a] Urban regions are as geographically defined in 2000. Population is based on a United States total of 287 million (Series D) on April 1, 2000.
[b] Total urban region population in United States and Mexico is over 1 million. Other international urban regions contiguous with United States: Canadian Metropolitan Belt; Lower Fraser Valley (with Puget Sound); Baja California (extension of California U.R. into Mexico).
[c] Excluding Alaska, which has no urban regions.

Within individual metropolitan and urban areas is an equally large opportunity for the time-series analysis of population change and movement; the evolution of so-called "urban ghettos" of the poor; the growth and settlement of urban and suburban zones of distinct social and economic character; the rapid spreading of "economic urbanization" and of commuting beyond the physical boundaries of the urban mass.

A growing body of materials deals with aspects of metropolitan and urban evolution. Data handling capabilities were never better. We could use more long-term analyses to improve our comprehension of the urbanization processes. This would provide significant new and improved information for shaping present and future urban policies [Table 5].

2
THE *WAR* ON CITIES
James Q. Wilson

What, indeed, is the "urban problem"? The language of crisis with which this subject is normally discussed—"sick cities," "the urban crisis," "spreading blight"—is singularly unilluminating. I doubt that most residents of most American cities would recognize in such terms a fair description of the conditions in their communities. Since such words are usually uttered or printed in Washington, D.C., or New York City, perhaps the most we can infer is that life is tough in these two places—though the staggering expense the authors of such words are willing to incur in order to live in the very center of these cities suggests that the "crisis" is at least bearable.

Viewed in historical perspective, and taking American cities as a whole, the conditions of urban life have, by most measures, been getting steadily better, not worse. Nationally, the proportion of families under the poverty line—for purposes of argument, let us take that as a family income of $3000 a year in constant dollars—declined from 31 percent to 19 percent between 1950 and 1963, and the decline was the greatest in the cities (in the rural areas of our country, by contrast, about *half* the families still live at or near the poverty line). Since the Second World War, there has been a more or less steady decline in the proportion of housing units that are substandard; this improvement has been greatest in the cities, least in the rural areas. (In 1960, less than 3 percent of the dwelling units in cities of 50,000

Reprinted with omissions from *Public Interest,* No. 3 (Spring 1966) by permission of the publisher. Copyright © National Affairs, Inc. 1966.

population and over were dilapidated by Census Bureau standards.) The "flight to the suburbs" has made most people better off—the middle-income family finds the peace and privacy of a suburban home, the lower-income family takes over the larger, sounder structures vacated in the central city. The proportion of young people who drop out of school before getting a high school diploma has been declining steadily, both absolutely and relatively, for about the last twenty years. Certain forms of violent crime—murder and forcible rape—have declined in rate for the last several decades, though other forms of crime (assault, theft) may have increased (no one knows for certain, because crime statistics are neither completely reliable nor standardized for the changing age composition of the population).

American cities have fully participated in the prosperity of the country—indeed, they have participated more than the rural areas; and this no doubt accounts for the fact that, whatever problems the cities have, people are moving to the cities in very large numbers. But it would be a mistake to try to be unreservedly optimistic about these aggregate trends. Certain classes of people within cities continue to confront problems, and these problems vary with the size and kind of the city in question. Three of these problems are especially noteworthy.

HIGH EXPECTATIONS

First, there is what might be called the "psychological urban problem"; that is, our expectations are increasing faster than our achievements. As more affluent suburbs spring up, with neat lawns and good schools, the apparent gap between the quality of life in the central city and at the periphery increases. The suburbanites, adjusting rapidly to residential comfort, become more discontented with the conditions that surround the places where they work in the central city, even though these conditions are also (on the average) improving. Those city dwellers who cannot, for reasons of income or race, move to the suburbs, grow increasingly envious of those who can; the prizes of worldly success are held up before their eyes but out of their reach.

Because whites are gaining, in income and housing, faster than Negroes (though they are gaining also), the gap between the two groups is widening. (The full-employment economy of World War II narrowed the gap because of the need to fill manpower shortages; the underemployment prosperity of the fifties widened the gap; a continued Vietnamese war and the reemergence of labor shortages may once again reduce the gap.) Moreover, within the Negro community itself, greater progress is being made in schooling than in income. The fact of Negro life is that a high school diploma is worth less to a Negro than to a white person, and the disparity is most obvious precisely where educational progress has been the greatest—in the cities.

In addition, the central city has remained the place where important members of the commercial and intellectual elite live. This is the group which, more than any other, sets the tone and provides the rhetoric of public discussion on "urban problems." By habit and tradition, it prizes the cultural amenities of the large central city and it tends to resent the spread of lower-class people into areas where these cultural and commercial institutions are established—even though that spread has been caused by the very increases in freedom and prosperity which the elite itself values. In the resulting distress, we see the conflict between the 2 major functions of the central city: on the one hand, the maintenance of a highly urbane style of life and of a concentrated and diverse market for the exchange of wealth and ideas; on the other hand, the provision of a place in which the lower classes, especially the immigrant lower classes, are housed, employed, educated, and by slow degrees assimilated to the standards of civility of American society. It is no longer possible to keep these 2 functions geographically separate within the central city, because it is no longer possible to confine the lower classes to high-density ghettoes—they have moved out into low-density ghettoes, thereby consuming much more land area than before, including land around or near the city's universities, hospitals, museums, and theaters.

The psychological urban problem cannot be solved, it can only be coped with. Indeed, it has been caused precisely because so many other problems *have* been coped with, if not solved. Efforts to lessen the gap between expectations and achievements will, in the short run, only make the discontent produced by that gap more acute. That is one of the inevitable tensions in a society committed to self-improvement.

TECHNICAL PROBLEMS, POLITICAL SOLUTIONS

The second kind of urban problem might be called the "technical" problem. By this I mean both that the problems are created because people are living in highly interdependent, dense settlements in an industrial society and that the solutions to these problems are technically feasible. If the problems are not solved, it is not for lack of knowledge. It might be more meaningful, indeed, to call them "political" problems, inasmuch as the obstacles to their solution are largely political.

These problems result partly from the fact that we are constantly getting in each other's way or otherwise committing various nuisances. We pollute the air with soft coal soot and with hydrocarbons from automobile exhausts; we pollute rivers and lakes with industrial and residential sewage; we congest city streets with cars, and sidewalks with pedestrians. The problems are also in part the result of consuming natural resources; for example, open space and park land—and of making future generations bear the cost of this consumption. (Or to say the same thing in other words: We spend less on urban and suburban beauty than would be spent if everyone who will at some time enjoy that beauty were here now to vote on the matter.) Finally, the "technical" problem is also the result of an imbalance between the costs and benefits of various essential local services—education, police protection, welfare, and the like. Everyone would agree that supplying such services is a common responsibility which one should not be able to escape simply by moving away from the place where such facilities are maintained. Yet this is exactly what many of us do when we leave the central city for the suburbs. If the central city is to continue to perform its traditional function of housing, employing, educating, policing, and supporting the poor and the disadvantaged (and the only alternative is to spread the poor and the disadvantaged throughout the suburbs), then it must be able to tap the taxable wealth of all of us.

What all these problems—nuisances, scarce collective resources, fiscal imbalance—have in common is that they result from a situation in which the costs and benefits of urban life are imperfectly related. People who get the benefits of consuming attractive land, driving cars on city streets, or cheaply disposing of waste products and junked cars, do not pay their fair share of the costs of vital central city services. Similarly, people who inhale the foul air, gaze at the ruined landscape or the junked cars, or put up with the traffic congestion, have no way of being reimbursed for having these annoyances inflicted on them.

There is no reason in principle why these problems cannot be solved or significantly alleviated. We know, or can discover, techniques for stopping pollution; the crucial task is devising an appropriate combination of legal sanctions, tax policies, and incentives that will make these techniques effective. Open space and other unique natural resources can be conserved by public purchase, by easements, and by tax policies. Those persons who are determined to produce ugliness in parts of the city where ugliness is out of place (and this is not everywhere; every city, like every home, ought to have some place—the equivalent of Fibber McGee's closet—where we can store necessary ugliness) can be restrained by fines, taxes, and laws from carrying on those activities, or can be induced by subsidies to hide the ugliness by appropriate devices. There is nothing very difficult about hiding or getting rid of junked automobiles, provided that the people who are pleased by the absence of junk are willing to share the necessary cost of achieving the result. Even the design of private buildings can be improved by rewarding builders who leave open spaces around their buildings and who hire good architects and artists. The fiscal imbalance between public needs and public resources in the central city can be corrected by using a combination of transfer payments and user charges to insure that the suburbanite who uses the central city pays his fair share of the cost of that use and that everyone, regardless of whether he uses the facilities, pays his fair share of the cost of supplying essential common services such as education, police protection, and the like.

Traffic congestion is a somewhat more complicated matter, for it is not obvious in what precise sense it constitutes a problem. Congestion arises because many people want to use limited space; in a sense, as Martin Meyerson and Edward Banfield point out (Boston: The Job Ahead), congestion is a means by which we ration access to a scarce resource (that is, a desirable central city location) just as the price system is a way we ration the enjoyment of most other commodities (for example, Cadillacs). The only way congestion could be eliminated entirely is to reduce the attractiveness of a given location to the point that no one will want to go to any one place any more than he will want to go to any other. Clearly this is both impossible and undesirable—central locations are central precisely because there are certain things people want to do in the company of large numbers of other people, or because large numbers of customers or workers are necessary to carry on various activities.

But congestion can be reduced if we provide other ways of rationing access besides traffic jams. One way—politically risky, but nonetheless likely to grow in favor—is to assess a charge on automobiles driven into central city locations, the amount of such a charge either to be based on the full cost of accommodating the car (parking space, police and fire protection, road use), in which case it is simply a user charge, or to reflect some penalty cost selected to deter the use of cars rather than merely to finance their accommodation.

The other strategy to deal with congestion is, of course, to subsidize mass transit facilities. The enthusiasm with which this proposal has been embraced by most public spokesmen suggests that their advocacy is based as much on an emotional dislike for automobiles (especially those parts made of chromium) as it is on a sober assessment of the comparative costs and benefits of various transportation programs. There are no doubt communities where the development of this kind of mass transit makes sense, either because of the population densities involved, or the investment already sunk in train tracks and equipment, or both. It is also perfectly clear, as John Meyer, John Kain, and Martin Wohl point out in their comprehensive study, *The Urban Transportation Problem,* that the vast majority of American cities could not possibly support a rail-based system without staggering subsidies. In fact, most communities would be better served by a mixed transportation plan that relied on a combination of user charges on automobiles entering the central city, high-speed bus service in reserved lanes on existing roadways, and various mechanical devices to regulate the flow of cars on and off expressways. The prosperity that produced the massive shift away from the train and bus and to the private car cannot be reversed by public policy; its effects, however, can be regulated.

THE NEGROES IN THE CITY

The third sense in which there is an urban problem is the most important. It results from the fact that the large central cities are where the immigrant lower classes congregate.

Today, with Negroes constituting the most important part of the urban lower class, the challenge to the central city is greater than ever before, because the Negroes create a unique set of problems. Unlike most previous migrants, they are marked by color. Furthermore, the Negro came originally from a slave culture in which he had no opportunity to acquire a complete range of political, economic, and social skills, and in which his family was subjected to systematic disruption and abuse. Unlike other immigrants—even other colored immigrants, such as the Chinese and Japanese—the Negro began his migration to the central city lacking the relevant skills and experience, and with a weakened family structure. Urbanization, of course, places further strains on community and family ties. The result is a central-city population with little money, few skills, a weakened capacity to cope with large bureaucratic institutions, and high rates of social disorder—crime, broken homes, alcoholism, narcotics addiction, illegitimacy, delinquency, and unemployment.

The argument over the details of the Moynihan Report on the Negro family has to some extent obscured its most important implication, which I cannot believe anyone will reject: If all Negroes were turned white tomorrow, they would still have serious problems. Whether these problems are more the result of a weak family structure, or of the impact of urbanization, or of the past history of discrimination, or of a depressed economic position, is very hard to say. But I suspect that whatever the cause, there are few aspects of this problem which will not be cured—or will not cure themselves—in time.

In time. In how much time? And what does one do in the meantime? I incline to the view that in the long run the acculturational problem of the Negro, that is, the problem of being unable, as an individual or a family, and as compared with previous migrants to the cities, to cope with the fact of poverty—will be reduced by improvements in income and education; habits will change as class changes, though more slowly. Perhaps I say this because it is easier to think of changing class position than cultural values, though altering the former is hard enough. Perhaps I say it because of the great and obvious differences between middle-class and lower-class Negroes, differences much greater than those between middle-class and lower-class whites. And perhaps I am wrong.

But whatever the strategic factor is, we cannot as yet say we have discovered it. The best that can be said in our favor is that we are perhaps the only free society which has ever tried to change a large racial minority by massively upgrading its condition. The debate about what the goal of "equality" means—whether a random distribution of Negroes throughout the city and the social structure, or a distinctive Negro enclave with guaranteed rights of entry and departure, or some combination of the two—is less interesting to me than the fact that, wherever we want to go, we don't know how to get there. And for the present, the urban Negro is, in a fundamental sense, *the* "urban problem."

If there were no Negroes in our large cities, or if the only difference between Negroes and whites were the accident of skin color, the rate of serious crime in our cities would immediately be cut by about a third. The welfare rolls would be cut by a like amount. The population of our state prisons would be cut by more than one-fourth. No one can be sure how many fewer narcotics addicts or alcoholics there would be, but no one could argue the reduction would be negligible. The number of "dilapidated" homes would be further reduced by about 30 percent.

WHAT WE DON'T KNOW

If solutions to the technical problems facing our cities are impeded because our motivation does not yet equal our knowledge, then solutions to our fundamental problems are impeded because our understanding does not yet match our motivation. A dramatic crisis—an epidemic of deaths resulting from smog, for example—will quickly produce the motivation necessary to move swiftly on many of the technical problems. But we have already had our crises with respect to the fundamental problems—Watts, for example—and the result has only been a frantic and futile search for "answers." There is no ready-made knowledge stored up in our universities or foundations on how to prevent a Watts, or even on what causes a Watts. The malaise of lower-class life in the central cities has been a matter of scholarly concern for several decades, but there is not much scholarly wisdom to show for it, except a general—and probably sound—belief that higher incomes, more education, and less discrimination are desirable things. For 30 years, various experiments have been conducted in an effort to reduce juvenile delinquency; although we have occasionally been successful in eliminating gang warfare (primarily by disarming and policing the gangs), no one has been able to reduce the apparent rates of the most common form of delinquency, theft. We know that the rates of certain "private" crimes—murder, for example—cannot be changed no matter what tactics the police may use. We suspect that certain "street" crimes (auto theft, or purse snatching) can be reduced by "saturation" police patrol, but no one knows whether what occurs is actually a reduction or simply a displacement of the crime to other parts of the city—or, if a reduction, whether it can be made permanent. No one is yet precisely certain what effect segregated schools have on Negro children, or how much of the slower rates of learning of these children is the result of family background (which is very hard to change) or of the school experience (which is somewhat easier to change). We do not even know how much narcotics addiction there is, much less what to do about it on any large scale. Above all, we do not know how much urban pathology is in some sense inevitable and how much space, therefore, our central cities must expect to reserve for the derelicts, the alienated, and the unaspiring poor.

One would suppose that we know most about one prerequisite for progress among the lower classes—employment opportunities. Yet, although the debate between the proponents of achieving full employment by stimulating aggregate demand and those who insist that we need structural change (job retraining, family allowances, vocational education, public works) has been raging for a decade or more, neither side has convinced the other. More importantly, *neither* strategy has been seriously tried. Until the war in Vietnam required a greater use of our industrial capacity, the federal government did not attempt as vigorously as it might, through tax and fiscal policies, to create a full employment economy—in part from fear of inflation, in part from a concern over the international balance of payments. Nor have the structuralists tried a program of public works, guaranteed incomes, worker resettlement, and vocational education on a scale sufficient to test the feasibility of eliminating the so-called "pockets of poverty." The war on poverty contains some of the elements of a "structuralist" strategy—

for example, the Job Corps as a way of developing skills and motivation, and Project Head Start as a long-term attack on rates of learning—but it will be some time before we know how successful they are and to what extent such methods can be generalized.

Federal policies have moved only by halting steps in a direction that acknowledges that the "urban problem" is not primarily, or even significantly, a housing problem. The rent supplement program is a recognition of the need to deal directly with the cause of slum housing; that is, the fact that there are people who cannot afford nonslum housing. The call for legislation to bar discrimination in the housing market is a recognition of the need to reduce the inflated prices of Negro housing by giving Negroes access to the entire housing market. (Although the principle is sound, not much is likely to happen as a result of such a statute; open occupancy laws already on the books in many states and cities have not broken up the Negro enclaves, partly because housing outside such enclaves sometimes costs more than housing inside them.) But for the present, these and other modifications are largely frosting on a tasteless cake. The major thrust of federal policy is now, and always has been, a commitment to maintain and enhance the physical shells of existing American cities—adding, where appropriate, a few new towns to handle the overflow. The desire to make all American cities "livable" not only exaggerates the extent to which cities are now "unlivable," but it thoughtlessly lumps together all cities—whether or not they continue to serve any functions, whether or not there is any rational grounds for conserving them at public expense, and even whether or not the local leadership conceives of urban conservation as driving the poor across the city line into somebody else's city.

It was long argued that urban interests deserved a cabinet department, just as agricultural interests had one. It is a disturbing analogy. For 30 years, the Department of Agriculture has, in effect, been committed to the preservation of farms regardless of how inefficient or economically unsound they became. Now there are signs that pressure from mayors and downtown business interests may move the Department of Housing and Urban Development even farther toward a policy of guaranteeing the perpetual existence of the central business district of every American city, no matter how inefficient or economically unsound they may become.

There is nothing sacrosanct about the present patterns or functions of urban life; cities, like people, pass through life cycles during which their values and functions change. But the implicit commitment of our new Department to physical structures, rather than to concrete human needs, makes it almost impossible for it to distinguish between cities which need help and cities which do not; any city "needs" help if it says it does. The result is that while the rhetoric of the "urban crisis" is aimed at the great national and regional centers of commerce, culture, education, and government—Washington, New York, Philadelphia, Boston, Los Angeles—the reality of federal programs can be found in Barre, Vermont, and Wink, Texas. *Over half of all cities with urban renewal projects have populations of less than 25,000* (in this respect, HUD is more democratic than the Department of Agriculture; whereas the latter was of more help to the big than to the small farmer, the former is subsidizing the smaller as well as the larger cities.)

There is an alternative policy which could direct federal activities. It would require, not the scrapping of existing federal programs, but only their redirection. Such a policy would begin with a recognition of the different kinds of "urban problems"—some of which, like poverty, are as much rural as urban problems, and others of which, like the gap between expectations and achievements, are not problems that government can do anything about. Such a policy would, I suggest, contain the following elements:

First, the federal government would assume responsibility for placing a floor under the capacity of Americans to acquire a minimally satisfactory level of personal and family amenities—housing, food, clothing, medical care. Where possible, guaranteeing such resources to every family would be done by combining aggregate fiscal policies which produce full employment with direct income transfers—in the form, say, of a negative income tax, family allowances, or rent subsidies—such that each family has maximum free choice as to the type and location of its housing. Some conservatives will of course object that this is a "dole," productive of moral debilitation. I submit that, unless we are willing to tolerate privation, we of necessity must have some sort of dole; the real question is whether it will be one which minimizes choice and maximizes bureaucratic intervention in private lives (as is the case with public housing projects and many welfare programs) or one with the opposite characteristics. As far as moral debilitation is concerned, I have found no compelling psychological or theological evidence that the souls of the poor are in greater danger from government subsidies than are the souls of businessmen, intellectuals, and farmers, all of whom have been enjoying government largesse for some time.

I am under no illusion that the problems of the central-city poor, white and Negro, will vanish because we adopt an income maintenance strategy. All I am suggesting is that whatever else must be done to cope with poverty, there will be little progress unless the one indisputable component of poverty—low incomes—is dealt with by methods more effective and less debasing than those which require husbands to first desert their wives and children before these latter can appy for welfare.

Second, public power and public funds would be used to provide those common benefits (or, as the economists say, collective goods) which are enjoyed, and thus must be paid for, by everybody. Fresh air, pure water, open spaces, park land, and police protection are the most common examples of indivisible benefits, to achieve which public powers must be exercised. Ironically, it is in this area (where even in the days of Adam Smith it was agreed that public intervention was required) that federal action has been the slowest in developing. The reason, of course, is understandable enough; most collective goods require control over those aspects of community life—the education of the young, the policing of the city, and the use of land—which Americans have long insisted be kept in local hands. So long as most of us lived and worked in the same place—that is, the central city—purely local control of these matters may have made sense. What services we used as we travelled to and from work we also paid for through taxes. Upper-middle-class citizens with a strong interest in (and a healthy capacity to pay for) common benefits, such as parks and the like, lived in—and often governed—the central city. With the exodus to the suburbs, and our self-segregation into radically different kinds of communities on the periphery, differences in preferences and income which used to coexist within a single taxing authority now are separated by political boundaries. If the incidence of costs and benefits of various collective goods is to be equalized throughout the metropolitan area, some higher taxing authority must assume responsibility for transfer payments. There are only two such authorities—the state and the federal government.

Third, where possible, central cities facing a fiscal crisis ought to receive block grants from state or federal governments in order to help defray the cost of servicing the poor, providing decent education and police protection, and so on. At the present time, cities must commit themselves to a whole range of federally conceived programs in order to get money they urgently need, even though many of these programs may be either irrelevant or harmful to the interests of parts of the city's population. Cities with an eroding tax base seize upon urban renewal as the only way to get federal support for that tax base, even though it is a clumsy and inefficient way—it requires destroying homes or businesses, allowing land to lie vacant for long periods of time, and pushing people who consume high levels of local services into neighboring cities where they cause the whole dreary cycle to be repeated. The already-enacted federal aid to education program is a step in the right direction, though the amounts will surely have to be increased. Even if one were to accept the dubious proposition that the cities could be rebuilt to retain or lure back the middle classes—a proposition that lies at the bottom of much of the urban renewal strategy—any but the most blind partisans ought to concede that what drives the middle classes out of the city in the first place may have much less to do with the physical condition of the buildings than with the quality of the public schools and the level of public safety. Subsidizing these institutions, rather than the rents the middle classes have to pay, strikes me as both fairer (since it will help the poor as well as the better off) and more likely to produce results.

Fourth, the federal government ought to encourage, through special incentives, cities to experiment with various user charges as a way of making certain that nonresidents pay their fair share of the services they use in the cities where they work or shop, and that residents have a more precise and personal way than voting for or against the mayor to indicate how much of a particular local service they really desire for themselves. At the present time, large groups of people get something for nothing—nonresidents who park on the city's streets, for example, or residents who, owning no taxable property, enthusiastically vote for more and more free public facilities. The whole burden is thrown on the property-tax payer, and he cannot sustain it.

Fifth, urban renewal and other land clearance programs can be used as a tool to aid in providing common benefits (by assembling land and financing good design for public buildings, schools, and the like) and as a way of eliminating hazardous or unsalvageable structures. If renewal is to do more than this, then to insure against the excesses of the past it ought to be hedged about with the most explicit restrictions. If decent low-cost housing is to be torn down for high-cost housing, then it should be done only when either a clear collective benefit (for example, a new park) will result or when surplus low-cost housing can be removed. The latter would require a prior showing that the vacancy rate among low-cost housing units in that city or area is high enough to make possible the absorption of displaced families without serious economic loss, and that a close study of the social structure of the affected neighborhood reveals it to be primarily a place with high transiency rates where strong family life and neighborhood ties have not developed. And if a subsidy is conferred on the developer and his new upper-income tenants, then provision ought to be made to recapture that subsidy over time—perhaps by making the federal contribution a long-term loan rather than a grant (this was actually proposed when the original legislation was first debated in Congress) or by allowing the city to adopt special tax measures to recover the subsidy for itself.

3
EXTERNALITIES
AND THE CITY
Joan G. Haworth

Solutions to urban problems are made more difficult by the inter-dependence of the economic activities in the modern city. This paper is concerned with one important set of these interactions which are commonly called "externalities"[1] or, in Mishan's more descriptive ter-minology, "spillover effects." These economic activities are character-ized by a lack of full compensation, either to the producer or to the user, in a situation where one person's actions benefit or cost another per-son. In such a situation the market mechanism fails to account for the interaction between persons in a complete way.

In every economic transaction each person involved incurs costs in order to receive some type of benefit. In the "normal" situation the purchaser pays the full cost of the item and expects to obtain full possession of the good or service. Sometimes, however, the purchasers pay for an item but do not receive all of its benefits; that is, there are "free riders" who share in the benefits but not in the costs. A home-owner may pay for extermination to prevent rats from living in his home. His neighbors do not share in the costs of that extermination program, but they may share in its benefits through the decrease in the neighbor-hood rat population. The neighbors have gained by means of this exter-nality which resulted from the single homeowner participating in a pest-extermination program.

---

[1] The name "externalities" is given because these effects are external to the market and, hence, not fully compensated for.

This essay was prepared for this volume.

Externalities may also be present when the item is a collective good rather than a private good. In this case many people can use the good without changing its economic value. For example, a lighthouse may be erected by a group of fishermen who are concerned about a particularly dangerous stretch of shore. The cost of the lighthouse construction and its maintenance will be shared by the fishermen who saw the need for the lighthouse and mobilized their resources to meet this need. However, once the lighthouse is in operation, any boat owner who operates in the area can make use of this safety factor. These "free riders" do not pay for their use of the facility but their use of the lighthouse does not affect its ability to be used by the fishermen.

External diseconomies also exist. They occur when the purchaser's payment does not cover the complete cost of the item. The owners of a factory that belches noxious smoke in the course of producing paper is not paying all the costs of paper production. Nearby residents suffer from the smoke, but they are not compensated for their discomfort. The discomfort is a cost of paper production as much as electricity, labor, or pulp are costs. However the discomfort cost is borne by residents downwind of the paper factory and is not included in the cost calculations made by the paper manufacturer. Hence, it is not a factor in the market determination of the quantity of paper produced.[2]

In either of these situations the market system is inefficient. In the first case, too little pest control is produced. If each neighbor paid for the reduction of rats in his house, the increased sum of money would have lowered the rat population further. Similarly, if the fishermen had been unable to cooperate and produce a lighthouse, this collective good would have been under produced in terms of safety requirements. In the external diseconomy case too much paper is produced. If the paper manufacturer's costs are increased by compensating others for the noxious smoke, he would produce less paper.

These are the unintended consequences of some economic activities that lead to overproduction of some goods and services and underproduction of others. Whenever this over- or underproduction results from a market failure, resources have been misallocated. For example, too many resources have been devoted to producing paper and not enough resources to rat extermination. This misallocation of resources has implications for public policy.

In the densely populated modern city many resources are in short supply. Too many people need to use the resources available in a limited geographic area. If the paper manufacturer were on an island

---

[2] This cost, like many other external diseconomies, could be internalized if legal action allows the transfer of socially born costs to the producer. For example, the downwind residents might successfully sue a paper producer for compensation for their discomfort.

in the Pacific, the misused air resources would be unimportant. In the modern city the resources being misused are scarce and their misallocation demands a solution.

Many of the resource allocation decisions within a city, both private and collective decisions, are distorted because of externalities. When a person knows that he will not receive complete possession of the good he buys, he is less likely to buy the product. In the case of slum landlords, when one landlord improves his building by painting, remodeling or modernizing, the surrounding landlords gain by the increased value of their buildings in this neighborhood. However, the landlord who improved his property is not compensated for the increase in the value of surrounding property. Consequently, he is unlikely to expend resources to improve his property when the returns are modest and do not fully compensate him for its benefits to society. Similarly, those goods which produce external diseconomies, such as air, water, or noise pollution, are overproduced by the private firms because there is no incentive to limit their production.

Those who wait for the market mechanism to correct the ills of the city will continue to wait until all markets are perfect and all external economies are internalized.[3] They are "waiting for Godot."

---

[3] For a further discussion of externalities, see Ezra J. Mishan, *Technology and Growth* (New York: Praeger, 1970).

4
THE CHANGING USES OF THE CITY
John Dyckman

INTRODUCTION: FORCES INFLUENCING THE CHANGING CITY

There is some evidence that men took to the city slowly. The early cities of Eastern culture were built by villagers as sacred centers for religious or ritual retreat. Eventually, the villager moved into the city with the concentration of agricultural surplus, the extended specialization of consumption, the assembly of a labor pool, and the growing economies of scale and social overhead as the urbanites developed technology. Thereafter, the momentum of urbanization took over on its own, freed for action by facilitating noneconomic institutions. Today, when the old economies of the city are dwindling in importance in the wealthiest industrial countries, metropolitan growth rushes on. But the urbanites, some of whom remain in village-like pockets in the hearts of the cities, show signs of resuming the village roots in the new suburbia.

Bertrand Russell once observed, in comment on Lloyd Morgan's optimistic doctrine of emergent evolution, "If indeed the world in which we live has been produced in accordance with a Plan, we shall have to reckon Nero a Saint in comparison with the Author of that Plan." Our emerging metropolitan civilization at times inspires similar sentiments in the hearts of its would-be planners. But if our cities have been produced by neither human nor divine plan, they are nonetheless a faithful mirror of our culture.

In contemporary America, the forces exerting the greatest influence

Reprinted by permission of *Daedalus,* Journal of the American Academy of Arts and Sciences, Boston, Mass., Winter 1961, *The Future Metropolis.*

on the changing city are so pervasive they sometimes escape attention. Among them we should surely include:

(1) The late-industrial technology, fed by the rapid leaps of modern science rather than the old painfully wrought steps of the industrial arts.

(2) The ubiquitous growth of socioeconomic *organization,* manifest in the form of
  (a) continuation of the long-time trend to "bigness";
  (b) extension of process of specialization, with its interdependence and hierarchical ordering of parts;
  (c) development of a self-conscious management rationale and an embryonic theory and science of organization.

(3) In the advanced industrial economies, the early signs of the first appearance of a sufficiently large societal surplus to permit the widespread weakening of old economic drives and motivation (this development has thus far been disguised by noneconomic military priorities).

(4) A rapid leap in communication facilities and the subsequent growth of world-wide communication (including the upsurge in literacy and shared symbols) which has made the world functionally "smaller" and has raised the potential for changing old boundaries and old definitions of community.

(5) The deepening awareness of cultural impoverishment relative to American material prosperity. The task of raising mass culture above the levels of its present vulgarity is inseparable from the awakening of mass interest in public canons of consumption. Respect for the communal arts and public services is a prerequisite for the development of public tastes. So far this awareness is confined to intellectuals, but with the aid of communication resources at their command, they may bring it to broader public attention.

One would wish to add a sixth force, that of a rising concern with organized city planning, but the evidence for it is not yet strong.

These developments are so closely interwoven that it is impossible to separate their contributions to the changing physical form and the changing cultural image of the city. Nonetheless, we shall indulge in some speculation about their individual and combined impact on the urban innovations ahead.

Late industrial technology and the physical city

In the early stages of the evolution of the city, industrialization, though only one of many social changes, was the decisive one. Without it the metropolis would have been impossible; without it the metropolis would have been unnecessary. The city, in turn, was an important artifact in the creation of an industrial civilization. Now, however, the marriage faces possible dissolution. For one thing, industry is freer than it has ever been to set up outside the city. For another, both the "city" and "industry" are less clearly defined. The former has been submerged in a tide of urbanization which does not respect clear-cut boundaries. The latter has evolved from recognizable processes of shaping and

fabricating materials to a range of activities shading almost impercepti-
bly in some cases from pure science to manipulation of human motives.
The change from the technology of steam, coal and iron to electric
power has not produced the dirt-free, decentralized city of the Geddes-
Mumford[1] dream, but there are few now who would feel it to be impossible. Newer power sources, most notably solar energy, may carry out
the job which the gasoline engine has crudely and imperfectly begun.[2]

These developments, of course, will be applied, if they are applied,
at first only on the margins. Like progressive education, they will be
debated and even superseded long before they have received widespread application. And in the meantime, our cities continue to feel the
full impact of the older technology and still reap the whirlwind of its
transformation of an agricultural society. Living with this heritage, the
contemporary city dweller hopes to escape from the uglier by-products,
or waits for "renewal." It is hard for him to see anything in his organiza-
tional role that is helping to bring about new living forms which will be
free of the mills that usurp the river banks and pollute the lakes, the
congestion that burns up a cloud of smog, and the waves of rural
workers moving into a chaos of residential decay. But if the city still
means excitement, ideas, and license to him, he will not—in the absence of suitable alternatives—want to be far away from it, either. This
is the limbo in which the half-empowered city dweller of today finds
himself, and the halfway solutions which he seeks in suburbia are familiar to all.

TECHNOLOGY AND POPULATION DISTRIBUTION

Cheaper, faster transport is potentially decentralizing (and given the
same population, density reducing) since it permits workers to achieve
the same real costs of travel to work at greater distance from the job.
When an improvement of transport technology cuts the costs of assembly and distribution significantly, it may reduce pressure to achieve
economies by a particular location, that is, it may leave the activity less
space-tied. On the other hand, engineering improvements in site utilization (for example, storage capacity) increase the ability of a site to
provide services at a given transport cost, and so may have a potentially
centralizing effect.

Thus in a rapidly changing technology conditions are being created
which may make both higher densities and lower densities more economic. Since technological innovations are themselves selected by economic factors, however, consumer demand plays a part in making its
own bed. The dispersal attained with the relatively costly auto commu-

tation is an indicator of the direction in which that demand leans. Decentralization trends may be boosted further by the exhaustion of the fossil fuels such as coal and petroleum, and their replacement by the direct utilization of solar energy.[3] The amount of space required per unit, the freedom of units from fixed power sources, and the requisite spacing of units indicate a relatively low density of development for residence using this type of energy.

The use of atomic power may serve to postpone this decentralization. The economic size of an atomic power plant is currently very large, and while the plant itself should not, for obvious reasons, be located in the heart of a major population center, it can most efficiently serve a large, concentrated market at some point nearby. Strides in the improvement of space-utilization in buildings are also possible, thus permitting the more intensive use of space "at the center of things." Microfilm, magnetic tapes, transistors, and other devices are achieving this effect in many kinds of data storage essential to business. In a much smaller way, urban renewal has worked to this end in the residential sector by replacing large but inefficient units with smaller and more "functional" ones. Measured in terms of the volume of activity taking place at a given point, rather than by the persons assembled, the capacity of land in our central places has been increased enormously in recent years, though this change has been disguised in central office districts by a more lavish use of space.

At the same time, individuals are less rooted to any one place. With more free time and more income in his hands, the individual's travel costs become relatively smaller. The range of activities within his grasp becomes larger. Under these circumstances, it is not unlikely that the extent and variety of spaces "consumed" by the individual should increase, and that his use of space should become more functionally specialized. This has long been an observable characteristic of the well-to-do, some of whom keep a separate apartment or house for such diverse functions as dwelling, work, theater going, duck shooting, and winter and summer vacationing. On a more significant scale, a limited variant of this kind of special purpose use of place and structure might be made available to large numbers of persons with technological developments which would make both the individual units and the travel to reach them cheaper.

A nondiscriminating technology, making possible both greater centralization and greater decentralization, might be turned to both uses simultaneously by a wealthy, pragmatic nation. One possible outcome is a kind of permanent oscillation between the dense city center and the sparsely settled outer suburbia; between a tiny but well-equipped cubicle (one-upping the "beats," a super-functional "pad") and a virtually portable solar-powered house. If the style of life of the multitudes who are electing to live in Southern California at the rate of a thousand a day is symptomatic of a deep American wish, provisions ought also to be made for long periods of living in a boat or trailer.

CENTRALIZATION, DECENTRALIZATION, AND DENSITY

Density of settlement and the spacing of persons, according to persistent beliefs, materially affect the quality of life. In the early industrial era, when the close quarters of the industrial towns were accompanied by bad diet, poor sanitary engineering, little knowledge of the transmission of disease and the low immunity to these hazards of a recently rural labor force, the rapid increase of urban density nearly proved a total disaster. In the later stages of the growth of the city, density has acquired a connotation of urbanity, and has thereby come to be associated with social development and intellectual awareness. Especially when contrasted with a peasant countryside, the city has been championed as the natural habitat of learning and the richest soil for cultural flowering.

It is no longer appropriate to associate high density with plagues, but it may be equally ill-fitting to correlate low density with "the idiocy of the countryside." The distinctions between city and country are in need of revision to fit the realities of present possibilities. Further, the vices and virtues attributed to the city were never wholly assignable to density per se. We still know little of the safely realizable densities of human congregation and of their effects on human performance.

Biological populations seem to show some "critical mass" beyond which the individual, as well as the group, exhibits malfunction and breakdown. The National Institute of Mental Health, in its researches, has shown a disposition to attempt to extend the findings on various animal populations to human groups by analogy. While human groups need not suffer as a group from being of a size that presses on a local food supply (at least in United States society), one suspects the existence of some more subtle stresses on the individual under certain conditions. Support for this view is supplied indirectly by recent biological research on the causes of disease and mass "neuroses" in rodents.[4]

At the same time, there is evidence of strong congregating tendencies in human populations, including a tendency to congestion even where space is available, free, and riskless.[5] The possibilities for an efficient storage of information and activity, and so for greater concentrations of persons, are implicit in much of our new communications technology, which tends to be "space" as well as "weight-losing."

Given the trends in world urbanization, one does not need a concept of "pathological togetherness"[6] to suggest that we will have much greater massing in future cities than in the present.

Will we then find a way to adjust our rhythm of life to swing gracefully between dense massings and lonely retreat? If this chameleon society should develop, constantly adjusting "tension gates" might need to be developed as part of man's psychosomatic regulation, permitting him to.raise or lower the bars to reception of stimuli under dramatically different environmental conditions.

CITIZENS OF A CHANGING CITY

The present effort at urban renewal may, in the long view, appear as the last-ditch attempt to save the old form of the city and the style of life it supported. Paradoxically, the mobilized corporate effort necessary for the large changes has in this instance been devoted to the braking of change. The individuals in the market, voting with their dollars and their feet, have shown little of this nostalgia for the old forms. What is more, the people who show the greatest enthusiasm for the new forms of urban living—the suburban and exurban varieties—are drawn from the ranks of the conformist, security-oriented "organization men." This suggests that there is a covert understanding that the dominant corporate image is favorable to the new forms, despite a token allegiance to the old city.

The visible changes in the city may suggest a deeper social change than has actually taken place. Middle-class Americans take their style of life with them, with only minor alterations, through various zones of suburbia. The heralded changes in the political affiliations of city workers which were expected to attend their increasing moves to mass suburbia and home ownership have been small. No doubt differences in the superficial aspects of culture, in the traditional symbols of class, nationality, or ethnic group, are reduced in the suburban resettlement of old working-class neighborhoods. But these changes are small compared with those still being experienced by rural in-migrants entering the oldest sectors of the city.

Both these movements, by reducing the backlog of differences, diminish the potential for future change. The long march of the underemployed rural labor force to the city, when seen through the glass of the once proud middle-class neighborhoods in its path, appears precipitate and devastating. It must be remembered, however, that these are the last throes of the change. The new urban recruits are being drawn from the most culturally remote areas, long-bypassed. These laborers in the vineyard will be the last, barring open-door immigration, for whom the move to the city will be a great cultural, social, and economic leap.

At the same time as the last pockets of rural isolation are being rooted out and incorporated into the disciplined organization of urban society, that organization is changing its rules of enlistment. The transition from an industrial to a "technological" organization has altered the requirements for education, social recruitment, and class distinctions, has changed the meaning of work, has robbed leisure of its release, and cloaked status in more obscure symbols.

The migrant from the subsistence economy of the hills always found it difficult to adjust to the industrial discipline of the factory system. Now that work is further depersonalized, the relation of worker to output less apparent, individual craftsmanship less applicable, and control more remote, the personal impact of the change is staggering. Neither the independence of the mountain man nor the social cohesion of the Puerto Rican villager is a usable resource in this new situation.

Even the children of veteran urbanites, the wise young of the cities, find important sources of meaningful activity draining away, as some novelist-critics have underlined.[7] The elaboration of the uses of the automobile, along with hi-fi, boats, and so on, is not only a cultivation of the garden of craftsmanship in a desert of routine, but serves even more importantly to give the user a power over the environment which is otherwise denied him even in his work. One need only look to the developing economies of Asia, Africa, and Latin America to see that it is the promise of self-determination contained in technology, not the exercise of a new craft, that beguiles them.

ALIENATION IN THE CITY

The greater separation of the place of residence from the place of work (a hallmark of the modern city) accentuates the separation of man from his productive activity. In space as well as in function, his leisure is freed from the taint of work (the exceptions are the activities of some writers, advertisers, salesmen and communication executives whose work is wrapped around the exploitation of others' leisure). Efforts to reestablish contact through "do-it-yourself" projects are not convincing.

Atomized leisure activities have failed to fuse into any satisfying esthetic of consumption. As Riesman has pointed out, conspicuous consumption (which bequeathed us many of our contemporary antiques and much of the monumental architecture and urban sculpture so revered by city planners) has declined as an avenue to status and has been largely usurped by the corporations.[8] Architectural historians of the future will have to write chapters on clients like Socony, Inland Steel, Crown-Zellerbach and Manufacturers Trust.

The leisure of the old urban villager was meaningful chiefly as a release from work as a physical break. The leisure of the new suburban villager has increasingly become a status-conferring device. For some contemporaries, the functional uses of leisure, as in business golf, have completely obliterated the old distinctions between leisure and work. For a few, leisure means a search for the ancient meanings of recreation in some forms of self-fulfillment. This last-mentioned constructive leisure, however, is denied all but a few intellectuals in our society. We have invented no goals which would make such an activity truly meaningful for most people.

If the city of today is liberated from the old use of the surplus which created it, the citizens of the United States city find themselves buried under the burden of finding meaningful consumption. J. K. Galbraith, who was an ardent Keynesian in a time when employment and production were faltering in America, has since found the stimulation of employment and output a counsel of aimlessness in an affluent America.[9] To salvage meaning for his economic policy, he proposes using government spending to jack up lagging collective consumption and to redress the balance between "private opulence and public squalor." Private satisfaction from public achievement is little developed in the United States. Perhaps city planning can confer this kind of satisfaction. The task implies vast consumer education as well as proportionate ingenuity and creativity.

THE LEVELING OF URBAN CULTURE

In an environment in which work is meaningless and consumption needs to be constantly refurnished with gimmicks to be acceptable, the rate of the absorption of novelty is terrifying. Television has virtually given up trying for new plots, and has settled down with Westerns, a form of morality tale in which plot is unimportant. The tourism of Americans with money is reaching staggering proportions, expressed in dizzying itineraries in which new places are gobbled up at the rate of one or more a day. We are destined to exhaust our supply of "quaint" places as the speed and availability of transport makes "neighbors" out of the "foreigners."

Perhaps when the visible differences between places have disappeared (in Burchard's words, when the world is "one great Conrad Hilton chain") more subtle distinctions will be cultivated by the natives of the various cities in order to set the home town apart. But it is also possible that man's identification with a particular place will be weakened. Allegiance to a city or state is even now weaker for many than allegiance to a corporation, a profession, or a voluntary association. National allegiances survive because they have stronger functional implications—political system, economy, money, language, arms, and so on. As long as one watches his clues to class and style, he can move from one American city to another with virtually no change in environment, as W. H. Whyte, Jr., has demonstrated.[10]

The second law of urban dynamics, were it written, would postulate that urban variety is running down fast. (Even now old-timers can acquire a semblance of distinction by picturing the "Old Tokyo" or "Old Bombay" before their Westernization.) The leveling has been most marked, not in the matters of subway systems, sewers, and skyscrapers, but in the whiskey-drinking habits of rising young French businessmen and the Coca-Cola breaks of the shop girls; it shows in the "beat" coffee shops of Japan and the omnipresent rock 'n roll of teen-agers everywhere—an ironic comment on the slow progress of jazz up the Mississippi from New Orleans to Chicago in World War I America. Clearly, we have entered on an information-organization drive for the whole world that dwarfs the old task of taking the message to the small towns. Cities play a convenient role in this process, as the metropolis continues to provide a favorable habitat for a large volume of interchanges of information, but they are no longer essential to the task.

THE AUTONOMOUS GROWTH OF ORGANIZATION

Social as well as physical systems usually start out smaller than optimum size, and so can improve their efficiency by growth for a time. Efficiencies of various kinds provide the main impetus for organizations to "grow big." After a certain scale is reached, however, the original functions of the organization may change. For at the "optimum scale" either a decline in efficiency sets in, or new tasks, appropriate to even greater size, are found.[11] The bigness in city forms, which is manifest in expressways and skyscrapers, housing projects and superschools, supermarkets and chain stores, is paralleled by bigger metropolitan systems formed by the inclusion of more and more urban units. Within these systems, the individual units have changed many of their functions.

The extension of metropolitan organization to the relatively unorganized environs has been accompanied by restructuring and greater specialization. Settlements caught up on the wake have changed from market or retail centers to dormitories; local transport and utility systems have either been integrated into metropolitan systems or have disappeared in many instances. Most important, the small places have lost much of their sense of self-determination.

New York is the locale of an increasingly large proportion of the nation's economic decisions. Its relative importance as a setting for economic decision is enhanced by two important trends in the growth of economic organization: (1) the consolidations, mergers, and combinations which are grouping many "local" companies in single national organizations,[12] and (2) the extension of the market of regional producers to a national scale, facilitated by the improvement of interregional communication and transport and by the homogenization of regional tastes.

The corporation, which dominates American economic life, is not bound by local restraints. It moves freely across city and state lines. To grow bigger, it must extend its markets. When it extends them geographically, the dependence on any one place becomes relatively weaker.

THE DECLINING SOCIAL IMPORTANCE OF PLACE

To Plato, Aristotle, and Augustine, the "city" was a synonym for the ruling political and social organization of human relations and for the governing of man. In contemporary America, the corporation has largely usurped that image. Scott Buchanan has suggested that the corporation is the archetype of organization itself in our society, and its rules are the guide for the evolving form of our political relations.[13] To the extent that this is so, the concept of place, around which utopian reformers have woven the tapestry of the good life, will lose some of its meaning.

Corporations form larger organizations out of the amalgamation of smaller ones. Within the larger unit there is, after each addition, a careful preservation of the unity of direction. Decisions formerly made in Chicago or Boston must now emanate from New York.[14] Disappearing, together with some of the local-market direction of the society is its counterpart, the local town-meeting democracy. Each now exists in isolated fringes only. Modified versions of local representation may well disappear as the cities themselves lose their old reasons for being. If cities become so specialized in function that citizens are members of the polity only on a part-time basis, while they are making economic decisions, working on a productive process, attending a conference, or vacationing (each in a different city), the old geographical basis for representation will have had the *coup de grâce.* For the wealthiest, most powerful, or most privileged of our society, this is already the case; their influence is exerted through "corporate," not geographical channels, and it tends to gain primacy thereby.

Margaret Mead's picture of a future studded with highly specialized functional places, and a population traveling, as the occasion and interest demanded, from place to place among them for special-purpose conferences,[15] might well be the outcome of the high degree of wealth and transportation which made this movement possible, and of a social and political organization of our society which stripped the local places of any other reason for existence. Men, who came into the city to live only after a period of enjoying it from the relative freedom of afar, might now return to the wilds without giving up the city. What then would be the hold of any particular city?

THE CONSTRUCTIVE CITY

The cosmopolitan skimming of many cities is reserved for the world of affairs and power, for intellectuals and executives. The world of most others is still tied more closely to a single city. The marginal people in our society need the city and its supports, and they cannot afford isolation. For them community has come to mean the city. The aged, the handicapped, and the 20 to 30 percent of our youth who will never get higher education in our time need to be in the mainstream of our society, not isolated from it. Idleness is an affront to their capacities and a barrier to self-esteem. Working mothers who need assistance in child care, minority groups, and deviants of all kinds seek tolerance, understanding and assistance in the city. Our era's rejection of the city is also a symptom of its rejection of the productively underprivileged. The exurban drift of the more able is the fruit of a philosophy of individual survival.

Wherever industrial societies have not rejected the city, or have not used it badly, they have quarantined it. There is a present tendency for societies to turn the old city sections into living museums, as in the old walled center of Krakow.

The real challenge of the constructive city runs deeper than the preservation of medieval town centers girdled by green belts. It lies in the reconstruction of some of the sense of community which previously characterized the town and which inspires a good deal of the nostalgia with which the town is still regarded by some. It is too late to get this community back by any return to the soil or to handicrafts, or by some combination of these earlier technologies, in the manner suggested by Arthur Morgan or Ralph Borsodi or the Hassidic collectives of Israel.

Nor is it very constructive to propose a city in which communities are confined by social walls, with bazaar-like meeting places. The ghetto and the bazaar belong to an earlier society. Urbanization and industrialization have destroyed the old communal and feudal structures of social organization. As they come to maturity, they produce mass societies, pluralistic societies, or totalitarian societies, according to Kornhauser. To the extent that United States society is both pluralistic and organized into collateral systems, the old simple unity of communal life is gone. The community of place is also gone. Even the old pluralistic community of the marketplace has been broken down and replaced by the organization of corporate planning. We reject the corporate state of the totalitarian examples, but we have nothing to put in its place except empty statements about national purpose. National purpose can be immediate rather than remote; it can be addressed to the reconstruction of the world in which most Americans now live—the world of the metropolitan area. The strength of our productive power has prevented neither alienation nor impoverishment of opportunity. The logical heirs-apparent of the task of constructing cities to meet this challenge are the city planners. By tradition and temperament they are dreamers in the grand manner.

But the American city-planning movement has spent so much of its still young history trying to "get its feet on the ground" of local government that it is painfully space-bound. It is tied to the use of land and finds it difficult to rise to legitimate flights of fancy. It is hard pressed to utilize the findings of the army of analysts who have come into the movement to provide it with batteries of forecasts. Meier observes, "Often the study of a single innovation by itself, carrying through all the projections that are associated with it, leads to the conclusion that it should have a trivial impact and that the decisions concerning it should be relatively unimportant. However, it is not uncommon that two or three streams of small-scale innovation converge and a transition with major consequences results."[16]

As an aid to the necessary anticipatory thinking, Meier suggests the use of the fictional constructs employed by H. G. Wells and Edward Bellamy and by many lesser science-fiction writers. If they are to play the wholly warranted utopian role which has been left them by default, the city planners would do well to take up this challenge. Without attempting so ambitious an undertaking here, I would like to list a few of the concerns which might be treated in an imaginative picture of the constructive city of the future.

THE EDUCATIVE CITY

The leitmotiv that might be played throughout the picture is "The City as a Place of Learning." It seems that learning has always been the most powerful lure of the city; the city as a work place was expected to inculcate skills, and the city as a play place was expected to provide vices that were at least slightly instructive. The city as a show place was a place to wander about in, and gape at, and be shown.

The educative uses of the city have always been too numerous to be comprised in the curricula of the schools, but organized education has shown a marked affinity for the urban setting. In its medieval beginnings, the university was a creature of the city. The schools themselves cannot be ignored in the planning of the city. In addition, however, a wide variation in institutional auspices, ranging from the university through adult education and extension to the museums, libraries, and public places of the city, will house the total educational experience of the citizens. The public school itself extends over many of these phases, and our concept of the "common education" can be extended to more of them.

A few years ago a group of architects and educators got together to work out a picture of the school of the future.[17] Their solution was a system in which the school was brought into the city, and the latter was turned into a total campus. This idea received the share of attention given to most novel school proposals, and then receded at the usual rate. It is unlikely that most educators interpreted it as anything more than a scheme for a wider use of field trips, for the proponents left enough conventional props of the school lying around to encourage this notion. But interpreted in more dynamic fashion, the scheme provides a beginning for an exploration of the potential dissolution of the barriers between school and city.

A more radical version of the educators' proposal would undertake the conscious design of the metropolis as an educational experience, rather than on the adaptive use of it. The aim would be to turn the city into an educational construct, with a view to providing a constant presence of meaning and a democratized form of learning.

The city that is devoted to the extension of opportunity would necessarily be an educative city. In the past, the extension of education, particularly to adults, has been aimed at facilitating social assimilation and upward mobility, and at remedying occupational deficiencies. For the genuinely underprivileged, our environment should continually be organized to these ends. But alienation is more widespread, reaching even into the economically more able. Here, education for noneconomic compensation must be extended. For these, it is not the education of the school, but the education of life experience which is most important. No sages can be found who can wisely prescribe the content of such experience; the best we can hope to do is to organize the opportunities for variety.

We live in an era in which formal schooling has largely supplanted apprenticeship, and the demands of skilled jobs have shifted from an emphasis on artistry to an emphasis on scientific literacy and communication skills so standardized that they can best be taught in school. The early contact with the world of real work cannot be reestablished by occasional field trips. For the many who, for reasons of poverty of experience or other handicaps, cannot bridge the great gap between the arid abstractions of school and the conquest of the world of materials and men, schools that are truly "open" to the world and do not shut it out must be devised. If there are not apprenticeships left in industry, law schools, and architects' offices, there is still room for first-hand learning in citizenship, social relations, mass culture, and the management of one's affairs. The great advantage of cities at "human scale," or organized in comprehensible communities, is that an overview of the range of activities of a society is accessible.[18]

The problem, of course, would be more than an exercise in physical design; it would be a challenge to administrative ingenuity and social imagination. It would not do just to provide art and artifacts in ingenious arrangements. Means must be found for dislodging the presently frozen constellations of the urban ecology. For example, access to the educational experience of the *whole* city would have to be provided for all. In today's city, only a small part of the population experiences the whole city; slum dwellers are notoriously rooted to the corners and blocks of the small ethnic slum world, while the cosmopolitan professional middle class ranges the entire city. Free public transit would be an essential minimum step in the educational city. (The partial subsidy of the subway system by New York City makes Manhattan possible; the potential for an extension of this relation is untapped.)

Freedom to experience the city and learn its lessons is more than a matter of transit fares. It is a question of real freedom of choice, of power and acceptability. The West Side Puerto Rican or the Harlem Negro knows that he does not have access to the full meaning of the city of New York. Both the physical space apprehended by the individual and the Lewinian "life space" would have to be expanded. We make much of the city as a center of communication, but the information in the messages is received by a few, while to the many the communication content is chiefly noise.

It will be argued that most inhabitants of the city lack the equipment to receive this information and that their isolation in "ghettos" is self-imposed, a protective device against the confusion, stresses, and possible breakdown from this communication bombardment. There is no evidence, however, that the ordinary urbanite is at the limit of his information-handling capacity. Extension of this capacity is itself a major utopian goal in the constructive city.

Whatever is done, the city will be an instructional milieu. Anyone doubting this should reflect that it is the educative force of the city that many of our families now flee, for it is in the city that plural or strange values are taught their children. Families who would guard the education of their children fear this influence. Only when interclass and interethnic differences in value have been reduced somewhat will communication flow more freely.

THE OPEN CITY

Even the communication specialists will at times find the information interchanges of the city a strain. They will seek escape to relative privacy. Traditionally, it was available in the city, but even the golf course is a major center for information and decision in America. Abercrombie's plan for London sought to accommodate to this condition by providing a precinctal organization of the city along functional and occupational lines. In typical English fashion, these precincts were to offer some of the sociability of the club with a protected, inward-turning privacy, while permitting business to be carried on as usual.

It would be more typically American, however, to provide a truly open city. The open city would not be in the political grip of local cliques. It would be the antithesis of the old-time, one-industry, company town. In fact, in an era of truly cheap transport there is no need for conventional kinds of production to be in the city, and there is no need for people to live full time near their work. The open city belongs to the citizens who participate in its works.

There are many ways in which citizens can participate in experiments in the working of the city if the city is willing to experiment freely. For example, citizens can experience almost any day what it means to overload a highway system; the same lessons can be extended to other workings of the physical city and to its very government. "Tryout" stations can be set up for various kinds of urban apparatus from conveyor sidewalks to expandable houses. The city government can rotate certain civic duties, like dining-room assignments at a boys' camp. It has been seriously suggested recently that citizens be deputized freely for the control of traffic violations. Such an action would be in the tradition of the colonial fire guards and citizen patrols who guarded the city at night. The losses in efficiency from the employment of less than optimum resources would not be crucial in an economy in which these resources were superabundant. It is important, however, that the civic duties in question be more than merely honorific; they must be functional in tangible respects.

Neither is there any need for the city to be the man's world while the suburbs belong to women, as is the case in America today. Only a relatively small part of the time charged to production in the city actually goes for that purpose. Much of the rest goes to a way of life, to the "business game." There is no need, other than the psychic requirements of the players, for maintaining this trend. Given greater choice, women might increasingly reject the exclusive role of consumer-specialist. As a society gets more remote from want, consumption as a class of activity loses importance and prestige. There are also signs that women of the leadership group, upper-middle-class style, are tending to a greater participation in politics. Business and politics, the great games of the city, should be opened to all its citizens.

The home—distant in psychological space and ground space but not in time from the city—would take less of a woman's day. Social planners have been slow to react to the steadily diminishing proportions of the average woman's life that are devoted to childbearing and infant care.[19] Housewives frequently complain that the advent of a new household technology has actually lengthened their workday, but some of the additional work is managerial, and some is self-imposed to fill the void left by labor-saving devices. Given a chance to play more meaningful managerial roles, women would be able to divert sizable amounts of household time to the affairs of the city.

The open city is not, by contemporary standards, an efficient city. For a considerable time it would be a difficult and costly place to get things done. Such an open city could come about only as the result of the conscious choice of placing participation above product. Our town-meeting tradition even now does not work in big cities; but it continues to hold a place in our atavistic longings, and might be even more attractive if it could be rescued from the parochialism of suburbia or the dullness of the small town.

The productive technology, which grew in an intimate interdependence with the overhead economies of urbanization, has outstripped these facilitating arrangements and has become independent of them. The urban style of life of a growing proportion of the population has fed the demand for services, private and public. The old forms of the city are no longer needed, but the services the city provides are more than ever in demand. As these demands grow, it is necessary to devise means for "taking in each other's washing." One way to do this is to make rewarding leisure out of community service.

Unfortunately, the ingrained American respect for work and productivity not only prevents us from developing a genuine culture of community leisure but also robs us of respect for activities whose productive consequences are not apparent. This outlook, which is manifest in our treatment of the aged, the infirm, and the intellectually underprivileged, inhibits the full use of national energies and prevents those who cannot master the socially approved developmental tasks from experiencing full adulthood. As we face the prospect of an increasing difficulty in placing new entrants in the labor force,[20] it behooves us to consider some alternatives to the empty extension of education. Instead of brushing the youth out of sight in rural C.C.C. camps, let us consider placing them in the service of the city.

CONCLUSION

The exciting new cities of our time have virtually nothing to do with the old economies of city founding. Brasilia is as much a temple city, remote from the habitat and business of its people, as ancient Edith Shar. Chandigarh is as unessential to the economy of India as Mohenjo Daro. If cities can be built today as monumental symbols of national aspiration in countries poor by our standards, it is not so implausible to consider that we might build cities for our present needs and desired uses. At times cities are turned to vital uses in spite of the intentions of their builders, like the California town which started out to ape Venice and wound up, against its will, as a playground for motorcyclists.

The American construction industry is the world's most efficient, but the imaginative use we have found for it is the building of longer and better autobahns than were built by Hitler. We are unable to renew cities, not for lack of land planning but for lack of economic planning, and, more broadly, social policy. Looking at our metropolitan life, we find a deepened stratification, in social communication even more than in social ecology; a city in which management is in the hands of a meritocracy[21] recruited from the top fifteen percent of the youth (the percent of high-school students who now elect the academic major); a city in which a sizable part of the work force is in actual or disguised idleness but in which there are virtually no skills or traditions for making this idleness personally meaningful; a city in which there is a glut of goods and a paucity of public services.

Democracy cannot function where most of the demos is not needed, save as customer or ward. Yet democratic participation may actually get in the way of the functioning of our present cities, as C. Northcote Parkinson has suggested.[22] The answer need not be that of chucking local democracy; it may well be that of recasting our cities. But it is naïve to think that local democracy need be organized around the old notions of place-belonging, just as it is an oversimplification to believe that a physical relocation of the population will solve the functional problems of democracy in our industrial world.

Social invention and innovation in design need to converge on this task. The life style itself would be changed. Traditionally, these patterns are obdurate; but one may easily overestimate the resistance of Americans to a change in life style. Spicer has noted the existence of a marked bias toward imputing such resistance to others on the part of those who are engaged in trying to bring about change or who are especially conscious of cultural differences.[23] People do resist change when it threatens their security; the change in the physical arrangements of city life would have to bulwark security rather than menace it. People tend to resist changes whose implications and workings they do not understand; the "new" forms must have elements of an earlier style (as the suburbs are related to rural small towns) which preserves some continuity. People may resist change if it is too abruptly and forcibly imposed; this is the hardest part of the process, for it requires involvement in change on the part of people who may lack the equipment desired, and so it means a willingness to pay high frictional costs.

Utopian thinking has a place in this process, not only in painting the consequences of failing to alter the present course, as Young recently, and Orwell, Huxley, and Ignatius Donnelley much earlier, have done, but also in sketching the possibilities of what might be, as Bellamy tried to do. Clearly, here is meaningful work enough for generations of American urbanists, if they can find in it the reward that will sustain them.

REFERENCES

1. The expected transition to a neotechnic complex, earlier formulated by Kropotkin and by Geddes, was applied by Mumford in *Technics and Civilization* (New York: Harcourt Brace Jovanovich, 1934) and *The Culture of Cities* (New York: Harcourt Brace Jovanovich, 1938).
2. It is worth noting that the forecaster who was guided by considerations of engineering efficiency would never have acknowledged the potential since realized by the gas-driven auto. Only by blending in liberal amounts of judgment on income levels, social and individual motivation could he have come to an accurate forecast.

3. As a recent handbook points out, "Solar energy arrives in the neighborhood of the Earth at the rate of about 1.35 kilowatts per square meter." The capture of this energy for heat and power is the task of a new technology. Direct conversion of this energy into electricity via solar batteries, or into heat through some intermediate fluid or salt, makes possible an "emancipated" unit in which the power plant and the consumer are one. With adjustments in the collectors and the use of some standby conventional sources, this energy is available virtually everywhere.

4. EDWARD S. DEEVEY, "The Harte and the Haruspex," *The Yale Review* (Winter 1960), pp. 161–179.

5. *Ibid.*

6. Kingsley Davis in a recent paper for a seminar on urbanization in India at the University of California, Berkeley (June 1960), painted the possibility of cities in India reaching a size of 60 million within the range of present forecasts.

7. Most recently, Paul Goodman, Harvey Swados, and others have updated this Veblenian theme. See Goodman's article, "Youth and Organized Society," *Commentary* (February 1960).

8. DAVID RIESMAN, "New Standards for Old," reprinted in *Individualism Reconsidered* (New York: The Free Press, 1954), p. 228.

9. J. K. GALBRAITH, *The Affluent Society* (Boston: Houghton Mifflin, 1958).

10. W. H. WHYTE, JR., *The Organization Man* (New York: Simon and Schuster, 1956).

11. The less flexible species in history often perished from gigantism, particularly as their size reached the point where it generated demands the environment could not meet. As H. G. Wells remarked, "In the record of the rocks it is always the gigantic individuals who appear at the end of each chapter." *Mind at the End of Its Tether* (New York: Didier Publishers, 1946), p. 25.

12. "Between 1949 and 1954, the number of mergers tripled. In recent years, two-thirds of all mergers have been of small companies into larger ones with assets of over $10 million." David T. Bazelon, "Facts and Fictions of U.S. Capitalism," *The Reporter*, 17 (September 1959), p. 47.

13. SCOTT BUCHANAN, *The Corporation and the Republic* (New York: Fund for the Republic, 1959).

14. The firm for which my grandfather worked, which by virtue of its product, building materials, was both locally oriented and politically committed, is a good case. Whereas once it could not afford to be far from the meeting places of Chicago politicians, it has since grown big enough to acquire a different orientation, and recently merged with a firm operating largely in the field of defense contracts requiring it to be close to Washington decision-makers. The head offices of the combine will undoubtedly be in New York, where the nucleus of national decision-making is found.

15. MARGARET MEAD, "Values for Urban Living," *The Annals* (November 1957), pp. 10–14.

16. R. L. MEIER, "Analysis of the Social Consequences of Scientific Discovery," *The American Journal of Physics*, 25 (1957), p. 611.

17. "Random Falls," feature article in *The School Executive* (March 1956).
18. The important point in this overview is not a mystical one of any special *Gestalt*, but resides in the power to choose more confidently when the alternatives are comprehensible.
19. Writing of British experience, Titmuss observed that at the beginning of the century, when the life expectation of a woman aged twenty was forty-six years, about one-third of this life expectancy would be destined for these activities. In 1956, however, when the life expectancy of a woman aged twenty was fifty-five years, only about 7 percent of this life would be concerned with childbearing and maternal care. R. Titmuss, *Essays on the Welfare State* (London: Allen & Unwin, 1958), p. 91.
20. In recent months (as of June, 1960) there has been some evidence that the seasonal peak in unemployment beginning with the end of the school term has been sharper than usual, and in some areas more than half the unemployed labor force is under 24 years of age. Within the next few years, employment prospects for new graduates are expected to become increasingly gray.
21. Michael Young, in his *The Rise of the Meritocracy 1870–2033* (London: Thames and Hudson, 1958) has sketched the consequences of such a tendency in Britain in a social-fiction exercise much like that proposed here.
22. C. Northcote Parkinson, in an address at a national conference of the American Institute of Architects, San Francisco, 21 April, 1960.
23. E. H. Spicer, *Introduction to Human Problems in Technological Change* (New York: Russell Sage Foundation, 1952), pp. 18–19.

part 2 INCOME DISTRIBUTION

Poverty is not unique to the city—indeed a higher percentage of rural residents have incomes below poverty levels. But it is in the city that one finds concentrations of poverty in stark contrast to affluence. Many of the most frequently cited urban problems are attributable, at least in part, to the existence of poverty in metropolitan areas. Crime, a declining tax base in the central city, flight to the suburbs, school segregation, and inadequate housing are all related to the large number of poor in the central city.

The selections have a twofold purpose. The first is to extend the reader's knowledge and understanding of the phenomenon of poverty. It is obvious that to be poor in India or Burma is different from being poor in the United States; there is no absolute living standard which provides a unique poverty level for all countries. However, the working definition used in the United States is based upon an estimated minimum requirement of nutrition, clothing, and shelter. With this oper-

51

ational definition, the incidence of poverty among different groups can be analyzed. Carolyn Jackson and Terri Velten provide statistics on the different degrees and incidence of poverty among whites and nonwhites, aged and nonaged, as well as urban and rural residence.

The second purpose of this part is to provide insights into the causes of poverty and the feasibility of policies that attempt to alleviate poverty. David W. Rasmussen investigates the popular belief that general business conditions are one of the most important determinants of the relative income of nonwhites. The other two selections focus directly on an aspect of poverty that is amenable to local public policy—residential segregation. Edward D. Kalachek investigates the impact of residential segregation upon the employment opportunities for the ghetto dweller. The *Manpower Report of the President* describes the effect of the irregular economy, found in the slums, on the integration of its residents into the mainstream of economic life.

5
RESIDENCE, RACE, AND AGE OF POOR FAMILIES IN 1966
Carolyn Jackson and Terri Velten

In recent years much research in the United States has been devoted to the study of poverty. Certain broad characteristics have emerged from the aggregate poverty data.[1] These generalities are well-known to the reader: Disproportionate numbers of the poor are elderly, beyond their working years. Although most poor people are white, nonwhite families are far more likely to be poor than are white families. About half the families counted poor in 1966 were headed by women with children, by the aged, or by the disabled.[2]

This article seeks other insights on poverty. Specifically, analysis is made of data on race and economic status in conjunction with the residential locale of families. What do the data tell us about where nonwhite families and white families live? Does the evidence on residence confirm or contradict common assumptions about poverty based on such factors as age, work experience, and family income? What relevance do these findings have for planners and administrators of antipoverty programs?

The limited information available on residence of families in 1967, by economic status, reveals that nonwhite families are divided between metropolitan and nonmetropolitan areas in a different manner than white families (Table 1).[3] The nonpoor families, unlike the poor, are more concentrated inside metropolitan areas than outside. And it continues to be more likely that the nonwhite rather than the white family will be poor. The following figures show, for families in the United States in 1967, the proportions that were poor, classified by race and by area of residence.

[Numbers of families are percentages]

Area of residence	All families	White families	Non-white families
United States	10.7	8.4	30.7
Metropolitan	8.1	6.2	23.6
In central cities	10.9	7.8	24.2
Outside central cities	5.8	5.0	21.4
Nonmetropolitan	15.3	12.4	48.4
Nonfarm	15.1	12.2	48.0
Farm	16.5	13.3	51.4

Because detailed data for 1967 are not yet available, most of the discussion in this article refers to data for the income year 1966 collected by the Bureau of the Census in the Current Population Survey for March 1967. The standard metropolitan statistical areas[4] have been subdivided into "central city" and "fringe" areas. The largest city (or cities) in the SMSA is the central city, and the areas not included in the central city are the fringe areas. The term fringe is often used interchangeably with the term suburb. Residents of SMSA's are considered the metropolitan population. Most metropolitan residents are urban dwellers, but some of them live on farms and in other rural places inside SMSA's. For this report, however, farm residents within the SMSA's have been excluded from the count of the metropolitan population and are counted with the nonmetropolitan farm population.

People living outside SMSA's have been classified as urban, rural nonfarm, or farm residents. Together they comprise the nonmetropolitan population. An urban area is a village, town, or city of at least 2500

---

[3] See also Bureau of the Census, "Trends in Social and Economic Conditions in Metropolitan Areas," *Current Population Reports: Special Studies*, P-23, No. 27 (February 7, 1969).

[4] The Bureau of the Census defines a standard metropolitan statistical area (SMSA) as a county or group of counties that contains at least one city of 50,000 inhabitants or more or twin cities with a combined population of at least 50,000. See Bureau of the Census, "Income in 1964 of Families and Unrelated Individuals by Metropolitan-Nonmetropolitan Residence," *Current Population Reports: Consumer Income*, P-60, No. 48, pp. 7–8.

TABLE 1. Number and percentage distribution of families by income below and above the SSA poverty level, race, and residence in 1967

Residence	All Families			White Families			Nonwhite Families		
	Total	Poor	Nonpoor	Total	Poor	Nonpoor	Total	Poor	Nonpoor
				Number (in thousands)					
United States	49,834	5303	44,525	44,814	3766	41,048	5020	1543	3477
Metropolitan	32,226	2603	29,617	28,646	1763	26,884	3579	845	2734
In central cities	14,629	1597	13,032	11,844	920	10,924	2784	675	2109
Outside central cities	17,597	1013	16,584	16,802	843	15,959	796	170	626
Nonmetropolitan	17,608	2701	14,907	16,168	2003	14,165	1440	698	742
Nonfarm	15,165	2297	12,868	13,933	1706	12,277	1232	591	641
Farm	2443	404	2039	2235	297	1938	208	107	101
				Percentage distribution					
United States	100.0	100.0	100.0	100.0	100.0	100.0	100.0	100.0	100.0
Metropolitan	64.7	49.1	66.5	63.9	46.8	65.5	71.3	54.8	78.6
In central cities	29.4	30.1	29.3	26.4	24.4	26.6	55.5	43.7	60.7
Outside central cities	35.3	19.1	37.2	37.5	22.4	38.9	15.9	11.0	18.0
Nonmetropolitan	35.3	50.9	33.5	36.1	53.2	34.5	28.7	45.2	21.3
Nonfarm	30.4	43.3	28.9	31.1	45.3	29.8	24.5	38.3	18.4
Farm	4.9	7.6	4.6	5.0	7.9	4.7	4.1	6.9	2.9

SOURCE: Derived from special tabulations of the Current Population Survey, March 1968, prepared by the Bureau of the Census.

inhabitants. The rural nonfarm population includes those persons who live outside SMSA's, are not in urban areas, and do not maintain farm residence. Farm residence is determined by the land area on which farm products are produced for sale and by the yearly income from these sales.

For the purpose of this discussion, rural nonfarm and farm data have been combined to form a rural category where the farm population is too small to constitute a meaningful unit. With Negroes constituting more than 90 percent of the nonwhite poor and at least 80 percent of the nonwhite population above the poverty level in 1967, the terms Negro and nonwhite are used interchangeably here.

INCIDENCE OF POVERTY

Age of family head

The age of the family head is an important factor in any analysis concerned with the poor and in policy decisions determining antipoverty strategies. If the head of a poor household is young, educable, and with many remaining years of earnings potential, solutions to the family's poverty will be different than if the "head of the house" is a senior citizen whose income is limited by retirement from the labor force or derives in whole or in part from public income-maintenance programs.

In 1966 approximately 12 percent of all families in the United States were poor. Among families headed by a person aged 65 or older, the percentage poor was double that for younger families. This disparity was more pronounced among white families than among nonwhite families and larger in rural areas than in central cities (Table 2). The greater incidence of poverty among the aged was most marked in the suburbs, reflecting the large proportion of white families living there.

Race

Differences between white families and nonwhite families in poverty rates were more pronounced for those under age 65 than for the older groups.[5] In the United States as a whole, only 8 percent of the white families headed by a person under age 65, compared with 33 percent of the nonwhite families, were poor. Where the family head was aged 65 or older, 20 percent of the white families and 47 percent of the

[5] See Mollie Orshansky, "The Aged Negro and His Income," *Social Security Bulletin* (February 1964).

TABLE 2. Number and percent of families below SSA poverty level in 1966 by race and age of head and area of residence [number of families in thousands]

Characteristic	All Families			White Families			Nonwhite Families		
	Total, all ages	Under age 65	Aged 65 and over	Total, all ages	Under age 65	Aged 65 and over	Total, all ages	Under age 65	Aged 65 and over
All families, number	48,923	41,995	6928	44,017	37,646	6371	4906	4348	557
Poor:									
Number	6086	4548	1538	4375	3098	1277	1711	1450	261
Percent	12.4	10.8	22.2	9.9	8.2	20.0	34.9	33.3	46.8
Inside SMSA	31,680	27,633	4047	28,210	24,470	3740	3470	3163	307
Central city, number	14,699	12,493	2206	11,944	9989	1955	2755	2505	250
Poor:									
Number	1819	1431	388	1066	765	301	753	666	87
Percent	12.3	11.5	17.6	8.9	7.7	15.4	27.3	26.6	34.8
Fringe, number	16,981	15,140	1841	16,266	14,482	1784	715	658	57
Poor:									
Number	1249	912	337	1080	768	312	169	144	25
Percent	7.4	6.0	18.3	6.8	5.3	17.5	23.6	21.9	a
Outside SMSA	17,243	14,364	2880	15,807	13,175	2632	1437	1187	250
Urban, number	6507	5440	1067	5961	4980	981	545	459	86
Poor:									
Number	951	706	245	644	462	202	286	243	43
Percent	14.6	13.0	23.0	11.1	9.3	20.6	52.5	52.9	a
Rural, number	10,737	8824	1813	9845	8194	1651	891	728	163
Poor:									
Number	2068	1500	568	1566	1105	461	502	395	107
Percent	19.3	15.8	31.3	15.9	13.5	27.9	56.3	54.3	65.6

a Not shown for base less than 100,000.
SOURCE: Derived from special tabulations of the Current Population Survey, March 1967, prepared by the Bureau of the Census for the Social Security Administration and the Office of Economic Opportunity.

nonwhite families were poor. The reliance on retirement income by families past their working years undoubtedly reduces—but does not eliminate—the economic advantage of the white over the nonwhite.

Racial differences were sharpest among the younger families living outside SMSA's, particularly in urban areas, where the poverty rate for nonwhite families was 6 times greater than that for white families.

Residence

In considering the prevalence of poverty in relation to residence, it should be pointed out that, though money income tends to be lower in small towns and rural areas, the Social Security Administration poverty index assumes the same minimum cash requirement except on farms. If the poverty index were adapted to reflect greater cost-of-living differences between large and small places, some nonmetropolitan residents might no longer be classed as poor.

On the other hand, the income of some poor families is so low that a modest reduction in the poverty standard would not lift them into the nonpoor classification, and there is very little information about the geographic differences in costs at a level of living as low as that presumed by the poverty index.

In any case, under the existing definitions, poverty rates reflect the combination of demographic factors such as age and race in the different areas. In Table 2, for example, the poverty rate for all families does not show a sharp urban-rural contrast. A contrast is presented in the detail on race and age, however.

RESIDENTIAL PATTERNS AMONG THE POOR AND THE NONPOOR

The primary concern throughout this analysis is with three broad age groups of family heads: aged 22–54, aged 55–64, and aged 65 and over. The fact that residence patterns differ markedly among families with the head in these age groups can materially affect the utility of specific antipoverty measures.

Patterns among the poor

Residential patterns among poor white families did not vary greatly in 1966 with age of the head (Table 3). Approximately 50 percent of all such families lived inside metropolitan areas, equally divided between central cities and suburbs. The proportion living outside nonmetropolitan areas was about the same for each age group. The principal distinc-

TABLE 3. Distribution of families by area of residence, race and age of head, and economic status in 1966

Percentage Distribution

Race and Age of Head	Number of families (in thousands)	Inside SMSA			Outside SMSA		Rural		
		Total	Central city	Fringe	Total	Urban	Total	Nonfarm	Farm
Poor									
White[a]	4375	49.1	24.4	24.7	51.0	15.2	35.8	27.8	8.0
22–54	2371	50.7	24.8	25.9	49.3	15.6	33.7	25.6	8.1
55–64	558	42.0	23.7	18.3	58.0	10.9	47.1	33.5	13.6
65 and over	1277	48.0	23.6	24.4	51.9	15.8	36.1	30.2	5.9
Nonwhite[a]	1711	53.9	44.0	9.9	46.0	16.7	29.3	21.3	8.1
22–54	1151	58.6	48.5	10.1	41.3	16.5	24.8	18.3	6.5
55–64	243	37.9	29.2	8.2	62.2	20.6	41.6	27.2	14.4
65 and over	261	42.5	33.3	9.6	57.5	16.5	41.0	31.4	9.6
Nonpoor									
White[a]	39,641	65.7	27.4	38.3	34.3	13.4	20.9	15.5	5.4
22–54	27,586	66.9	25.6	41.3	33.1	12.8	20.3	15.9	4.4
55–64	6393	64.7	31.1	33.6	35.3	13.7	21.6	13.9	7.7
65 and over	5094	61.4	32.5	28.9	38.7	15.3	23.4	15.2	8.2
Nonwhite[a]	3195	73.8	62.7	17.1	20.3	8.1	12.2	10.1	2.1
22–54	2336	82.4	64.5	17.9	17.6	7.2	10.4	8.9	1.6
55–64	497	74.2	56.9	17.3	25.8	8.5	17.3	14.9	2.4
65 and over	296	66.2	55.4	10.8	33.8	14.9	18.9	12.8	6.1

[a] Includes families with a head under age 22, not shown separately.
SOURCE: See Table 2.

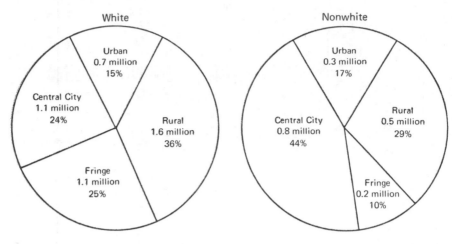

FIGURE 1. Number and Percentage Distribution of Poor Families in 1966, by Area of Residence.

tion in the general pattern for these families was that for families headed by a person aged 55–64 the proportion living in rural areas was much greater than it was for families older or younger.

Poor nonwhite families displayed a sharply contrasting pattern. Close to 60 percent of the younger Negro families lived inside metropolitan areas, mostly in central cities. But where the nonwhite family head was over age 54, 60 percent of them lived outside metropolitan areas and the majority were rural dwellers.

The most striking feature about the residential location of poor Negro families—young and old—was that only 10 percent lived in the suburbs.

Patterns among the nonpoor

Other insights into the nature of poverty may be gained by looking beyond the poor to the other side of the poverty line. Families above the poverty line display many differences, both from one another and from the poor.

Among these nonpoor families, white families were spread in a completely different manner from the nonwhite. Two-thirds of the white families lived within the metropolitan areas, with a majority in the suburbs; only 20 percent were in rural areas—5 percent on farms. Within metropolitan areas, white families with a head under age 55 were more likely to be in suburbs than older families were, particularly if the head was aged 65 or over. Moreover, a higher than average percentage of the family heads aged 55 or older were farmers.

Contrast this pattern of residential location to that for the nonwhite above the poverty level. Eighty percent of these families were inside SMSA's, predominantly in central cities. Only 2 percent were on farms. Among the younger, nonpoor Negro families—those with a head aged 22–54—barely 10 percent lived in rural areas, farm or nonfarm. But almost 20 percent of the older Negro family heads were rural residents.

Another aspect of residential dispersion of these young, better-off nonwhite families was the relatively small number in towns outside SMSA's, a fact that probably reflects lack of job opportunities or suitable housing and little or no personal or family experience with such communities.

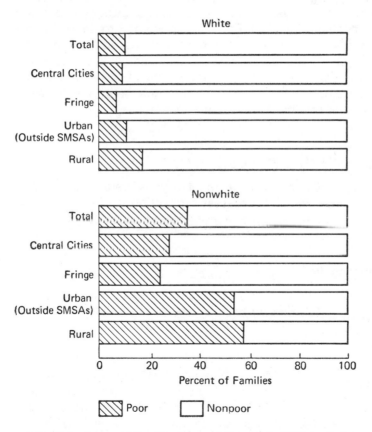

FIGURE 2. Percent of Families Poor and Nonpoor in 1966, by Race and Area of Residence.

Comparison of patterns for poor and nonpoor families

About 63 percent of the nonwhite families above poverty lived in central cities, and just 18 percent were in suburbs. By contrast, among the white nonpoor 27 percent lived in central cities and 38 percent resided in the suburbs.

Among nonpoor families with an aged head there was more similarity in area of residence. For white and nonwhite aged families the proportions inside metropolitan areas were 61 percent and 66 percent, respectively.

In general, outside metropolitan areas poor families, regardless of race, tended to have a common pattern of residence (Table 3). That is, nonmetropolitan poor families who were white were distributed in cities, small towns, and farms in a pattern more like that for poor Negro families of the same age than that for white families above the poverty line. The relationship between economic status and residence was also strong among nonwhite families: For corresponding groups of Negro families, the residential pattern for the nonpoor differed from that for the poor. The basic difference between families above and below the poverty line was that a much larger proportion of those above the line—particularly among the nonwhite—lived inside metropolitan areas and a much smaller proportion were rural residents.

COMPARISON OF AREAS BY AGE OF FAMILY HEAD

In 1966 little over two-thirds of all family heads were aged 22–54 (Table 4). The locale with the greatest proportion of these younger families was the suburbs, and the farming area had the largest share of families with an aged head.

Heads of poor families

Inside SMSA's. Of the 6 million poor families, half lived inside metropolitan areas. Central cities were the home of more than 1.8 million of these families—1.1 million of whom were white and 0.7 million nonwhite.

A closer look at the poor families within central cities shows that about 55 percent of the white families had a head aged 22–54 and 30 percent had an aged head. The Negro poor in central cities were younger than their white counterparts. Almost 75 percent of these Negro families were headed by a person aged 22–54, and barely 12 percent had a head aged 65 or older. The age of the head has direct bearing on family economic status because many old people no longer work regularly. Poor families that include potential earners, for example, may be able to escape from poverty as a result of industrial development within the central cities or their suburbs.

Outside SMSA's.   There were 3 million poor families in areas outside SMSA's: 1 million living in urban places, more than 1½ million living in rural nonfarm areas, and almost one-half million on farms.

Rural nonfarm areas were the locale with the largest number of poor white families and the second largest number of poor Negro families. Half the white and 58 percent of the Negro families were headed by a person aged 22–54. Half a million poor families lived on farms—350,000 of them white, 140,000 nonwhite. And regardless of race, about 45 percent of these farm families had a person aged 55 or older as its head.

Thus, when nonfarm and farm areas are considered as a whole the economic health of rural communities may require about as much emphasis on income support for the aged and "nearly aged" as it does on education or training of potentially fully employed family heads.

WORK AS AN ESCAPE FROM POVERTY

It is often asserted that a sure avenue for rising above poverty is through income from employment. The data indicate, however, that for many this route is not at all certain.

Work experience

Among younger families with a male head, most of the men worked The poor were no exception. In all residential areas at least 80 percent of the poor male family heads worked some time during the survey year (Table 5). Inside SMSA's, 90 percent of the men heading white families worked and 95 percent of the nonwhite men.

Most of these men worked at least 40 weeks out of the year (Table 6).[6] Of all families in poverty that were headed by an employed man aged 22–54, close to 70 percent of the white men and 75 percent of the nonwhite men worked at least 40 weeks. Among these family heads, considerable racial difference is found in central cities, where about 60 percent of the white men and 75 percent of the nonwhite worked for 40 or more weeks.

The heads of nonpoor families had different work experience. About

---

[6] In this report, a person working 40 weeks or more, at least 35 hours a week, is considered to be working full time.

TABLE 4. Distribution of families by race and age of head, area of residence, and economic status in 1966

Race and Age of Head	Number of Families (in thousands)						Percentage Distribution					
	All families	Inside SMSA		Outside SMSA			All families	Inside SMSA		Outside SMSA		
		Central city	Fringe	Urban	Rural			Central city	Fringe	Urban	Rural	
					Nonfarm	Farm					Nonfarm	Farm
All families												
All families	48,923	14,699	16,981	6507	8040	2697	100.0	100.0	100.0	100.0	100.0	100.0
22–54	33,444	9712	12,534	4269	5398	1530	68.4	66.1	73.8	65.6	67.1	56.7
55–64	7690	2477	2358	1028	1215	615	15.7	16.9	13.9	15.8	15.1	22.8
65 and over	6928	2206	1841	1067	1280	533	14.2	15.0	10.8	16.4	15.9	19.8
White[a]												
White[a]	44,016	11,945	16,266	5961	7354	2491	100.0	100.0	100.0	100.0	100.0	100.0
22–54	29,957	7649	12,000	3911	4980	1417	68.1	64.0	73.8	65.6	67.7	56.9
55–64	6951	2122	2249	936	1074	568	15.8	17.8	13.8	15.7	14.6	22.8
65 and over	6371	1955	1784	980	1160	491	14.5	16.4	11.0	16.4	15.8	19.7
Nonwhite[a]												
Nonwhite[a]	4906	2755	714	545	686	205	100.0	100.0	100.0	100.0	100.0	100.0
22–54	3487	2064	535	358	418	112	71.1	74.9	74.9	65.7	60.9	54.6
55–64	740	354	106	92	140	47	15.1	12.8	14.8	16.9	20.4	22.9
65 and over	557	251	57	87	120	43	11.4	9.1	8.0	16.0	17.5	21.0
Poor												
All families	6086	1819	1249	951	1580	488	100.0	100.0	100.0	100.0	100.0	100.0
22–54	3522	1145	731	562	817	268	57.9	62.9	58.5	59.1	51.7	54.9
55–64	801	203	122	111	253	111	13.2	11.2	9.8	11.7	16.0	22.7
65 and over	1538	388	337	245	468	100	25.3	21.3	27.0	25.8	29.6	20.5

	Number (thousands)						Percent					
White[a]	4375	1066	1081	664	1216	350	100.0	100.0	100.0	100.0	100.0	100.0
22–54	2371	587	615	371	606	192	54.2	55.1	56.9	55.9	49.8	54.9
55–64	558	132	102	61	187	76	12.8	12.4	9.4	9.2	15.4	21.7
65 and over	1277	301	312	202	386	75	29.2	28.2	28.9	30.4	31.7	21.4
Nonwhite[a]	1711	753	169	286	364	138	100.0	100.0	100.0	100.0	100.0	100.0
22–54	1151	558	116	190	211	75	67.3	74.1	68.6	66.4	58.0	54.3
55–64	243	71	b	b	66	b	14.2	9.4	11.8	17.5	18.1	25.4
65 and over	261	87	b	50	82	b	15.3	11.6	14.8	15.0	22.5	18.1

Nonpoor

	Number (thousands)						Percent					
All families	42,836	12,881	15,732	5556	6460	2208	100.0	100.0	100.0	100.0	100.0	100.0
22–54	29,922	8567	11,804	3709	4581	1263	69.9	66.5	75.0	66.8	70.9	57.2
55–64	6890	2274	2233	916	962	504	16.1	17.7	14.2	16.5	14.9	22.8
65 and over	5390	1818	1504	822	812	433	12.6	14.1	9.6	14.8	12.6	19.6
White[a]	39,641	10,879	15,186	5297	6138	2141	100.0	100.0	100.0	100.0	100.0	100.0
22–54	27,586	7062	11,385	3540	4374	1225	69.6	64.9	75.0	66.8	71.3	57.2
55–64	6393	1990	2147	875	887	492	16.1	18.3	14.1	16.5	14.5	23.0
65 and over	5094	1654	1472	778	774	416	12.9	15.2	9.7	14.7	12.6	19.4
Nonwhite[a]	3195	2002	545	259	322	67	100.0	100.0	100.0	100.0	100.0	c
22–54	2336	1506	419	168	207	b	73.1	75.2	76.9	64.9	64.3	c
55–64	497	283	86	b	74	b	15.6	14.1	15.8	16.2	23.0	c
65 and over	296	164	b	b	b	b	9.3	8.2	5.9	17.0	11.8	c

[a] Includes families with a head under age 22, not shown separately.
[b] Not shown for less than 50,000.
[c] Not shown for base less than 100,000.
SOURCE: See Table 2.

TABLE 5. Percent of families with a male head aged 22–54 who worked in 1966, by economic status, race of head, and area of residence

Area of Residence	Nonpoor		Poor	
	White	Non-white	White	Non-white
Total	96.4	95.7	86.7	91.4
Inside SMSA	96.5	96.3	82.5	88.1
Central city	97.1	97.4	85.4	89.7
Fringe	96.0	92.5	80.1	b
Outside SMSA*ª*	96.2	92.9	89.9	94.8
Urban	96.7	96.6	92.3	b
Rural nonfarm	95.1	88.8	86.0	95.9

ª Includes farm, not shown separately.
b Not shown for base less than 100,000.
SOURCE: See Table 2.

TABLE 6. Percent of all working male family heads aged 22–54 who worked at least 40 weeks full time in 1966, by economic status, race of head, and area of residence

Area of Residence	Nonpoor		Poor	
	White	Non-white	White	Non-white
Total*ª*	93.9	89.5	68.0	74.3
Inside SMSA	93.9	89.1	63.2	73.4
Central city	93.0	90.2	61.6	76.2
Fringe	94.5	85.2	64.6	b
Outside SMSA*ª*	93.9	91.5	71.4	75.1
Urban	94.3	90.8	65.6	b
Rural nonfarm	93.5	91.4	69.5	72.1

ª Includes farm, not shown separately.
b Not shown for base less than 100,000.
SOURCE: See Table 1.

90 percent of the Negro men and 95 percent of the white men who headed these families worked 40–52 weeks during the year. The disparity in the work experience of poor and nonpoor white family heads was greater than it was among corresponding groups of nonwhite families.

In each type of area a larger proportion of the younger men heading nonpoor families worked for 40–52 weeks than did poor family heads.

Underemployment in terms of weeks worked was thus a serious handicap to the poor. It was more of a problem among white families than it was among the nonwhite.

One-third of the poor white men who had employment worked less than 40 weeks, but only about one-fourth of the poor nonwhite men had that little work. For many of the poor, the problem was low earnings coupled with a large family to support, as well as the inability to find work.

Earnings of family head

The earnings of young family heads who worked for 40 weeks or more differed with respect to area of residence and race (Table 7). The

TABLE 7. Average earnings of head, average family income, and percent of income earned by a male head aged 22–54 who worked 40–52 weeks full time in 1966, by economic status, race of head, and nonfarm residence

Area of Residence	Nonpoor		Poor	
	White	Non-white	White	Non-white
Earnings of head				
Inside SMSA	$8829	$6081	$2188	$2699
Central city	8327	5996	2451	2782
Fringe	9128	6407	1962	a
Outside SMSA	7299	4525	2394	2438
Urban	7590	4668	2440	a
Nonfarm	7062	4410	2372	2441
Family income				
Inside SMSA	$10,910	$8407	$2667	$3150
Central city	10,497	8361	2975	3207
Fringe	11,157	8682	2403	a
Outside SMSA	9142	6767	2760	2871
Urban	9593	6868	2750	a
Nonfarm	8775	6685	2765	2863
Percent of family income earned by head				
Inside SMSA	80.9	72.3	82.0	85.7
Central city	79.3	71.7	82.4	86.7
Fringe	81.8	74.7	81.6	a
Outside SMSA	79.8	66.9	86.7	84.9
Urban	79.1	68.0	88.7	a
Nonfarm	80.5	66.0	85.8	85.3

a Not shown for base less than 100,000.
SOURCE: See Table 2.

TABLE 8. Relationship of earnings of head and income
of family for nonpoor families with a male
head aged 22–54 who worked 40–52 weeks
full time in 1966, by race of head and area
of residence

Area of Residence	White	Nonwhite	Nonwhite as Percent of White
Average earnings of head			
Inside SMSA			
Central city	$8327	$5996	72.0
Fringe	9128	6407	70.2
Outside SMSA			
Urban	$7590	$4668	61.5
Rural nonfarm	7062	4410	62.4
Average family income			
Inside SMSA			
Central city	$10,497	$8361	79.7
Fringe	11,157	8582	76.9
Outside SMSA			
Urban	$9593	$6868	71.6
Rural nonfarm	8775	6685	76.2

SOURCE: See Table 2.

earnings pattern of the poor also differed from that of the nonpoor in
these respects. The earnings of the poor were highest in the central
cities, lowest in the suburbs. Regardless of race, the nonpoor workers
who lived in the suburbs earned the most; those living in rural nonfarm
areas earned least.

Among families above the poverty level, white men "outearned" Negro men, no matter where they lived. The disparity was greater outside
metropolitan areas. There, Negro men earned little better than 60 percent of what their white counterparts earned (Table 8). Inside SMSA's
the ratio was about 70 percent.

Both white and nonwhite men who headed nonpoor families in the
suburbs earned about $2000 a year more than those whose families
were in rural nonfarm areas, though the level of average earnings for
the nonwhite was much lower. Thus the Negro male family head in the
suburbs earned 45-percent more than his counterpart in rural nonfarm
areas, but the comparable difference for white men was less than 30
percent. On the other hand, difference in earnings between residents
of central cities and those in suburbs was greater for white families than
for nonwhite families. For nonmetropolitan residents the same situation
existed: White men living in small cities earned proportionately more,

compared with those in rural nonfarm areas, than was true for the corresponding groups of nonwhite men.

FAMILY INCOME

Relation to earnings of head

The poor man aged 22–54 with a family, like the nonpoor family head, earned most of the family income (Table 7). Except for those living in the suburbs, men who headed a poor family earned a larger percentage of the family income than did men with a family above the poverty line.

The nonpoor were more apt to have, in addition to the earnings of a full-time male worker, other sources of income. In young families, most of the family income not earned by the man at the head was probably earned by the wife.[7]

Negro families above the poverty level, to a greater extent than white families, have had more than one earner. The Negro man heading a nonpoor family no matter where he lived earned a smaller porportion of the family income than the men heading other families. Only those who lived in the suburbs earned as much as three-fourths of the family income; outside metropolitan areas, the proportion was about two-thirds. By contrast, the earnings of white men heading nonpoor families constituted about 80 percent of the family income in all areas.

Except in central cities, the family income of Negroes above the poverty level—even with more than one earner—fell short, on the average, of the earnings of the white man heading a family above the poverty level.

Income other than earnings of head

Among the poor, "other" income for families headed by nonaged men would, of course, be small, as the following tabulation shows. On the other hand, among the nonpoor, the amount of income other than earnings of the family head was considerable. On the average, this additional income almost equaled the average earnings of the head in poor families.

Income other than earnings of the man heading the family was great-

---

[7] For husband-wife families in 1966, 14 percent of the wives in poor white families and 33 percent in poor nonwhite families worked. Comparable percentages for the nonpoor were 36 percent in white families and 53 percent in Negro families. See Mollie Orshansky, *op. cit., Social Security Bulletin* (March 1968), pp. 12–13.

est for those in central cities. White families in rural nonfarm areas had the least income from other sources. For Negro families, it was those in the suburbs who had the least.

Area of Residence	Nonpoor		Poor	
	White	Non-white	White	Non-white
Inside SMSA	$2081	$2326	$479	$451
Central cities	2170	2365	524	425
Fringe	2029	2175	441	582
Outside SMSA	1843	2242	366	433
Urban	2003	2200	310	446
Rural nonfarm	1713	2275	393	422

CONCLUSION

Poverty among white families merits concern because of the large number involved—3.7 million families in 1967. Poverty among non-white families is of even greater concern in that it affects 1 family in 3 in this group.

Poverty is a widely dispersed problem afflicting both cities and rural areas. In 1966, as in earlier years, nonwhite families below the poverty level were concentrated in the central cities and to a lesser degree in rural areas. Poor white families, on the other hand, lived primarily in the rural areas but also in the central cities and in the suburbs.

All the information on families indicates that, both for the central cities and the rural areas, concentrated efforts to find solutions to the poverty problems are urgently needed. The improvement of employment possibilities for those of working age and provisions for adequate retirement income would have an important impact.

The employment data for metropolitan and nonmetropolitan areas support the view currently gaining wider recognition that underemployment in addition to unemployment is a factor in the persistence of poverty for men heading poor families.[8] Although the majority of male family heads among the poor work all year, they do not earn enough to bring the family income above the poverty level.

[8] For discussion on this subject, see Department of Labor, *A Sharper Look at Unemployment in U.S. Cities and Slums;* Bureau of the Census, "The Extent of Poverty in the United States," *Current Population Reports,* P–60, No. 34 (May 31, 1968), pp. 3, 6–7; and *Social Security Bulletin* (March 1968), p. 15.

Programs aimed at alleviating poverty for the aged will contribute to the well-being of a greater percentage of the white poor than of the nonwhite poor, since for white families poverty is more concentrated among the aged. The nonwhite poor will benefit proportionately more than the white poor from programs that improve employment opportunities.

Poverty is not restricted to any particular age, race, or type of community. Opportunities for an adequate income are often limited by obstacles over which individuals have no control. Antipoverty efforts must therefore be directed toward providing the means by which anyone can surmount these obstacles and join the more fortunate majority of Americans.

6
GHETTO DWELLERS, TRANSPORTATION AND EMPLOYMENT
Edward D. Kalachek

Generally tight labor markets during the past several years have alleviated but far from eliminated the heavy concentration of unemployment among core city residents and among Negroes. In the first 9 months of 1967, for instance, the unemployment rate in the central city of 9 major SMSA's was 4.7 percent; in the outer range of these SMSA's, it was only 3.5 percent.[1] If we draw geographic boundaries in a more pertinent fashion and consider only the poverty areas of big cities, the unemployment rate in early 1966 was 7.5 percent, about double the rate for the nation as a whole.[2] As is well known, Negroes experience considerably more unemployment than whites. In 1967, the unemployment rate was 6.0 percent for nonwhite males, as compared with 2.7 percent among white males. Among nonwhite teenagers unemployment is particularly high, 26.3 percent in 1967, and exhibits quite adverse time trends. Since labor force participation among these high unemployment groups is below the national norm, all of these comparisons understate the differential difficulties of finding and maintaining employment.

Why do central city residents and Negroes experience such high unemployment even in times when the overall demand for labor is

[1] Paul O. Flaim, "Unemployment in 15 Metropolitan Areas," U.S. Department of Labor, Bureau of Labor Statistics, *Employment and Earnings* (January 1968).

[2] Susan S. Holland, "The Employment Situation for Negroes," U.S. Department of Labor, Bureau of Labor Statistics, *Employment and Earnings* (September 1967).

A Paper Prepared For The Transportation and Poverty Conference of The American Academy of Arts and Sciences, June 7-8, 1968.

strong and hiring standards are consequently quite relaxed? Inferior quantity and quality of education, poor health, low motivation, and racial discrimination are the traditional explanations. Recently, an additional hypothesis has been advanced suggesting that the location of jobs and workers and the existing transportation network within metropolitan labor markets may also play a culprit role. The availability, speed and price of public transportation facilities may significantly and adversely affect employment opportunities for Negroes and others at the bottom end of the income distribution. This problem is a relatively new one, resulting from the suburbanization of industry, primary reliance on the privately owned automobile as a means of reaching suburban work sites, and residential segregation.

An appreciable proportion of new manufacturing plants and retail centers is being constructed in the suburbs.[3] The central business district and its contiguous zones is declining in relative, and frequently also in absolute importance, as a source of trade and manufacturing employment. The causes of the suburbanization of industry have been well documented.[4] Retail trade in moving outward is following its customers to the suburbs. In many manufacturing industries new technology can be operated most efficiently with large, one-story buildings. Since the proximity to railroad lines is not as important as it once was, and since the need for land area is greater, manufacturing firms find it increasingly profitable to take advantage of the cheaper land costs and lower taxes to be found in the suburbs. This outward migration of industry seems likely to continue and to lead to an increasingly perverse specialization of population and of work functions between central cities and suburbs. The trade and manufacturing establishments that provide a sizable proportion of the low-skill jobs that can be rapidly taught to workers with modest amounts of education are migrating to the suburbs. So are the middle- and upper-income families who provide employment opportunities for maids, gardeners, handymen, and other lower-skilled service workers. At the same time, central cities are tending more and more to specialize in control, consultation and communication functions—in activities that require chiefly professional, technical, and highly trained clerical workers. As the sophistication of their industry rises, central cities are finding themselves increasingly populated by workers with relatively limited amounts of education and skills.

---

[3] "Between 1954 and 1965 more than half of all new industrial buildings and stores were built outside the central city of the nation's metropolitan areas. Sixty-two percent of the valuation permits authorized for new industrial building in standard metropolitan areas were for the suburbs from 1960 to 1965." See Louis Buckley, "The Manpower Revolution in the Central City," mimeographed.

[4] See J. R. Meyer, J. F. Kain, and M. Wohl, *The Urban Transportation Problem* (Cambridge: Harvard University Press, 1965).

Between 1950 and 1960, the central cities of the 24 major metropolitan areas lost nearly 1 1/2 million white residents, and gained nearly 2 million nonwhite residents.[5]

This suggests the development of intricate patterns of crosscommuting. Higher level white-collar workers would reside in the suburbs and work in the cities. Many blue-collar and lower level service and trade workers would live in the central city and work in the suburbs. Such crosscommuting patterns by themselves would not be impediments to employment. The impediments appear to lie in residential discrimination and in the limitations of the public transportation system. Existing public transit facilities were designed primarily to bring residents of outlying areas to the employment concentration found in the central business district. In contrast, suburban employment concentrations are being developed during an era of widespread private ownership of automobiles. They rely on their employees commuting to work by private automobile and are generally poorly serviced by public transit if serviced at all. Of course many suburban residents working in the central city do live beyond easy access to public transit facilities and commute by automobile. This is a matter of free choice. Suburban residents can be assumed to have chosen their residences, and accordingly the distance between residences and work, in a fashion designed to maximize their net satisfactions. The ownership of a private automobile has enabled them to live at a greater distance from their jobs, trading off the cost or inconvenience of travel over space against savings on the cost of housing and the advantages of noncongestion. Central city residents, particularly lower-income residents and Negroes are more constrained. Since the incidence of private automobile ownership is relatively low among central city residents, they may find suburban employment centers difficult or expensive to reach. In such circumstances a normal expedient is to relocate one's residence near the area of current or prospective employment. However, residential segregation may prevent nonwhites from engaging in such relocation. These factors interact to form a pattern of foreclosure of opportunity. Suburban employment centers are generally not serviced by public transit convenient to downtown residents; many Negroes do not own automobiles and residential relocation near preferred work sites is frequently not possible.

The labor market imperfections identified here may play a key role in keeping unemployed workers and unfilled jobs apart. If so, improving transportation services, or lowering their costs, or relocating industry

[5] John F. Kain, "Housing Segregation, Negro Employment and Metropolitan Decentralization," Program on Regional and Urban Economics Discussion Paper No. 14, Harvard University, Cambridge, Mass. (July 1967).

back to the city, or encouraging the free relocation of residents, or halting in-migration would have a significantly favorable impact on central city unemployment. Then again, these imperfections may be of such trivial importance that they are best disregarded and attention focused on more important causes of unemployment or nonlabor force participation.[6] The information necessary for choosing between these alternatives is lacking.[7] In its absence, the spelling out of the channels through which an inconvenient or protracted or expensive journey to the actual or prospective work site could deter employment, and the specification of the groups most likely to be adversely affected may assist in the forming of qualitative judgments. There are two reasons for expecting adverse employment effects. First, an undesirable journey to work will diminish work incentives. Second, it will make both job hunting and job maintenance more arduous.

We can begin by analyzing the incentive effect within the context of the work-leisure decision. The amount of work people are willing to perform for pay depends on the wage rate, given such other factors as tastes for work and leisure, nonwork-related sources of income, and productivity outside of the market place. Wage-rate changes result in both substitution and income effects. Leisure becomes a more expensive good as wage rates increase and people substitute against it by working more. As wage rates rise, however, so does potential income, and at higher income levels, people buy more of all normal goods, including leisure. There is no a priori basis for determining the relative importance of the income and substitution effects. As an empirical matter both time series and cross-sectional data suggest a predominance of the income effect, leading to a decline in hours worked as wage rates rise.

Without doing violence to reality, all of the inconvenience of any journey to work within a metropolitan area can be subsumed into time and money costs. Even for those who do not own automobiles or have access to car pools, there is no such thing as a physically inaccessible job. All jobs are potentially reachable from any residence either on foot or by taxicab. The time, energy and inconvenience required by the journey to work will affect work-leisure choices. Commuting time

[6] Even if they do not have an important impact on employment, residential segregation and deficiencies in public transportation still reinforce poverty. The unwished distance between residence and work, and the necessity to live in areas of greater congestion, undoubtedly represents a reduction in real psychic income for Negroes. The narrowness of the geographic area where it is feasible or convenient to hunt for employment results in lower average earnings.

[7] The only relevant information available is contained in an important study by John Kain, cited above, which demonstrates for Chicago and Detroit that the Negro proportion of employment declines with the distance from the ghetto and suggests that Negro employment would increase significantly if the Negro population were evenly distributed throughout the metropolitan area.

clearly must be considered part of the working day. An 8-hour job which pays $16 affords an effective hourly wage of $2 if transportation time is zero, of $1.78 if an hour is required to get to-and-from work, and of $1.60 if 2 hours are required. Likewise the pertinent wage is net of transportation and other work-associated costs. Changes in the money costs of transportation will have both income and substitution effects and consequently an unpredictable impact on willingness to work. Changes in travel time will, however, have only a substitution effect. A longer journey to work will reduce, and a shorter journey will increase, the number of hours offered for work in the market place.

The journey from the central city to the suburban work site is frequently time consuming and expensive. Dorothy Newman estimates that a minimum of $3 a week, plus more than an hour a day, including transferring and waiting time, is involved in commuting from the typical core city to the suburbs with actual experience being frequently considerably more expensive and time consuming than this minimum.[8] This will deter some from seeking work in the suburbs. The ranks of the discouraged, however, should include very few married adult men, living with their families, and capable of securing full-time employment. The social and economic incentives for adult men to find and maintain full-time employment are too strong for labor-force participation to be very sensitive to 10 or 20 percent changes in effective wage rates. Hours of work should also be unaffected, at least up to the length of the standard work week, since on most full-time jobs, hours are not at the discretion of the employee.[9] Further, a sizeable proportion of suburban manufacturing jobs are located in the factories of large, multiestablishment, unionized firms. It is normal for even relatively unskilled workers employed on a full-time basis in such factories to earn at least $80–$100 a week and often significantly more. At this income level, $4000–$5000 a year and up, car ownership is both feasible and usual, so that once a central city resident becomes a permanent manufacturing employee, the absence of direct access transportation may cease to be a major problem.

Discouragement is far more likely among single persons, teenagers and married women. Among such persons, compulsions to work are generally not so acute and total or partial withdrawal from the labor force is a more feasible option. Women and teenagers tend to work

---

[8] Dorothy K. Newman, "The Decentralization of Jobs," *Monthly Labor Review* (May, 1967).

[9] Significant negative incentive effects could be expected only if the money cost of transportation were so high as to reduce effective income close to the levels which could be obtained from relief or illegal activities.

[10] During 1967 average hourly earnings were $2.57 in nondurable goods manufacturing and $3.00 in durable goods manufacturing.

part-year or part-time and have considerable latitude for varying the amount of their labor input. A woman working as a maid or retail clerk can seek work for 1 day a week or 6. A teenager can work after school or on weekends or both, during part or all of the summer, or given the availability of free room and board, not at all. Further, women, teenagers and those single or older men who work part-time or part-year in service and trade activities are likely to be permanently dependent on public transportation, since their jobs generally result in annual incomes too low to warrant automobile ownership. A good deal of anecdotal or impressionistic evidence is available to support the contention that the willingness of Negro secondary labor-force members to work may be quite sensitive to wage changes and that the journey to work may be a particularly time consuming and expensive problem for them.[11] The fact that adverse incentive effects are probably heavily concentrated among secondary labor-force members does not mean the effects are of negligible social importance. Many families enjoy income above poverty levels only because of multiple earnings, while the employment experiences of teenagers may appreciably affect their subsequent attitudes and productivity as adult labor force members.

The duration and expense of the journey to work may still reduce the probability of employment for married adult males even though it does not have significant incentive effects. The distance barrier may substantially increase the difficulty of finding a job and of surviving the probationary period.[12] This adverse effect cannot always be attributed solely to the expense and inconvenience imposed by distance from work but rather, is frequently due to its interaction with the processes of information dissemination, and with job hunters who may be more lethargic and unimaginative than most.

There are a variety of ways in which distance, information deficiencies, and lethargies can combine to reduce the probabilities of employment. Information about job vacancies is disseminated through a considerable number of organized channels. They include the United States

[11] See Charles E. Silberman, "What Hit the Teenagers," Fortune (April 1965) and "Beware the Day They Change Their Minds," Fortune (November 1965) for some discussion of the relationship between reservation wages and high unemployment among Negro teenagers. As for maids, dwellers in the far suburbs appear to pay higher wages than near-in residents, frequently provide transportation to public transit stops, and nonetheless appear to experience above-average difficulties in securing help. In Los Angeles, the contact and transportation problems are such that private services are able to recruit and transport maids to households in affluent residential areas, charging the household $16 per day and paying the maid $10.

[12] The willingness of some employers in labor-short areas to underwrite charter bus service from central cities to industrial parks in the suburbs demonstrates that the absence of direct access public transit can impede the matching of jobs and workers. The fact that so few suburban employers have seen fit to underwrite such services indicates that not many large employers are burdened by the persistence of job vacancies for which they regard central city residents as suitable applicants.

Employment Service, private employment agencies, and help-wanted advertisements in newspapers and on radio. Nonetheless, all studies indicate that job information is primarily disseminated through friends, relatives, and other informal channels. This is because informal channels are superior mechanisms for conveying some types of information. They are more believable authorities on subjects like, "What really are my chances of being hired, how good really is the job?," and so on.[13] So long as relatively few central city residents have secured work in suburban plants, the existence of jobs in these plants will not very frequently come to the attention of other central city residents. Although they may formally hear of these jobs, they may not perceive of them as being actually available.

In some instances, particularly when public transportation does not run directly to the hiring office, central city residents may not be able to afford the quite substantial transportation expense involved in thorough job hunting, or may regard the probability of securing a job as being so low as not to warrant the expense or the potential psychic disappointment resulting from refusal. In some factories, personnel officers ask job applicants to fill out an application form at home and return it the next day. The willingness to make the return trip is taken as an indication of the intensity of applicant interest. This procedure has a legitimate rationale. It permits personnel officers to restrict the coverage of their open files to applicants with a greater than tangential interest. However, the end result may be the discouragement of those applicants who find the trip to be highly time consuming or expensive, and who may be dubious as to the probability of securing a job.[14] In other instances, transportation may be sufficiently time consuming that central city residents arrive at the hiring office when the morning is well advanced. This may be fatal where personnel officers regard early arrival as proof of the proper work attitude and hire accordingly. In still other instances, employers restrict hiring to workers who own automobiles or have guaranteed access to existing car pools.

Finally, the central city resident who manages to secure a job in a suburban factory may still face significant transportation problems. His income will frequently permit the eventual purchase of an automobile but financing may not be forthcoming until the completion of the probationary period. During the early stage of employment, he may have to rely on car pools or on public transportation (which, in some instances, might involve several transfers plus some walking or the use of taxis). This may result in tardiness or in absence from work. Since employers

[13] Albert Rees, "Information Networks in Labor Markets," *American Economic Review* (May 1966).

[14] William L. Yancey, "Intervention Research: A Strategy of Social Inquiry" (Doctoral dissertation, Washington University, 1967).

in mass production industries place a high premium on punctuality and on the avoidance of absenteeism, the consequence may be dismissal before the end of the probationary period.

The knowledge myth is quite fashionable among analysts of social problems. If a direction of effect can be determined, either by casual empirical observation or on a priori grounds, the effect is described as though it were of considerable significance, meriting a prompt and substantial policy response. I will eschew that type of mythology here. Our survey of the channels through which an expensive or inconvenient or time consuming journey to work might adversely affect employment does not suggest that this is likely to be the major explanation for differentially lower employment rates among Negroes and central city residents. Still, there is good reason for thinking that spatial barriers may be an important contributor, either by themselves or in collaboration with information deficiencies and lethargies. Controlled social experiments are the surest and most efficient technique for assessing the importance of this negative contribution. What is needed are pilot programs designed both to alter the environment by lowering the cost or reducing the duration of the journey to work, and to collect information on the results. Fortunately, a number of such mass transportation demonstration projects are currently underway.

If such transportation programs (as distinct from auxiliary efforts to motivate either jobless Negroes or their potential employers) do have a significant impact on Negro employment, they will open a rich menu of policy choices. Should the transportation network be altered, or is it preferable to relocate workers or jobs? Residential relocation may be ideologically preferable but a fully adequate relocation cannot realistically be expected for some years. In the interim, the choice would be between subsidizing transportation and subsidizing work site location. Transportation seems the preferable tool. It deals with the needs of secondary as well as primary workers. It will not tend to reinforce current dwelling patterns. It does not represent an effort to offset comparative advantage. If the policy is based on some element of error, or if need alters, it is quickly reversible.

What type of transportation changes should be subsidized depends on the nature of the barriers and on the groups adversely affected. It may be that improvements in transportation have a beneficial impact but only if they are accompanied by programs to improve the dissemination of job information or to increase motivation or to persuade employers to alter hiring standards. If the limited route structure of public transportation impedes job hunting or the successful weathering of the probationary period, but those who obtain jobs ultimately buy automobiles or join car pools or change residential locations, then a transportation line which successfully increased the number of central city residents employed in suburban factories might find itself without many customers. This would suggest that it might be most profitable socially to subsidize small flexible vehicles without standardized routes, or buses whose routings might be changed frequently depending on what plants were currently engaged in new hiring. On the other hand, if the income derived from the new jobs does not warrant automobile ownership, and if relocation is not feasible, standardized route public transit will be required. The best locations for new public transit routes will depend on whether the groups most adversely affected are secondary workers or prime working age men. If it were prime working age men, this would suggest a limited number of routes to major industrial concentrations. If it were women, teenagers, and older men, routes might better be directed toward shopping centers, and it might be appropriate to experiment with lower fares in addition to or even as a possible substitute for more service.

7
CHANGES IN THE RELATIVE INCOME OF NONWHITE MALES, 1948-1970
David W. Rasmussen

I. INTRODUCTION

In recent years there has been much debate as to the economic gains nonwhites (particularly Negroes) have realized, both absolutely and relative to whites. Until very recently, the data have been so thin that few scientific hypotheses could be verified. In "The Decline in the Relative Income of Negro Men," Alan Batchelder investigated the income data available in the 1950 and 1960 decennial census, concluding that the 1950s were characterized by a downward trend in the nonwhite-white male income ratio.[1] Furthermore, he hypothesized that increases in the ratio during the 1960s would be a result of civil rights action or a return to high levels of aggregate demand. Using more recent data, Rashi Fein reported that the income ratio rose considerably by 1964, suggesting that this increase was in fact related to the overall performance of the economy.[2]

The purpose of this paper is to investigate how fluctuations in aggregate economic activity affect the nonwhite-white income ratio. Second, the change in the relative economic well-being of nonwhite males is analyzed in order to verify Batchelder's conclusion that the 1950s were

---

[1] *The Quarterly Journal of Economics,* 78 (November 1964), pp. 525–548.

[2] Rashi Fein, "Relative Income of Negro Men, Some Recent Data," *The Quarterly Journal of Economics,* 80 (May 1966), p. 80.

This article is a revised version (prepared for this volume) of an article by David W. Rasmussen, "A Note on the Relative Income of Nonwhite Men, 1948–1964" which appeared in *The Quarterly Journal of Economics,* 84 (February 1970), pp. 168–172.

characterized by a decline in the income ratio. More recent evidence suggests that the nonwhite-white income ratio has in fact increased throughout the post–World War II period.

II. THE TREND: 1948–1970

The values of the nonwhite-white male income ratio from 1939 to 1970 are recorded in Table 1. Assuming that the 1939 value accurately reflects the relative income of nonwhites in the pre–World War

TABLE 1. Trends in the median male income ratio: 1939–1964 (in constant 1964 dollars)

Year	Nonwhite Income	White Income	Nonwhite-White Income Ratio
1939[a]	$ 460	$1112	0.414
1948	1765	3258	.542
1949	1563	3222	.485
1950	1904	3502	.544
1951	2044	3701	.552
1952	2088	3812	.548
1953	2151	3926	.548
1954	1945	3894	.499
1955	2165	4117	.526
1956	2269	4366	.520
1957	2247	4296	.523
1958	2130	4246	.502
1959	2119	4487	.472
1960	2369	4511	.525
1961	2378	4610	.516
1962	2359	4785	.493
1963	2558	4880	.524
1964	2798	4936	.567
1965	2791	5186	.538
1966	2938	5306	.554
1967	3263	5551	.588
1968	3537	5791	.611
1969	3498	6013	.582
1970	3565	6013	.593

SOURCES: United States Bureau of the Census, *Trends in the Income of Families and Persons in the United States: 1947 to 1964,* Technical Paper No. 17, Washington, D.C., U.S. Government Printing Office, 1967, and *Current Population Reports,* P–60, Nos. 69, 75, and 80.
[a] Includes wage and salary income only. Since the wage and salary nonwhite-white income ratio is closer to unity than all income, this figure may have an upward bias. See Elton Rayack, "Discrimination and the Occupational Progress of Negroes," *Review of Economics and Statistics,* XLIII (May 1961), p. 211.

II period, there appears to have been a dramatic increase since that time.

There is a widespread agreement among economists that the non-white-white income ratio fluctuates with variations in aggregate economic activity. When GNP is growing rapidly and there are low levels of unemployment in the economy, the economic well-being of non-whites rises relative to whites. Nonwhite males suffer a decline in relative income in times of economic contraction, the losses being regained in times of expansion. Hence, a successful anticyclical policy contributes significantly to the welfare of nonwhites.

This is not to suggest, however, that the use of buoyant demand is an effective policy tool with which to achieve long-term increases in the relative economic well-being of nonwhites. The most ideal state of the economy is one in which GNP grows at a steady rate and unemployment is kept at a minimum. (In such a situation there are no increases in economic growth and no declines in unemployment, the conditions that are required for increases in the nonwhite-white income ratio.) This suggests that recessions will hurt minority groups but that continued and steady economic growth will not yield long run increases in the nonwhite-white income ratio. This result is not surprising since productivity and prejudice would be the primary determinants of nonwhite income and these are not related to the business cycle.

Once the business cycle is accounted for, regression analysis can be employed to investigate secular trends in the nonwhite-white income ratio. Recent evidence indicates that the income ratio increases about one percentage point every three years.[3] For example, if the income ratio at a particular point on the business cycle was 0.543 in 1950, the ratio would be 0.609 in 1970 if economic conditions were identical to those of 1950.

Part of this secular increase in the income ratio may be due to the migration of nonwhites from small southern towns to northern metropolitan areas. It is often suggested that the latter region is less discriminatory than the South and thus the nonwhite population has improved economic opportunities. An alternative, although not mutually exclusive interpretation of the rising relative income of nonwhites that accompanies migration from the South to the North is that only money income rises, not real income. There is evidence that the cost of living is lower in small towns than it is in metropolitan areas. Further, it is less expensive to live in the South than in the North.[4] Hence when a black moves from a small southern town to a metropolitan area in the North,

[3] Rasmussen, *op. cit.*, p. 169.

[4] U.S. Department of Labor, Bureau of Labor Statistics, *Three Budgets for an Urban Family of Five Persons* (Washington: Government Printing Office, 1970).

he may experience a rise in money income but not an increase in purchasing power. Nonwhites become relatively more urbanized than whites during the 1950–1970 period, suggesting that the secular rise in the income ratio includes some of this "money illusion." Fifteen percent of the nonwhite population moved from small towns and rural areas to metropolitan areas from 1950 to 1970 compared to only 5 percent of the white population. Since the cost of living is about 12 percent higher in metropolitan areas than outlying areas, this suggests that 18 percent of the 0.066 secular increase is a result of money illusion.[5]

The 0.054 real increase in the income ratio from 1950 to 1970 was overshadowed by the increase in relative productivity of nonwhite males. It is generally held that age and education are the primary determinants of productivity. Changes in the age and education distributions between 1950 and 1960 have been used to determine changes in the relative productivity of nonwhites. The rising educational attainment of nonwhite males during the decade of the fifties resulted in a 2.2 percent increase in their productivity relative to whites. Using a similar technique for the 1960–1970 period suggests that the relative productivity of nonwhite males increased 4.2 percent.[6] Therefore, the relative productivity of nonwhite males rose approximately 6.4 percent in the two decades following 1950.

The fact that productivity increases exceeded the real rise in relative income can be explained in 2 ways. One is that discrimination increased during the post–World War II era. Gary Becker in the *Economics of Discrimination* has argued that white discrimination against nonwhites is positively correlated with the relative size of the nonwhite population.[7] Negroes as a percentage of total population in the United States rose from 9.8 percent in 1950 to 11.1 percent in 1970. If Becker were correct, this secular increase in the relative size of the nonwhite population should lower the income ratio over time and erode the nonwhite gains in productivity. However, civil rights activity during this period suggests that other factors may be responsible for the diminished impact of educational gains in the relative income of nonwhite males. Trends in technical change and residential segregation are two factors which may have had an adverse influence on the relative income of nonwhite males.

[5] Low-income budget indices for 1969 are 101 for metropolitan areas, 94 for nonmetropolitan areas and 89 for nonmetropolitan areas in the South. Corresponding figures for a moderate budget are 102, 90, and 85, respectively.

[6] This technique is described in Rasmussen, *op. cit.,* p. 170. Available data for 1970 only permit comparisons of education distributions. This is probably not a serious shortcoming since most of the variation in productivity between 1950 and 1960 was due to differences in educational achievement.

[7] (Chicago: University of Chicago Press, 1957), p. 98.

Technical change is usually thought to increase the demand for skilled labor and decrease that for unskilled labor. Gary Becker offers impressive evidence that this is in fact the case.[8] The private rate of return to college graduates was roughly constant from 1939 to 1962, while during the same period the return to those completing high school almost doubled. Since the relative supply of high school and college graduates approximately doubled during the same period, it is clear that demand shifted in favor of human capital relative to unskilled labor. Since the median nonwhite male in 1970 only completed an elementary education while his white counterpart was a high school graduate, this trend in technical change would tend to lower the income ratio of these median males.

Residential segregation of nonwhites may affect their income relative to whites inasmuch as public transportation to job sites is costly and time consuming while private (automobile) transportation is frequently beyond their income.[9] Segregation may also cause nonwhites to have inadequate information about the job market, especially if jobs are acquired through informal (personal contact) rather than formal (for example, newspaper advertising, employment agencies) channels of communication.[10]

The population trends in urban areas are well known: Nonwhites are concentrated in the central cities as an increasing proportion of the white population moves to the suburban ring. Further, the increasing suburbanization of job opportunities has been shown by John F. Kain.[11] To the degree that segregation influences nonwhite job opportunities adversely, its increase could work to lower the secular rise in the non-white-white income ratio.

III. CONCLUSION

Recent evidence suggests that the decline in the nonwhite-white income ratio from 1950 to 1960 observed by Batchelder was caused by fluctuations in economic activity and did not represent a secular trend. The relative income of nonwhite males appears to have in-

[8] Becker, *Human Capital* (New York: National Bureau of Economic Research, 1964), pp. 128–131.

[9] The impact of segregation on nonwhite income has been explored by Edward D. Kalachek, "Ghetto Dwellers, Transportation and Employment," Chapter 6 in this volume and J. D. Mooney, "Housing Segregation, Negro Employment and Metropolitan Decentralization," *The Quarterly Journal of Economics,* 83 (May 1969), pp. 299–311.

[10] Albert Rees, "Information Networks in Labor Markets," *American Economic Review,* 56 (May 1966), pp. 559–566.

[11] John F. Kain, "The Distribution and Movement of Jobs and Industry," in James Q. Wilson, *The Metropolitan Enigma* (Cambridge, Mass.: Harvard University Press, 1968).

creased from 1950 to 1970 although not as much as one measure of nonwhite productivity relative to whites. This may be a result of changes in the demand for labor caused by technical change and the increasing suburbanization of economic opportunities.

8
THE IRREGULAR ECONOMY OF POVERTY AREAS
Manpower Report of the President (1968)

The barriers which separate subemployed slum residents, nonwhite or white, from the mainstream of economic and social life have resulted in the creation of a separate economic world, which differs vitally, and in many ways, from the middle-class world surrounding the slums. This world has its own special values, its own strategies for survival, its own moral standards, its own criteria of success or failure.

The sources of income of the poor and dependent—those at the bottom one-fifth of the income distribution—are varied, and public policy is directed at altering them in many ways. When income from employment is low, unstable, and unpredictable, the traditional distinctions between employment and unemployment, work and welfare become blurred, and extra-legal sources of income may be sought.

The contrasts between this irregular economy[1] of the slums and the country's regular economy are sharp. In the regular economy, work offers opportunities for vertical mobility, a reasonably predictable pattern of wage improvement with increasing seniority and skill, and the possibility of stable employment. Jobs can be classified in terms of status, skill requirements, and level and stability of earnings—as white- or blue-collar, skilled or unskilled, salaried or paying an hourly wage. By contrast, the irregular economy is characterized by horizontal mobility,

[1] The irregular economy is discussed by Louis A. Ferman in an unpublished paper titled, "The Irregular Economy: Informal Work Patterns in the Urban Ghetto" (Ann Arbor: University of Michigan—Wayne State University, Institute of Labor and Industrial Relations, June 1967).

Reprinted from U.S. Department of Labor, *Manpower Report of the President* (1968).

erratic wage fluctuations, and overlap between the welfare and the wage systems. Jobs are better described as dead end, low wage, sporadic, extra-legal, and so forth.

The size, characteristics, and fluctuations of the irregular economy are not well known nor understood. How does this economy work? How does it overlap with the regular economy? What are its implications for public policy?

The irregular economy has many different income streams, which blend into economic sustenance for slumdwellers. Many people work in low-wage, part-time, marginal jobs that provide no ladder to better opportunities. The work may be physically exacting, job security low, and employment offered only on a short-time basis. In some jobs, the employer pays so little that employees have great temptation to steal from him in order to supplement their earnings. Occasionally, a criminal activity may be the source of income, but the situation is seldom so clear cut. A man may have his own type of "hustle"—an easy way to money, sometimes legitimate, sometimes partly not, that puts him in a quasientrepreneurial role. For example, he may discover where he can get a watch cheap—a "hot" watch—and then sell it to someone on his block. A woman may be on welfare for some months of the year and work in other months;[2] or she may receive welfare and at the same time work covertly; or a man may be living with a woman receiving welfare. As another alternative, a man may enroll in one of the training programs which pay stipends, in order to get funds to tide him over a lean period. Or he may borrow money, to be repaid when he gets a job or a hustle. Or he may decide to retire temporarily from the "scuffle" for a livelihood, and so swell the ranks of the jobless. However, many ghetto residents show high motivation and unusual resourcefulness and persistence in efforts to earn a living.

A possible basis of life for marginal workers is thus provided by the irregular economy. The variations of this world, its occasional excitement and flexibility, may have more appeal to many such workers than do low-paid, demanding, regular jobs. According to a recent study:

> the streetcorner man . . . knows the social value of the job by the amount of money the employer is willing to pay him for doing it. . . . every pay day, he counts . . . the value placed on the job by society at large. . . . Nor does the low-wage job offer prestige, respect, interesting work, opportunity for learning or advancement, or any other compensation . . . [The low-wage job in the regular economy is] hard, dirty, uninteresting and underpaid. The rest of society . . . holds the job of the dishwasher

---

[2] In 1966 about 12 percent of the case closings on AFDC were attributable to employment or increased earnings of the mothers.

or janitor or unskilled laborer in low esteem if not outright contempt. So does the streetcorner man. He cannot do otherwise. He cannot draw from a job those social values which other people do not put into it.[3]

The marginal economy develops a social psychology appropriate to its work world. As the streetcorner man views his future:

It is a future in which everything is uncertain except the ultimate destruction of his hopes and the eventual realization of his fears. . . . Thus, when Richard squanders a week's pay in two days it is not because . . . he is . . . unaware of or unconcerned with his future. He does so precisely because he is aware of the future and the hopelessness of it all.[4]

Since the jobs typically available to slum residents have no attraction in terms either of income or of the nature of the work, it is not surprising that many of these jobs are rejected or held for only short periods. A taxing regular job must offer higher income than the economic activities of the irregular economy to appear preferable to them. And it must offer compensation also for the strain of regular hours of work day in and day out, often in physically demanding or boring work, and of accommodating to supervisors.

There is evidence that many from poverty areas do not stay, even on better jobs. They may not know how to behave on such jobs or find it difficult to maintain the routine; or too much may be expected of them too soon; or their off-job situation may make it difficult to keep the job. For such workers, placement in jobs in the mainstream economy may not be enough; they will need assistance in handling and adjusting to the new jobs.

Employers and supervisors need to develop increased understanding of these workers' problems and to learn how they can be handled. When jobs are opened up for the disadvantaged, changes in the customary work patterns and in supervisory relationships are likely to be essential if the workers are to succeed in, and stay on, the job.

Furthermore, manpower and social policy must be concerned with the ways in which work-training and welfare programs influence the irregular economy. The more differentiated and partial the benefit system, the more opportunities for integration of this system with the irregular economy's other income sources. Programs which provide only marginal increases in an individual's income tend to reinforce this economy.

To challenge it effectively, more attractive alternatives must be provided. This can be done by helping private employers open reasonably

[3] Elliot Liebow, *Tally's Corner* (Boston: Little, Brown, 1967), pp. 57–59. This study describes the job and other experiences of the Negro marginal worker in a big city.
[4] Liebow, *op. cit.,* p. 66.

well-paying jobs in the regular economy to sub-employed workers. Many individuals who live in the irregular economy are eager to leave it, provided they have a chance to really advance their position in a society strongly oriented toward consumption. They would welcome an opportunity to move from a dead end job to a career opportunity, such as the New Careers Program is designed to offer.[5]

THE AFDC MOTHER—A CASE STUDY OF SUBEMPLOYMENT

Mothers receiving assistance through the federal program of Aid to Families with Dependent Children (AFDC) provide an illustrative case study of one group of subemployed in the irregular economy—their problems, their difficulties in meeting these problems, and the way in which they react not only to their individual situations but also to the economic opportunities available to them.

Many theories have been evolved, and myths created, about this relatively small group of the underprivileged. Recipients of AFDC have been widely regarded as caught in a chronic, static condition of dependency, handed down from one generation to the next. Welfare has been viewed as an alternative to work, increasingly unrelated to such economic factors as the general level of unemployment or the participation of women in the labor force. This discussion looks at some of these theories in the light of available evidence. Obviously, there are families whose members have been brought up with welfare support and then have gone on to raise their own families with such support. But there are also many families whose members are on welfare rolls for very short periods of time and never sever their connection with the labor force, even when they are on welfare.

AFDC recipients are encouraged by welfare agencies to find work. Their earnings are included in the total family income that is considered when the amount of welfare payment is determined. States may, however, disregard some part of the earnings of mothers in order to conserve them for the future needs of children.[6]

Each state sets its own cost standards for living requirements under AFDC. But many states also set arbitrary ceilings on the amount of assistance that will actually be paid—often well below the amount of determined need.

[5] For a discussion of this program, see the chapter on New Developments in Manpower Programs in U.S. Department of Labor, *Manpower Report of the President* (1968).

[6] The 1967 amendments liberalize somewhat the ar. ount of income which may be excluded in determining AFDC assistance. See *Summary of Social Security Amendments of 1967* (Washington, D.C.: 90th Cong., 1st sess., Committee on Finance of the U.S. Senate and Committee on Ways and Means of the U.S. House of Representatives, December 1967), p. 17.

Data for the analysis that follows are drawn largely from the only two available national studies of AFDC caseloads. A study sponsored by the American Public Welfare Association was based on a 1-in-3 sample of cases closed during the first 3 months of 1961;[7] a study sponsored by the Department of Health, Education and Welfare (HEW) covered a 1-percent sample of the cases currently active during the last 2 months of 1961.[8] The situation has undergone changes since that time—one of the most notable being the continuing increase in the AFDC caseload, despite the marked reduction in the overall rate of unemployment. The increased caseload is the result of many factors, including an increase in the numbers of young children, of female-headed households, and of children in such households; a relaxation in eligibility requirements in many states; and wider knowledge of the existence of the AFDC program. However, more recent evidence, including several studies of local situations, in general bears out the conclusions reached in the two nationwide surveys.

LENGTH OF TIME ON WELFARE

One way of exploring whether welfare is in fact a way of life, passed on from one generation to another, is to examine the length of time individual recipients remain on welfare. In 1961, the median length of time on AFDC was 27 months for currently active cases and 18 months for closed cases. But the length of time on assistance varied widely with both race and residence. For closed cases, the median time spent on assistance was higher for Negroes (22 months) than for whites (15 months) and lower in urban areas (16 months) than in rural areas (20 months). Periods of dependency tended to be longer in medium-sized cities (50,000 to 500,000) than in the largest cities. In general, however, the mothers in rural farm and nonfarm areas were those who spent the longest continuous periods of time on assistance.[9]

These figures on "continuous time" on assistance obscure the great turnover in the AFDC rolls. A recent analysis of case turnover showed that 584,000 cases were authorized and 508,000 cases were closed in calendar year 1966, while slightly more than 1 million were carried over from the preceding year. Averaged over the year, about 45,000

[7] M. Elaine Burgess and Daniel O. Price, *An American Dependency Challenge* (Chicago: American Public Welfare Association, 1963).

[8] *Study of Recipients of Aid to Families with Dependent Children, November–December 1961; National Cross-Tabulations* (Washington, D.C.: U.S. Department of Health, Education and Welfare, Welfare Administration, August 1965).

[9] Burgess and Price, *op. cit.,* p. 50.

new families were added to the rolls each month, while 41,000 left. Certain families have repeated periods on relief; of the cases added in 1966, about 34 percent had received assistance previously.[10]

Since individuals do go on and off welfare, cumulative data showing the total time spent on welfare by an AFDC mother and her children are important in determining how welfare fits into their life cycle. According to the study of cases closed in 1961, 10 percent of the Negro and 7 percent of the white mothers had spent 9 or more years on welfare. Nevertheless, in absolute terms, white families outnumbered Negro families among the very small minority of AFDC cases on assistance for as long as this.[11]

The proportion of their adult life that women spend on AFDC is another significant measure of their dependence on this assistance. A study based on a 1-percent random sample of AFDC cases in Philadelphia (drawn in 1959, and followed through to 1962) showed that the majority (60 percent) had spent slightly less than half (47 percent) of their adult life on welfare.[12] In at least one city, then, welfare was not a permanent or exclusive style of life for all of the women on AFDC during the time they raised their children.

Finally, intergenerational dependency on welfare can also be measured. In the cases closed during early 1961, less than a third both of the white and of the Negro mothers had grown up in families in which their parents had also been on assistance.[13] However, a study in the State of Washington in 1964 yielded a substantially higher figure. About 43 percent of the AFDC mothers in the sample reported that their parents had been on assistance—3 percent said their parents had been dependent for as long as they could remember; 27 percent said that they had been dependent for several years; and 13 percent said that they had received assistance for a brief period.[14]

Altogether, the generalization that welfare becomes a permanent

[10] Wilbur Cohen, testifying as Under Secretary of HEW, said that it would be a great mistake to think of the caseload as being static, with the same families continuing to receive assistance for long periods of time. *Social Security Amendments of 1967*, Hearings Before the Committee on Finance (Washington, D.C.: 90th Cong., 1st sess., U.S. Senate, Committee on Finance, 1967), H.R. 12080, pt. I, pp. 254 and 730.

[11] Burgess and Price, *op. cit.*, p. 49.

[12] Jane C. Kronick, "Family Life and Economic Dependency, A Report to the Welfare Administration" mimeographed (October 27, 1965). In addition, a special analysis of the relationship between welfare and work experience of AFDC families in Philadelphia was made for this report.

The age of the mothers is important since a high proportion of adult life can mean a short period of time in the case of young mothers. In the Philadelphia study, the average age of the mothers was 35, and as only a small proportion of young mothers was included, age bias does not appear important in this case.

[13] Burgess and Price, *op. cit.*, based on tables on pp. 258, 259, and 280.

[14] *Public Welfare, Poverty—Prevention or Perpetuation* (New York: Greenleigh Associates, December 1964), p. 32.

style of life for all or most AFDC recipients is not supported by the available evidence. The people on welfare are a varied group. Many of the families are not involved in long-term or intergenerational dependency. It must be recognized, however, that significant proportions of AFDC families do represent a second generation on welfare. This is one of the problems to which the program changes provided for by the 1967 amendments to the Social Security Act are addressed.

WELFARE AND WORK

Welfare and employment are widely regarded as alternative rather than complementary or overlapping sources of income. The AFDC caseload is generally seen as made up of nonworking mothers. This is consistent with the theory of public assistance embodied in the original Social Security Act of 1935, which assumed that social insurance protected members of the labor force when their income was interrupted, while federally financed social assistance was for the unemployable. The 1967 amendments to the Social Security Act are directed at promoting economic independence—a permanent or long-term break from the irregular economy—through a program of social services, job training, and cash incentives.[15]

The recent amendments are based on the assumption that AFDC mothers have been entirely outside the labor force and that, if adequate child-care facilities are made available, they can, through training and other services, be enabled to care for themselves and their families. But, in fact, AFDC mothers have frequently been active members of the subemployed labor force—the underemployed and low-wage workers. Public assistance often served as a form of wage supplementation for the low-paid, partially employed worker. Welfare status did not necessarily represent a sharp break with the labor force, as the theory of assistance would imply.

The study of AFDC cases closed in 1961 showed that about 26 percent of the white and 41 percent of the Negro children were in families where the mothers had maintained some degree of attachment to the labor force during the periods on AFDC. (See Table 1.) About half of the mothers had been regularly employed before receiving welfare and continued to be regularly employed after receipt of AFDC payments.[16]

[15] The new Work Incentives Program for welfare recipients (WIN) is discussed in more detail in the chapter on New Developments in Manpower Programs, U.S. Department of Labor, *Manpower Report of the President* (1968).

[16] Burgess and Price, *op. cit.*, pp. 28 and 250.

The HEW study of AFDC cases active in late 1961 showed the mother's employment status at a given point in time, rather than over a longer period. Of all AFDC mothers on the rolls at the time of the study, 14 percent were employed—including 11 percent of the white and 19 percent of the Negro mothers.[17]

The study of the AFDC caseload in Philadelphia in 1962 classified the work history of AFDC mothers in terms of their level of skill and job stability, based on information on their first job, their longest job, and their most recent job. About 40 percent of the women had a stable work history, and 47 percent an unstable one. Only 13 percent had no history of work. Of those with a work history, 40 percent had been employed in skilled or semiskilled jobs.

Thus, AFDC mothers can hardly be described as a group made up predominantly of "work-shy women" who inherited their welfare status. However, there appears to be a generational difference in these women's work histories. The older ones had the more stable work history but lower levels of skill, while the reverse was true for the younger women. These different work habits may have resulted from the nature of the job market at the time the women entered it. Older women had apparently been able to develop a pattern of stability in a job world which accepted their low level of skill, but younger women with higher education and somewhat more skill appeared unable to develop a pattern of work stability in the present, more demanding job market. In general, the women who were unskilled workers had spent less of their adult lives on assistance than had the more skilled.

In view of the generally higher overall rates of unemployment among unskilled than higher skilled workers, this is a rather significant finding. It underlines the special circumstances—social and psychological as well as economic—which affect the work situation of these subemployed women and other groups in the irregular economy.

The type of locality in which these mothers lived also had a marked effect on their pattern of employment. According to the study of cases closed in early 1961, the proportion of mothers who had been employed was lowest in large cities. This was true of both white and Negro mothers, but geographic location had a greater effect on the employment pattern of Negro women than on that of whites. Only about one-fourth of the Negro women in cities of over half a million had worked while on welfare, as compared with nearly 3 out of every 4 of those on farms. (See Table 2.)

---

[17] "Study of Recipients of Aid to Families with Dependent Children, November–December 1961," *National Cross-Tabulations,* table 25.

TABLE 1. Percent distribution of AFDC children by color and by employment status of homemaker during period on AFDC[a]

Employment Status of Homemaker	White	Negro
Total: Number	9629	4245
Percent	100.0	100.0
Employed	26.4	40.6
Full-time throughout period	3.0	5.4
Full-time most of period	4.5	4.4
Part-time throughout period	4.8	11.0
Part-time most of period	7.2	12.6
Other employment history	6.9	7.2
Not employed	73.2	58.8
Employment status unknown	0.4	0.6

[a] Based on a sample of cases closed in first 3 months of 1961; includes children born in wedlock only.
SOURCE: M. Elaine Burgess and Daniel O. Price, *An American Dependency Challenge* (Chicago: American Public Welfare Association, 1963), based on table on p. 268.

TABLE 2. Place of residence and employment status of homemaker during period on AFDC, by color[a]

Place of Residence	All AFDC Families[b] (percent distribution)	Percent with Homemaker Employed	
		White	Negro
Total	100.0	26.4	40.6
Metropolitan Counties			
City of 500,000 or more	25.3	16.4	23.5
City of 50,000 to 499,999	21.1	25.9	45.8
City of 2500 to 49,999	7.5	25.8	44.4
Rural nonfarm	4.4	25.6	56.5
Nonmetropolitan Counties			
City of 2500 to 49,999	19.4	33.2	57.6
Rural nonfarm	18.4	26.7	56.5
Farm	3.9	20.8	72.9

[a] Based on a sample of cases closed during first 3 months of 1961.
[b] A few families, 0.3 percent, were in farm areas of metropolitan counties.
SOURCE: M. Elaine Burgess and Daniel O. Price, *An American Dependency Challenge* (Chicago: American Public Welfare Association, 1963), based on table on pp. 264, 265, and 268.

SOME IMPLICATIONS AND PROGRAM DEVELOPMENTS

These findings cast some doubt on two of the dominant ideas which color much of the discussion about the public assistance program—that being on welfare generally becomes a permanent style of life and that the benefits it provides are an alternative to work. Employment and welfare are systems which mesh in complex ways. Welfare is a form of social provision when income is absent, interrupted, or inadequate, and not simply a cash transfer system operating outside the world of work.

Much more information is needed, however, about the interrelationships between work and welfare and, in particular, about why many AFDC mothers work. At present, there is no definitive information on this latter point. One can do little more than speculate regarding the factors that enter into the situation and even about how many mothers do and do not increase their total income through their work.

To throw light on these basic questions will require extensive study of the circumstances surrounding these women's employment, as well as analysis of their budgets. The need for such research is the more urgent because of the possible implications of the findings for current programs aimed at increasing employment of AFDC mothers.

It seems probable that, in many cases, monetary incentives may not be the crucial factor in the mothers' decisions to work. At the same time, it is likely to take more than minimum earnings to effect a real change in the status of AFDC recipients; this requires income adequate for upward mobility—for a takeoff from dependency to economic self-sufficiency.[18] Thus, programs of income incentives and work training may not reverse the upward trend in the welfare rolls, unless the training is designed to move clients to permanent employment at adequate wages. The new Work Incentive Program established under the 1967 Social Security Act amendments is aimed at precisely this objective.

An expansion of child-care facilities is also provided for by these amendments, on the assumption that lack of such facilities has been one of the factors which prevent AFDC mothers from seeking employment. The total capacity of licensed child-care facilities in the United States is placed presently at only 310,000 to 350,000. So the proportion of working women using such facilities is necessarily small. According to a 1965 study, only about 5 percent of all working mothers placed their children in group care. Of those with low incomes (under $3000), only 3 percent used such facilities.

In view of these findings, it is not clear how expansion of child-care facilities will affect the AFDC mother's entry into the labor force. But

[18] For a discussion of this issue, see Alvin L. Schorr, *Poor Kids* (New York: Basic Books, 1965).

whether or not the number of such mothers who become economically self-sufficient increases markedly, the provision of more good facilities for child care should help both the mothers and the children who use them. It may reasonably be expected that such services will ease the tensions of work for these women and reduce their absences from the job. They will also improve the situation of the children, who will benefit socially and educationally from organized programs of care.

part 3 THE LOCATION OF ECONOMIC ACTIVITY

Declining economic activity in the central city is often cited as a major component of the crisis in our cities. While virtually all central cities are losing employment and population relative to the suburban ring, most are not declining in absolute terms. Of the 45 metropolitan areas with more than 250,000 people in the central city, 21 actually lost population between 1950 and 1970. Thus less than one-half of the major metropolitan areas experienced a decline in population. Particularly vulnerable are older central cities which typically have a high population density. For example, of the 12 central cities that had more than 10,000 people living on each square mile, 11 lost population. The forces responsible for the absolute decline of some central cities and the relative decline of most are analyzed in this part.

In the first selection, Michael A. Goldberg synthesizes the literature on the relationship between land values and distance from the central city. To a large extent the transportation system determines this relationship. Land values and the accessibility provided by the transportation system influence the location of economic activity.

Edgar M. Hoover summarizes these influences and outlines some of the dynamic forces affecting the distribution of economic activity in our major metropolitan areas. In the concluding article, George Sternlieb suggests that the central city will soon be devoid of economic purpose unless one is fostered through public policy. Such a policy, according to Sternlieb, might reduce the rate of economic growth but is essential if all citizens are to have an opportunity for meaningful and useful lives.

9
TRANSPORTATION, URBAN LAND VALUES AND RENTS: A Synthesis
Michael A. Goldberg

The present study investigates the relationship between transportation, land values, rents and price elasticities of demand. The analysis draws heavily from earlier works, in the hope of providing a synthesis which overcomes the weaknesses of each contribution and maximizes the strengths inherent in them all.

The paper builds upon a framework introduced by Robert Murray Haig in 1926.[1] The basic concept put forward and elaborated upon by Haig was the interrelation between transportation and urban land values. Given a general transportation improvement, *all other things being constant*, there would result a decline in aggregate land values. This idea has attracted attention almost continually since 1926. The most recent writings on the subject are those of William Alonso[2] and Lowden Wingo.[3]

* The author wishes to express his gratitude to Professor Richard U. Ratcliff for comments and suggestions and above all for an understanding of the continuum we have come to call human knowledge.

[1] Robert Murray Haig, *Major Economic Factors in Metropolitan Growth and Arrangement* (New York: Regional Plan of New York and Its Environs, 1927).
[2] William Alonso, *Location and Land Use: Toward a General Theory of Land Rent* (Cambridge, Mass.: Harvard University Press, 1964).
[3] Lowden Wingo, *Transportation and Urban Land* (Washington, D.C.: Resources for the Future, 1961).

SOME ANTECEDENTS

By Haig's own admission,[4] his ideas can be traced back as far as Johann von Thunen in 1826.[5] A relatively complete and brief discussion of the history of these ideas can be found in Alonso's study.[6]

The Haig argument.[7]   The basic idea underlying Haig's reasoning is that a general improvement in transportation will tend to lower aggregate rents in a metropolitan area, *ceteris paribus*.

> Site rents and transportation costs are vitally connected through their relationship to the friction of space. While transportation overcomes friction, site rentals plus transportation costs represent the social cost of what friction remains. Obviously, an improvement in transportation, other things remaining the same, will mean a reduction in friction and consequently, the diminution of the aggregate sum of site rentals. The two elements, transportation costs and site rentals, may be termed the "costs of friction."

The costs of friction are the driving mechanism in Haig's theory of urban form and land use specialization. He goes on to suggest an hypothesis relating the costs of friction, and therefore indirectly transportation facilities, to the form of an urban area.

> It may be suggested as an hypothesis that the layout of a metropolis—the assignment of activities to areas—tends to be determined by a principle which may be termed the minimizing of the costs of friction. An economic activity in seeking a location finds that, as it approaches the center, site rents increase and transportation costs decline. As it retreats from the center, site rents decline and transportation costs increase. The sum of the two items, the costs of friction, is not constant, however.

Richard U. Ratcliff lends support to Haig's discussion of transportation costs and land values and rents and gives the following conclusions regarding the impact of the automobile on central business district rents. "Thus, the spread in the use of private automobiles has, in fact, tended to reduce site rents in central business locations by making outlying retail centers more generally accessible."[8]

Consider 2 extreme simplified models of cities. The first is an ideal state where there is no cost whatsoever in moving among the subareas of the urban region. In such a case no site has any particular advantage over any other as all sites are equally close.[9] The axioms of perfect

---

[4] Haig, *op. cit.*, p. 32.

[5] Johann von Thunen, *Der isolierte Staat in Beziehung auf Landwirtschaft und National Okonomie* (1826).

[6] Alonso, *op. cit.*, pp. 1–15.

[7] Haig, *op. cit.*, p. 39.

[8] Richard U. Ratcliff, *Urban Land Economics* (New York: McGraw-Hill, 1949), p. 372.

[9] Richard U. Ratcliff, "Commentary: On Wendt's Theory of Land Values," *Land Economics* (November 1957), p. 361. It should be noted here that this comment was in response to one of a series of

competition are satisfied: There are numerous sellers, selling an undifferentiated product (urban sites), and there is perfect information since people can travel among all the subareas without cost. In such a case perfect competition leads to an equilibrium where no firm (seller of land) earns any economic rent. This follows from the competition among sellers to attract buyers, which leads to a lowering of the price of the product (the site) until price equals marginal cost. If we assume the land is unimproved and lying on a homogeneous plain, then marginal cost is zero as is economic rent and site rent. This is a highly dispersed city.

At the opposite extreme, consider an urban region where transportation costs are prohibitively high. The cost of moving from home to work, and from home to shopping center is excessively high unless the work site-home site-shop site are coincident in location. In such a city, there exists only 1 site, and therefore a monopoly situation. Here, the seller makes monopoly profits and charges rents which are as high as the traffic will bear. The shape of this city will be a point. All activity will be concentrated at this point, with no activity away from it. This contrasts with the random distribution over the plain.

These abstractions from reality are extreme, with real cities falling somewhere between these two models. Cities which grew up under the influence of the automobile lie nearer the dispersed city, while those which grew up with older transportation technologies are closer to the point city. Los Angeles is an example of the former while New York and the older Eastern cities exemplify the latter.

The implication of the Haig hypothesis for city growth and structure is that people will locate so as to minimize total payments for rents and transportation. Again Ratcliff notes: "Each land use seeks the lowest total of rent and transportation costs. The opportunity to minimize the total is limited for any one land use by the competition of lower uses, which are willing to bid up to the savings in transportation costs that the use of the site will permit them."[10] This line of reasoning and its implications may be conveniently summed up again by Robert Murray Haig: "Of two cities, otherwise alike, the better planned, from the economic point of view, is the one in which the costs of friction are less. This will mean that the aggregate site rents are less or that the transportation is superior—or both."[11]

---

three articles by Professor Paul F. Wendt. Wendt criticized the Haig-Ely-Dorau-Ratcliff hypothesis concerning the relationship between land values and transportation improvements. The present articles overcomes some of Wendt's criticisms while being consistent with both Haig and Alonso. For a brief discussion of the issues in the Wendt-Ratcliff debate see Alonso, *op. cit.*, pp. 6–15.

[10] *Op. cit.*, p. 372.

[11] Haig, *op. cit.*, p. 39.

A NEW DIMENSION: ALONSO AND SIZE OF SITE

A new parameter was interjected into the above discussion with the publication of William Alonso's book, *Location and Land Use: Toward a General Theory of Land Rent.*[12] Alonso makes one very significant criticism of previous work in urban land economics: that the spatial aspects of the size of the site were ignored. The individual not only chooses a residential location so as to minimize the sum of rent and transportation costs but also to maximize the size of the site. Accordingly, there are three considerations in the location decision: rent, transportation costs (or accessibility), and size of the site. Individuals reach a locational equilibrium determined by their relative weights upon rent, site size, and accessibility or travel costs.

Alonso introduces the size of the site explicitly into the argument. The failure to recognize different land absorption rates at different locations was certainly a weakness of earlier work. This shortcoming had the effect of making previous location theories aspatial since locations were considered as points without any spatial extension.[13] Alonso says: "If the only criteria for residential location are accessibility to the centre and the minimizing of the costs of friction, and considerations of the size of the site are excluded, all residences would be clustered around the center of the city at a very high density."[14]

RECONCILING THE DIFFERENCES: THE SYNTHESIS

The hypothesis is: A general improvement in transportation, *ceteris paribus*, will result in a decline in *economic* rents in the aggregate. This, however, need not and probably will not lead to a decline in real property and site rents in the aggregate.[15] To examine this hypothesis requires first an intuitive understanding of the impact of transportation improvements on the urban environments. To clarify the argument assume a classical homogeneous featureless plain.

[12] Alonso, *op. cit.*

[13] See Alonso; also Michael A. Goldberg, *Intrametropolitan Industrial Location: Plant Size and the Theory of Production* (Berkeley, Calif.: Center for Real Estate and Urban Economics, University of California, 1969).

[14] Alonso, *op. cit.*, pp. 8–9.

[15] Economic rent is defined as the surplus over and above a "normal profit." A normal profit in turn can be thought of as the return accruing to the entrepreneur under perfect competition. In such a circumstance a normal profit would be equal to the going wage rate. Property or land rents are factor payments. They are payments for the use of an input to the productive process (or the personal utility function). Rent is the payment for land in this sense just as interest and dividends are payments for capital. This is the more common use of the concept of rent. Historically, however, the two concepts are related because the return to a gift of nature like land was considered economic rent due to the monopoly position in which the land holder was placed by the location of the land.

Such a simple conception of terrain allows the use of simple tools from geometry to illustrate the argument. Defining an urban region is difficult. A region might consist of all those places within M miles of the CBD of the city. Another variant of this definition of a region might be all those places within t minutes driving time of the same CBD. Finally, a slightly more general form of the same concept might be to include all those areas within a given accessibility band of the CBD. Accessibility has the advantage of being a useful concept under the more realistic assumption of a multinucleated urban realm. For present purposes accessibility is defined as:

$$A_1 = \sum_{j=1}^{j} \frac{\sum_{k=1}^{k} E_j^k}{D_{ij}^{\beta}}$$

where A_i is the accessibility of the ith area, E_j^k is the amount of activity k occurring in the j, D_{ij} is the distance (time, linear or otherwise) from i to j, and b is a coefficient representing the "friction of space." This gives us a measure of access to all the activities in the region suitably discounted by the distance from the subject area, i.

The simplest linear distance variant of the above definition of a region implies that, for a city with a 1-mile radius, there are 3.1 square miles of land area. Proportional changes in the radius of the city result in geometric increases in the area of the city and therefore its supply of land. Ratcliff observes the same relationship.

> Within 1 mile of the center there are 3.1 square miles of land in the circle; if you double the distance to 2 miles from the center, the area in the circle increases to a total of 12.6 square miles. With a 3-mile radius, the area is 28.3 square miles. Thus a city can expand to nine times the area with an extension of its boundaries to only three times the distance to the center.[16]

It is possible to relate improvements in the transportation system to increases in the effective size of the city region which is the relevant focus for a study of the land market and land value patterns. Assuming that people are unwilling to travel more than 30 minutes to work, we can define an urban region and therefore an urban land market as being all those places within 30 minutes of the city center. Assume that without any transportation improvements this 30-minute limit corresponds to a city with a 5-mile radius at rush hour. Such a city would have a land area of 78.54 square miles. Now assume the introduction of a transportation improvement (perhaps a beltway-radial system)

[16] Richard U. Ratcliff, *Real Estate Analysis* (New York: McGraw-Hill, 1949), p. 44.

which increases the distance travelled in 30 minutes at rush hour to 10 miles. The effective area of the city and land market would now be 314.16 square miles or a fourfold increase. The resulting increase in the supply of land (a 235.62-square-mile increment) has a very powerful impact on the structure of land prices in the urban area, and therefore on housing costs and rents as well. Competition is greatly increased among the sellers of land or land services, and prices, rents, and economic rents must decline.

Implicit in this result is the absolutely essential assumption that the price elasticity of demand for land is unitary. If it is not . . . then it need not follow that price per lot and rents must fall. If price falls under a price elastic demand, lot size will increase and total expenditure on land will also increase. Thus, price or rent per fixed unit area will decline with a transportation improvement but aggregate rents need not (nor must aggregate land values). The only quantity which must decline because of increased competition is aggregate *economic rent*.

10
THE EVOLVING FORM AND ORGANIZATION OF THE METROPOLIS
Edgar M. Hoover

I. PRINCIPAL LOCATION FACTORS

The first step in building a useful conceptual framework for understanding urban spatial patterns is to sort out the multifarious location factors that influence the preferences and placement of specific activities or types of decision units. What is suggested below is a logical way of reducing these factors to a manageably small number of groups.

"Given" locations

As already intimated, there are some kinds of locations within an urban area which are not determined primarily by where the other activities of the area are. Actually there are two distinct bases for exogenous determination of locations in an urban area.

For some kinds of activities, certain topographical or other natural site features are essential, which means that the lay of the land narrows down the choice to one or a very small number of locations. Ports for water traffic illustrate this, and there are some urban areas where the topography limits jet airport sites almost as drastically. In the past, defense considerations played a major part in locating the center of the city and the city itself. Localized recreational features such as beaches also illustrate this kind of factor, and in a few urban areas extractive

Reprinted with omissions from Harvey S. Perloff and Lowdon Wingo, Jr., eds., *Issues in Urban Economics* by permission of The Johns Hopkins Press for Resources for the Future, Inc., 1968.

industries (mainly mining) occur and are, of course, limited to certain special sites.

There is a further type of exogenously determined location where the independent influence arises not from site features so much as from the fact that the activity in question is primarily concerned with contact with the outside world. Not just water ports but all kinds of terminal and interarea transport activities come under this head. Since there are great economies of scale in interregional transport and in terminal handling of goods, the urban area's gateways to and from the outside world constitute a set of focal points whose locations within the area help to determine—rather than just being determined by—the other activities of the area. This does not, of course, mean that such terminal locations (unless constrained by natural site features) are absolutely and permanently unresponsive to the changing pattern of other activities in the area served: Such terminals are from time to time shifted to improve local accessibility or to make way for more insistent claimants for space. But the terminal locations do, in dynamic terms, play a primarily active role in shaping the pattern, and are to be viewed as part of the basic framework around which other activities are fitted.

Finally, in practice, we can generally take as given the focus of *maximum overall accessibility* within the urban area. If we think of that as, for example, the place at which all the people of the area could assemble with the least total man-miles of travel, it is simply the median center of population, depending upon where all of the various types of residence are located. But travel is cheaper and faster along developed routes, and the cost and layout of these are affected by scale (traffic volume) and topography. So, evaluated in terms of travel cost and time, the focal maximum-access point can be regarded as a quite stable datum, even though the extent and importance of its access advantage over other points can change radically. We find in major American urban areas that, despite great overall growth and far-reaching change and redistribution of activities, the focal point in this sense has usually shifted only a relatively short distance over periods measured in decades and generations, and that the earlier central foci are well within what we currently recognize as the central business district.

This concept of a single, most central focal point in an urban area is then significant and useful in developing simplified bases for understanding the overall pattern. Obviously it has limitations, some of which will be discussed later in this paper. In the first place, there is in principle a variety of distinguishable central points of this sort, depending on what kinds of people or things we are imagining to be assembled with a minimum of total expense or effort. The employed workers of the area are not distributed in quite the same pattern as the total population, the shopping population, the school-attending population, the office workers, the industrial blue-collar workers, the theater-going or the library-using population; there might be a different optimum location from the standpoint of access for each of these types of people. Where goods rather than people are moving (as for example in the case of wholesale activity or production serving local needs such as daily newspapers or bread) the transport conditions are different and this may again mean a different optimum-access point. Finally, we have to recognize that, in varying degrees, the concept of one single point serving as the origin or destination for all flows of a specified type may be unrealistic and defensible only as a convenient fiction. Thus, if we identify some central point as having best access to the homes of the entire clerical office force of an urban area, this does not imply that all offices should logically be concentrated there. What it does imply is that, solely from the standpoint of commuting access for the clerical workers and ignoring claims of alternative space uses, it would make sense for the density of clerical employment to peak at that point. The significance of the focal point is determined, then, by the extent to which the activity involved is dependent upon (1) concentration in a single small district, and (2) access to the flow in question.

Access linkages

Since the function of an urban concentration is to facilitate contacts, the most important class of location factors shaping in the spatial pattern involves the advantage of physical proximity as measured by the money and/or time saved. This applies to cases in which such costs are substantially increased by added distance. Where they are not, they have nothing to do with urban concentration. For example, information in a widening sense (now including not only the printed word but sounds and computer signals and various types of pictures) can now be transmitted electronically over long distances just as quickly as over short distances, and sometimes just as cheaply to the user. This kind of contact, then, does not in itself depend upon, nor help to maintain or explain, intraurban concentration.

Most relevant to the urban pattern are kinds of access for which costs are high and increase very rapidly with distance within the intraurban range of distances (ranging from next door to a few dozen miles). Access involving human travel belongs par excellence to this category. Human beings require more elaborate and expensive vehicles (in dollars per ton of freight) than almost anything else. And, in particular, the time cost becomes generally even more important than the actual transport cost.

For people and things alike, the time cost to the passenger or the owner of the cargo is essentially an "opportunity cost," measured in terms of what useful services the person or thing being transported might otherwise be yielding. For commodities, we can measure this crudely in terms of interest on the investment represented by the value of the goods tied up in transit. For human beings, a commonly used yardstick is the rate of earnings while at work.[1] Thus, a man who earns $5.00 an hour would consider the time cost of a half-hour trip to be $2.50. This rate of time cost equals the accrual of interest (at 5 percent per annum) on an investment of about $880,000. So, calculated on that basis, human freight carries a time cost equivalent to that of a commodity worth at least $300 an ounce—perhaps not "more precious than rubies," but somewhere in the range between gold and diamonds.

The locational importance of an access linkage—that is, the economic advantage of proximity—depends not only on how much the trip costs but also on how often the trip is made. Access to one's regular work place is likely to be a weighty consideration because it generally involves at least 5 round trips a week. It becomes somewhat less important if one shifts from a 6 day to a 5 day or shorter working week.

In the case of shopping trips, the costs of the trip should be related to the amount of the purchase order to get a measure of the proximity advantage. Thus, if 10 minutes' additional travel in each direction (20 minutes round trip) is valued at, say, $1.50, it would be worthwhile making the extra travel in order to save $1.50. That is 15 percent on the purchase of $10 worth of groceries, but only 1 percent on the purchase of a $100 television set. We could infer that it is logical to travel 10 times as far to shop for television sets as to shop for groceries, if the amounts of purchases stated are representative and if the price differentials among shopping places are about the same for both types of goods. Here again, only time costs are considered; but this illustration illustrates the wide variations in the strength of the proximity incentive, even within the limits of one category of relationship, like retail trade.

The various kinds of access linkage that tie together the urban complex can be meaningfully classified in a good many ways: for example, by mode of transport or communication, or according to whether the incentive toward proximity is thought to influence predominantly the location of the sender or that of the receiver of whatever is being

[1] This way of evaluating time cost is used for lack of anything better. We need more information on what value people of various sorts place upon time spent in transit under various circumstances.

transported. Perhaps as useful a classification as any other can be based on the distinction between households and other decision units—that is, between residential and nonresidential activities.

Access among nonresidential activities.   This involves in part interindustry transactions such as those recorded in an input-output table. Business firms have an incentive to locate with good access to their local suppliers and their local business customers. To that extent, an interindustry transactions table gives us an idea of the relative volume and importance of the flows of goods and services between establishments[2] of the same and different industries, though this does not go very far toward measuring the relative strengths of locational attraction. Nor do these input-output figures take account of some strong business proximity ties that do not directly involve transactions at all. Thus, local branch offices or outlets of a firm are presumably located with an eye to maintaining good access to the main local office, while at the same time avoiding overlap of the sublocal territories served by the branches (for example, the individual supermarkets of a chain or branch offices of a bank). There are strong access ties between the central office of a corporation and its main research laboratory, involving the frequent going and coming of highly paid personnel, but no entries in the input-output tables.[3]

Access among residential activities (interhousehold).   A significant proportion of journeys from homes are to the homes of others. Such trips are by nature almost exclusively social and thus involve people linked by family ties or closely similar tastes and interests. This suggests that the value of "interhousehold access" can also be expressed fairly accurately in terms of homogeneity preference—like seeks like. As we shall see later, however, the pressures toward neighborhood or "microspatial" homogeneity include a good many other factors in addition to simple access.

Access between residential and nonresidential activities.   This type of access is far and away the most conspicuous in the urban flow pattern.

---

[2] Although interindustry transaction (input-output) tables are organized in crosstabulations of *industries,* the basic unit is the industrial plant or other *establishment,* and interestablishment transactions within the same industry are shown in the diagonal cells of the table.

[3] It would be useful, I think, to try to construct tables showing the transport and communication charges incurred in the transaction flows between each pair of industries. This could lead to a still more useful cross-tabulation in which such charges were expressed as coefficients on a per-mile, per-unit-of-output basis. These coefficients would roughly measure the strength of spatial attraction between pairs of industries attributable to transport and communication costs. On this point, as on many others in the present paper, I am indebted to my colleague Professor David Houston for stimulating comments and discussion.

The entire labor force, with insignificant exceptions, is concerned with making the daily journey to work as quick and painless as possible. Such trips are much the largest single class of personal journeys within any urban area.[4] In addition, the distribution of goods and services at retail makes mutual proximity an advantage for both the distributors and the customers; some attention has already been paid here to the factors determining the relative strength of the attraction in the case of different types of goods and services. Trips to school, and for cultural and recreational purposes, make up most of the rest of the personal trip pattern. There is mutual advantage of proximity throughout: The nonresidential activities dealing with households are most advantageously placed when they are close to concentrations of population, and at the same time residential sites are preferred (other things being equal) when they are in convenient access to jobs, shopping districts, schools, and other destinations.

The way in which these mutual attractions shape the locational pattern of activities within the urban area depends not so much on the strength of the attraction as on the degree to which the nonresidential activity in question is concentrated at relatively few points (since almost any such activity is much less evenly diffused over the area than residence is). At one extreme, there are nonresidential activities that need access to a large fraction of the households of the urban area, but that are confined to one location, and perhaps one establishment or facility. Thus, a visit to a large department store or some kind of specialty shop, or to a main library, or to the opera, or to attend university classes may mean, in many urban areas, a visit to one specific location, without alternatives. All such trips within the area have a single common destination focus and the attraction, from the household side, is centripetal, or at least monocentric. From the standpoint of the nonresidential activity in question, optimum access means the choice of a point of minimum total travel time for all of the interested households in the area.

At the opposite extreme are activities not subject to any compelling scale economies or other economics of concentration, which can therefore have a dispersed or many-centered pattern. Drugstores, barbershops, branch banking offices, and the like are basically neighborhood-serving rather than catering to a broad citywide clientele. A good

---

[4] For relevant reference material, see J. R. Meyer, J. F. Kain, and M. Wohl, *The Urban Transportation Problem* (Cambridge, Mass.: Harvard University Press, 1965), and Louis K. Loewenstein, *The Location of Residences and Work Places in Urban Areas* (New York: Scarecrow Press, 1965). Also, for a primarily bibliographical survey of the whole question of access, see Gunnar Olsson, *Distance and Human Interaction: A Review and Bibliography*, Bibliography Series, No. 2 (Philadelphia: Regional Science Research Institute, 1965).

location is simply one in which there is a sufficient amount of business within a short distance. And the attraction of such activities to the householder is within rather than between neighborhoods, being measured in blocks rather than in miles. The gradient of access advantage is a local one, replicated many times over in all parts of the area, rather than a single one peaking at some one point.

Agglomerative factors

Access considerations involve a mutual attraction between complementary parties: stores and customers, employees and firms, pupils and schools. But there are also economic incentives favoring the concentration and clustering of identical or similar units of activity. The simplest case of this is perhaps that of scale economies. A large electric power plant is more efficient than a smaller one. A large store can, in addition to possible cost savings, provide more variety and thus enhance its attractiveness to buyers. As already suggested, some kinds of activities (such as opera performances) are subject to scale economies to the extent that only in the largest cities can more than one establishment be supported. Business corporations as a rule find that they can best concentrate their research laboratories at one location, and the same applies somewhat more obviously to their central offices.

A different and more subtle case involves the basis for clustering of many similar business firms or institutions. The classic case is the mid-Manhattan garment center, but analogous complexes are found in every city, such as "automobile rows," the financial district, and various types of specialized wholesale districts.[5]

If we inquire more deeply into the reasons for these clusterings we find that the establishments in the cluster are sharing some common advantage that is generally a pool of especially suitable labor, a variety of specialized business services, or the congregation of customers seeking to compare a variety of offerings. Sometimes two or all three of these kinds of external economy are involved. If the individual small firms in the cluster have good enough access to these external advantages, they themselves can specialize narrowly in functions not requiring large-scale operation, while at the same time having passed on to them the economies of a large labor market, a large concentration of buyers, and specialized business services produced on an efficiently large scale.

It appears, then, that these external economies of certain clustered

[5] Cf. Robert M. Lichtenberg, *One-Tenth of a Nation,* New York Metropolitan Regional Study (Cambridge, Mass.: Harvard University Press, 1960) for a penetrating analysis of the "external-economy" industries in New York.

activities are really based on two factors previously discussed: access, and economies of scale. What is new is the extension of the concept of scale economies to labor markets and shopping comparison markets as operating mechanisms.

Finally, the clustering of like activities can reflect immediate environmental interdependence. A site has value according to its access but also according to its physical features and to the character of its immediate surroundings. Neighborhood character in terms of cleanliness, smells, noise, traffic congestion, public safety, variety interest, and general appearance is important in attracting some kinds of use and repelling others. Prestige types of residence or business are of course particularly sensitive to this kind of advantage, which often is more important than any access consideration as such. A high-income householder may be willing to lengthen his work journey greatly for the sake of agreeable surroundings.

As has been suggested earlier, the usual effect of this type of consideration is to make neighborhoods more homogeneous within themselves, and more unlike other neighborhoods—a tendency toward areal specialization by uses, or segregation in the broad sense. With few exceptions, a given type of activity finds advantage in being in a neighborhood devoted to reasonably similar kinds of uses, and disadvantage in being in violent contrast to the neighborhood pattern. Zoning controls and planned street layouts play a part in reinforcing this tendency.

Competition for space: the cost of sites

I have cataloged above the various kinds of locational pulls and pushes that affect activities in an urban area. Most of the relationships mentioned are pulls—they involve a mutual locational attraction among complementary or similar units of activity. This reflects the underlying rationale of a city as a device effecting close contact and interaction on a grand scale.

But every land use needs some space or elbow room on which to operate, and the sites with best or environmental features command a high scarcity value. The market mechanism works (albeit imperfectly like most markets) to allocate locations to uses and users who can exploit them to best advantage as measured by what they are willing to bid for their use.

Simplification and synthesis

The various determinants of location in an urban area have been discussed above. In a really complex analysis, each could be broken down much further. But we seek simplification. It appears that basically there are just three kinds of considerations that determine the relative desirability of locations for particular decision units such as households or business establishments. These are (1) access, (2) environmental characteristics, and (3) cost. They reflect the fact that the user of a site is really involved with it in 3 different ways. He occupies it, as resident or producer, and is thus concerned with its site and neighborhood, or immediate environmental qualities. He and other persons and goods and services move between this site and others; he is therefore concerned with its convenience of access to other places. Finally, he has to pay for its use and is therefore concerned with its cost.

Ruthless simplification along these lines makes possible the useful step of building a conceptual model of the spatial structure of an urban economy. For example, in such a model we can reduce the complex factor of access to the simple form of access to a single given focal point, as if all intraurban journeys were to or from downtown and all shipments of goods also passed through downtown. We can in the interests of maximum simplicity even assume that the cost of transportation within the urban area is directly proportional to airline distance. Access is then measured simply in radial distance from the center.

We can assume away all differentiation of sites with respect to topography, amenity, and environmental advantage. These two simplifications also imply ignoring the manifold types of external-economy effects and environmental attractions and repulsions that have been discussed. In effect, we envisage each type of activity as *independently* attracted (by access considerations) toward the urban center; the only interdependence among the locations of the various activities arises, then, from the fact that they are bidding against one another for space.

It is also appropriate to develop a condensed classification of activities. No 2 households, factories, or other decision units are exactly alike in their location preferences, but they can be grouped into more or less homogeneous classes on the basis of similarity in access/space trade-off. Among households, for example, it appears from empirical studies that income level and family structure (presence or absence of young children) are the principal determinants of this trade-off.

With the above types of simplification as well as with others, it is possible to develop more or less systematic theories or frameworks of analysis for urban spatial patterns. Some of these patterns will be taken up here. It is sufficient here to note that most such models are partial in the sense that they attempt to explain or predict the location of 1 type of activity in terms of its adjustment to given or assumed locations of the other activities, including transportation services. Thus, a retailing location model may analyze the way in which retail stores locate in response to the advantages of access to the homes of consumers, a residential location model may analyze the way in which residences locate in response to the desire to shorten the journey to work, and so on.

II. GROWTH AND CHANGE

The remainder of this paper will focus on the dynamics of urban spatial structure, which up to this point has come in for only incidental attention. Most of our real problems involve dislocations (imperfect adjustments) which arise because of some change. Urban areas grow in size, they age, their populations achieve higher living standards and changed consumption patterns, the technology of production, transport, and exchange develops, and public action plays new roles.

We can start off by trying to isolate the effects of certain sources of change that seem relatively simple, one dimensional, and predictable. One of these is growth in size, with the related phenomenon of aging. Another is rising income levels as such, also a trend that we have become accustomed to taking for granted.

Growth

Some kinds of changes in spatial patterns in an urban area stem simply from increased size, independent of higher levels of income or technology. One appropriate way to shed light on the structural implications of pure size is to make cross-sectional comparisons among urban areas of different populations in the same country at the same time.

What differences, then, do we find associated with larger city size as such? Some of the most obvious ones can be rationalized in terms of the basic density gradient model of an urban area. Increased total size has both intensive and extensive impacts: the central densities or other measures of peak central intensity rise; in other parts of the area the intensity of land use increases. Residential densities in any given zone increase, except that the central nonresidential crater expands. Increases in density are greatest, percentage-wise, at the outer fringe of urban development.

We also envisage (as impacts of growth per se) the successive pushing out and widening of the various more or less concentric zones of activity, already discussed in the context of the original Burgess model. An increase in the length of all types of journeys and hauls of goods is likewise to be expected.

But as such journeys and shipments become lengthier and more expensive with expansion of the area, there are partially compensatory adjustments, representing responses to the increased incentive to keep travel time and cost from being excessive. Subcenters for various single activities or groups of activities play an increasing role in a larger urban area, because the total market in the area, for more and more kinds of goods and services, comes to be big enough to support two or more separate production or service centers at an efficient scale rather than just one. This is clearly pictured in the intraurban central-place schema. Thus, the hierarchy of central places in a small town consists of just a single order of activities, all concentrated on Main Street. In a larger place there may be two levels in the central-place hierarchy: downtown activities and neighborhood subcenters. In a still larger urban area there will be more levels: some kinds of activity being replicated in dozens or even hundreds of individual neighborhoods, others being replicated in a handful of big shopping centers serving a whole sector of the area, and still others serving the whole area from a single location (which, in the simplified central-place schema, is, of course, the central business district).[6]

It would appear, then, that growth as such helps to account for the flattening of density gradients that has characteristically shown up as a trend in our cities—though there are, of course, other and perhaps even more important reasons as well. And this growth impact, involving the development of more and more kinds of subcenters of nonresidential activity, comes in response to the enlarged total market in the area as a whole and the desire to keep length of journeys from increasing too much.

Finally, the larger size of the area, with its expanded and more variegated manpower, services, materials, and markets, provides the basis for an increasing number of noncentral-place subcenters as well—that is, off-center concentrations of nonresidential activity that are not simply oriented to the neighborhood consumer market but may serve the whole area and outside markets as well.

Thus, the picture of changing patterns in an urban area that is simply getting more populous, assuming no changes in the state of technology or level of income, is this: Development proceeds both vertically (that is, in terms of more intensive use of space) and horizontally (in terms

[6] There is plenty of empirical verification of the smaller relative importance of the central business district as a travel destination in larger cities. It appears further that the effect is more pronounced for nonwork journeys than for journeys to work. Cf. for example, Richard B. Andrews, *Urban Growth and Development* (New York: Simmons-Boardman, 1962), ch. 3, citing relevant evidence from U.S. Bureau of Public Roads, *Parking Guide for Cities* (Washington, D.C.: U.S. Government Printing Office, 1956), table 26, p. 29; D. L. Foley, "The Daily Movement of Population into Central Business Districts," *American Sociological Review*, 17 (October 1952), p. 541; and U.S. Census of Business.

of use of more space). Each specialized zone of activities widens and moves outward, encroaching on its outer neighbor and giving way to its inner neighbor. New types of central-place activities arise in the central area. The variety of types of activity and occupancy increases. Off-center foci of both central-place type and other activities increase in number, size, diversity, and importance. The gradient of residential densities becomes higher but flatter. The average length of journeys and total amount of travel and internal goods transfer increases, but not as much as it would if all nonresidential activity remained as highly concentrated at the center as it was originally. The pattern of transport flows becomes much more complex, with more criss-crossing and more nonradial traffic.

With the increased variety of activities, occupations, and styles of life represented in a larger area, and and the proliferation of more and more orders and types of subcenters, it is clear that size of an urban area is associated with a more elaborately differentiated pattern of land uses: more spatial division of labor and specialization of functions. This increased heterogeneity in the whole fosters, somewhat paradoxically at first sight, increased homogeneity within individual neighborhoods and other subareas, or segregation in the broad sense of the term. We have considered earlier the various pressures for microscale homogeneity within urban areas, and these pressures can operate to a much greater degree in the framework of a larger and more varied community complex. One manifestation of this is the magnitude of the problem of de facto racial segregation of schools (that is, reflecting neighborhood composition) in larger cities. Another is the problem (again, most in evidence in the larger cities) of accommodating intensely cohesive specialized business concentrations such as the Manhattan garment district and urban wholesale produce markets which are highly resistant to piecemeal moving or adjustment. A third manifestation is the problem (also more in evidence in the largest metropolitan areas) of political and economic conflict between the main central city and surrounding suburbs and the resistance of the latter to merger or basic coordination with the central city or with one another.

Thus, it appears that many of the most pressing problems of our larger urban areas today, ranging from traffic congestion to racial discord, city/suburb conflict, and the fiscal crises of central cities, can be traced in some part to sheer size. They are implicit in even the extremely simplified models of urban structure already discussed in this paper. Still more broadly, it is clear that larger agglomerations, as such, raise increasingly challenging problems of divergence of private from social (and local from overall) costs and benefits, in view of the intensified proximity impacts involving scarcity of space, pollution of water and air, environmental nuisances, and generally increased interdependence of interests. These problems are part of the quid pro quo for the economic and social advantages of greater diversity of contact and opportunity: the rationale of the city.

This hypothetical and mainly deductive picture of trends of change in a single growing area conforms very closely, as would be expected, with what we observe empirically in a cross-sectional comparison of urban areas of different sizes in one country at one time. Moreover, we recognize in the picture a great many familiar features corresponding to observed historical and current trends. We can infer that simple growth plays a part in accounting for them and can be expected to exert a similar influence in the future.

But in some ways the picture does not fit. Conspicuously unrealistic in relation to observed trends, for example, is the implied rise in the central density parameter of the residential density gradient. As we have seen, this figure has characteristically fallen off in the present century, at least in urban areas in the more developed countries. Influences other than growth per se must account for that phenomenon and for a great many other features of the actual evolution of urban spatial patterns.

Aging

The relative age of urban settlements, urban populations, neighborhoods, and structures is always identified as a significant factor accounting for different spatial patterns of development and a wide range of urban problems, in both empirical and theoretical analyses. As noted earlier, Berry, Muth, Schnore, and other research leaders in this field assign the aging factor a prominent role. It has been shown that significant further insights into differences observed in cross-sectional comparisons can be gained when the relative ages of the areas compared are introduced as an explanatory variable, and reasons have been put forward for this effect.

Aging in the literal sense implies simply the effect of the passage of time upon something (for example, a person, a firm, a building, a city) that retains its identity. This is not so simple a variable as might at first sight appear. The age of a person is of course reckoned from his birth, and that of a structure from its construction. But structures can be modified and renovated. Mark Twain used to refer to his favorite "old" jackknife, which had had several new blades and several new handles. And how old is a city?

Pragmatically, the age of a city has been measured by arbitrarily assigning as its date of birth the date at which it attained some specified minimum population, such as 50,000. If, at the same time, we are considering the current population of the area as in independent variable, the relation between the 2, of course, reflects the average rate of growth per annum since the assigned "birth date." In other words, size, growth, and age are rather tightly interdependent; we have really 2 variables rather than 3.

In the case of a region's population, the age structure reflects not the age of the region but essentially the previous rate of growth. A fast-growing urban area almost inevitably has a relatively young population, whether the growth comes from high birth rates or from net inmigration, and a slow-growing area is characterized by a relatively old population.[7]

There is a somewhat less direct relationship between the previous or current growth rate of an urban area and the degree to which its physical and human resources are "behind the times" or overage in an economic sense. The latter depends on the extent to which renewal has failed to keep pace with changing needs and conditions. Growth and change have a dual effect on obsolescence in this context. They influence both (1) the need and incentive, and (2) the economic capabilities for renewal and expansion.

This is well brought out in Ira S. Lowry's penetrating critique of the filter-down theory of the housing market.[8] That theory assumes or implies that housing depreciates inexorably with the sheer passage of time. Under that hypothesis, if the upper-income groups who can afford it indulge a preference for new housing, the same units will then over the course of time be passed on, at ever lower prices, to occupants with lower and lower income levels, and each stratum of urban society except the top will have access to the housing given up by the stratum above. Something like this appears to occur in the used car market, and Lowry's contention is that the analogy has been unwarrantedly assumed to apply to the housing market as well. The filter-down process does not actually operate very effectively in housing, he shows, because housing quality deterioration is not by any means so closely related to age as is the case with automobiles. Instead, it depends primarily on maintenance, the structure itself being almost indefinitely lasting if adequately maintained. Unless the owner can afford maintenance, the housing rather quickly loses both habitability and economic value.

---

[7] Some qualifications must be noted here. Mortality differentials among areas are ignored, and there is also the special case of the fast-growing "Senior Citizens" communities so common in Florida and the Southwest. It remains true, however, that the average age of an area's work force is inversely related to the previous rate of growth of employment in the area.

[8] Ira S. Lowry, "Filtering and Housing Standards: A Conceptual Analysis," in *Land Economics,* 36, No. 4 (November 1960), pp. 362–370.

Affluence

We complacently assume, in looking to the future, that we shall be ever more numerous and also ever richer. The latter effect has been shown to be mainly contingent on continuous advances in technology rather than the mere accumulation of a larger stock of capital per man;[9] but barring world holocaust we feel that such advance is now built in and dependable in the more fortunate developed nations, if not elsewhere. Certain kinds of technological change we shall have to discuss later in terms of their specific effects on the urban spatial pattern; but some observations can be made on the effects on that pattern stemming from rising levels of economic well-being as such.

A higher family income in real terms means more to spend on both living space and transportation, 2 kinds of expenditure that we have already identified as peculiarly significant in shaping urban residential patterns. It means also more to spend on a wider variety of other goods and services (including public services), and finally the opportunity to take some of the gains in the form of leisure and in a broad range of pursuits that combine both consumption and "investment in human capital" aspects, such as education and cultural activity. Which of these avenues of increased benefit will be emphasized (that is, the relative income elasticities of different kinds of expenditure plus leisure) is largely culturally determined; it had to be gauged from empirical evidence on actual behavior, and can change greatly.

Mention has been made of the fact that cross-sectional evidence (comparing the behavior of the poor and the rich at any one time) strongly suggests that rising income levels will go into the purchase or rental of more residential space and more daily travel in such a way that lot sizes and the length of intraurban journeys will continue to increase while residential densities and slopes of density gradients will continue to fall in our urban areas.[10]

The extent to which this trend will continue, however, cannot be

[9] Cf. Edward F. Denison, *The Sources of Economic Growth* (New York: Committee for Economic Development, 1962).

[10] This empirically substantiated phenomenon is sometimes characterized as showing that "access is an inferior good"; that is, as people get richer, they buy less access rather than more, because they prefer to spend their added incomes on something else; just as a Southern farmer might be expected to buy less grits, molasses, and corn liquor (and more beefsteak and bonded bourbon) if he struck oil on his land. The analogy is slippery and a bit misleading, however. What does buying more access mean in the urban context? If it means investing in a car that will quicken or ease or cheapen the journey to work, then it is clear that the income elasticity is strongly positive, not negative. Automobiles are not yet an "inferior good" as the term is used in economic analysis. If buying more access means moving closer to the work place, then it really means *reducing* transport cost and time and either reducing residential space or paying more for it. A further complication in integrating the access/space trade-off into rigorous analysis in terms of price and income elasticities is that access has to be conceived as some kind of inverse (perhaps a reciprocal of travel cost), of which one very important component (time) is appropriately imputed at a price depending on income.

predicted with confidence. Some of the outward movement of upper-income groups may be associated with the income difference as such, though (as suggested earlier) we do not seem to have any convincing deductive demonstration that this should be so. Some is without doubt due to greater automobile ownership, and in that respect we may expect differentials among income groups will diminish. Some reflects a preference for new housing against old, and that factor might conceivably change with a shift in tastes or in refurbishment technology. And some reflects a flight from proximity of low-income (particularly Negro) newcomers to the central city, who have so far been rather tightly concentrated there by sociopolitical as well as economic barriers. Arrest and substantial redress of the threatening drift toward a contrast of slum cities and all-white suburbs might well have cumulative equalizing effects in the long run. So might a sufficiently drastic enhancing of downtown amenities, that might make the central area something more than a destination for necessary work and special shopping trips.

It is pretty clear that a partial cause of the relative decline of the central areas of cities is the trend toward increased leisure, at least as embodied in the prevalence of the 5-day work week and longer vacations. It is generally assumed that still further reduction of work hours will, on balance, heighten people's appetite for spacious home sites and neighborhoods, if only because they can spend more time around home. Here again, there is a conceivable offset in the possibility that the central areas of cities will offer more tempting recreational, cultural, and other off-hours opportunities than they do now. But the only conclusion that has a really firm presumptive basis is that increased leisure will continue to mean a greater number and diversity of nonwork trips, probably averaging longer in distance and time. One may surmise that access to the central areas of cities is likely to diminish in importance relative to other access, though perhaps not nearly as rapidly as has happened in the past few decades.

Technological progress

It is both difficult and artificial to make any sharp separation between the impact of affluence and the impact of technological change upon ways of life and the urban spatial pattern. Greater affluence comes from technological change, and at the same time this change provides new kinds of goods and services for the more affluent society to buy.[11]

[11] For what is perhaps the best recent discussion of the role of technology and rising income levels in reshaping urban spatial patterns, with some predictions of future developments, the reader is referred to Meyer, Kain, and Wohl, *op. cit.*, chap. 2. The authors emphasize that, although transport and communications development, and particularly the private automobile, have played a leading role in the relative decline of urban central areas, a number of other factors have also been in part

Specific attention needs to be given, however, to technological changes in transport and communication in view of their direct relation to change in spatial patterns. Indeed, the impact of mass ownership of automobiles (particularly in suburbanization of industry and population) has been so evident and so copiously analyzed that there would be little point in belaboring it here. Quasiuniversal car ownership is indeed a fait accompli, and perhaps we should devote more attention to the future implications of a termination of the changeover rather than to the fairly long-standing experience of the changeover itself. More positively, we need to conjecture as to the nature and spatial impacts of whatever is the next step in urban transport progress. Innovations have a way of responding to persistent economic pressure, and some of the pressures are already clear. Chief of these is the more and more obvious conflict between effective realization of the access advantages of individualized transport in terms of flexibility and convenience, and the high space requirements of such transport in its present form. Despite (or might we better say, because of?) the zeal of public parking authorities and freeway promoters, and the persistence of use of curb space for parking at quite nominal fees, the private automobile has, in at least some cities, worn its welcome to the center pretty thin. The possible implications of a more efficient system for bringing large numbers of people into close contract in agreeable surroundings appear large in terms of revitalization of the urban mechanism at its most vital spot.

Much has been made, in some speculations about the urban future, of the idea that with improved facilities for transport and particularly communication, distance means less and less, and people's contacts and access cease to be closely associated with space or location.[12] It is clear that the typical household and business has had and will find it increasingly easy to develop and maintain ties with households and firms in other regions, and that such contacts will continue to increase. It is less clear, however, that this really has much bearing on the future of intraurban spatial patterns with which we are concerned. A more likely presumption is that these growing external contacts are simply in addition to, and not substitutes for, local contacts, which are likewise

---

responsible. These include (in addition to the effects of more income and leisure already discussed here) new technologies in materials handling and distribution that have radically changed factory and store layouts, mechanized and automated data processing, and television as a means of both entertainment and communication.

[12] For a discussion that emphasizes the potential effects of reduced transport and communication costs in terms of diminished rationale for concentration, lower land values, and substitution of amenity for access as the major location factor, see Melvin M. Webber, "Order in Diversity: Community Without Propinquity," in Lowdon Wingo, Jr., ed., Cities and Space: The Future Use of Urban Land (Baltimore: The Johns Hopkins Press for Resources for the Future, 1963), pp. 23–56.

becoming more numerous, convenient, and multifarious. And there is no reason to expect a radical change in space relations unless and until some essentially distance-free communication obviates the necessity for existing important access desires that do depend on distance. The telephone did not do away with either the business office or the shopping trip, and it is doubtful that it diminished social travel. It is not easy to envisage any other device doing so in the foreseeable future.

11
THE CITY AS SANDBOX
George Sternlieb

How is one to write about a Newark or a Youngstown? All the adjectives have been used up, as have all the warnings of disaster and dire happenings in the streets if "they" don't come across, all the stories of soaring syphilis rates, TB gone uncared for, children made vegetables by lead poisoning, rats running rampant, high infant mortality, increasing numbers of unwed mothers, schools and hospitals and garbage departments that don't work, or won't, and so on. The cries of "wolf" have become so plentiful that we no longer listen and may even have begun to lose our fear of the beast itself. Yet there is something to be learned from a reshuffling of these dying embers of old rhetorical fires. For the Newarks of America are a foretaste of things to come, and if we want to understand the probable future that faces many of our older cities, then we will first have to get clear on what is happening—has already happened—in a place like Newark.

The bitterness of political conflict in such cities, and the intensity of their citizens' demand for an expansion of public services and public funding, provide a major clue. Of all the things people are prepared to fight over, their property interests are perhaps the most important, or at any rate the first; and of all a man's property interests, that in his job is usually the most important. Especially in cities like Newark, where the public sector has grown immensely while the private sector has decreased, the property interest which people possess—or seek—in their jobs gives local politics a peculiar importance. At one level, of course, such politics is precisely what it appears to be—an effort to promote the public interest. Thus, a housing program is an effort to provide housing for the poor; school reform aims at improving the achievement of pupils; a health program may be measured by its effect in raising the level of health and care. But beneath this there is another level of reality—that of who gets the action. Who will get (or keep) the job, the patronage? Who is going to build the new school? Who is going to make those sandwiches for the lunch program? Who is going to give out the contracts? As the size of the public sector grows, such questions become increasingly important and therefore increasingly divisive, for they engage the property interests of more and more people. Why should there be a fight for community control in Ocean Hill-Brownsville or Newark? There are many reasons, but one of the simplest and most important is that, for more and more people, new government programs are the only game in town; there is little else worth fighting for. Thus, for those who remain in the central city, fighting for such new programs is the only realistic response to the economic sterility of their environment.

EXPLOITED—OR MERELY DEFUNCT?

It is often said that our older central cities are essentially colonies —areas rich in resources which are systematically exploited by the suburban hinterlands. The residents of the latter drive into the city in the morning, use its services all day, and then creep out at night, taking with them much of the city's income and wealth. In one or another variant, this is the vision subscribed to by most city leaders, and they find it a satisfying one, for it implies that the "Golden Return" is at hand if only the city is given justice. The city's lack of such equity, which creates all its problems, is the result of a short-sighted plot by "outside" interests. Let there be a reallocation of wealth, and all will be well again.

The only problem with this notion is that it is untrue. The size of the constituency which lives outside the cities but still wants to preserve them at any cost grows smaller day by day. It is not exploitation that the core areas must fear; it is indifference and abandonment. The crisis of the cities is a crisis of function. *The major problem of the core areas of our cities is simply their lack of economic value.*

For a long time, the principal role of our inner cities was as a staging area for the floods of immigrants who came from Europe and elsewhere. Cities provided jobs, schools, and an infrastructure which helped earlier groups of immigrants move upward and outward. Although each of these groups left a residue of those who didn't make it, on the whole the city was an extremely successful processing center. Now that these great migrant flows have been reduced to a comparative trickle, the city has lost its *raison d'être*. Formerly the focal point for cheap labor, uniquely amassable there in great volume, it now finds that competition from welfare payments keeps its labor far from cheap and that its traditional jobs have been taken over by Puerto Rico, Formosa, Hong Kong, Singapore, and the like. As its current group of immigrants begins to make it, they too are moving out; but because no new groups are moving in, the city emigrés leave behind a vacuum.

America's major cities are unique in that *they are losing population.* Everywhere else—in Moscow or Buenos Aires or Calcutta—the flow of the agrarian poor off the land to the big city is at its flood stage. We have already gone through that phase; we are now on uncharted territory. To be sure, the Puerto Rican migration may from time to time increase, depending on relative economic conditions, and small pockets of surplus population remain in the South. But for the most part, large-scale immigration to the city is a thing of the past, and much of the migration which does take place bypasses the older population centers for more promising areas.

The absence of replacements for the new emigrés from the city means that some of the first rungs in the nation's traditional ladder of upward mobility have been eliminated. The consequences of this development are already making themselves felt. One of the most common ways for earlier immigrant groups to accumulate capital was as slum landlords. They bought, as they could afford to buy, only the poorest and weakest of structures, which they would rent, at whatever they could get, to their immigrant successors. By trading up the real estate ladder to bigger and better properties, these slumlords became prominent sources of capital for the business-oriented among their own ethnic group. But today, there is no new immigrant group to exploit. Slum tenement ownership has become a dead end, instead of an avenue to wealth—a fact symbolized by the abandoned slum dwelling.

Another way for earlier ethnic groups to move upward and outward was the exploitation of their own countrymen. Members of the immigrant group could rise as brokers between their ethnic labor pool and the external economy. If one wanted to build a sidewalk a generation or 2 ago, the cheapest labor available was Italian. Because the people who wanted sidewalks built rarely spoke Italian themselves, they dealt with bilingual Italian brokers, who would assemble and supervise the strong backs that were needed for the job. That was the stuff general contractors were made of. Or, to take another case, two generations ago the cheapest needle workers available were non-English-speaking

Jews. Their labor was exploited by Jewish sweatshop owners, who served as go-betweens with the department stores of Grand Street. Of course the needle workers themselves had no chance to become rich; but the go-betweens did.

The need for strong backs and 15-hour-a-day sweated labor has been reduced to almost nothing by the transportation revolution, which has had the effect of homogenizing time and distance. Much of our labor-intensive work is now imported from abroad. Welfare legislation, minimum wages, maximum work hours, and the like have minimized the economic function of the conglomerations of poor-but-willing people in our cities. Similarly, the goad of hunger has been mitigated by the rising level of welfare payments. In Newark a woman with 3 children lives very badly on welfare payments, but these nevertheless average somewhere around $300 to $350 per month. To live at the same level, a man with a wife and 3 children would have to make about $5500 a year. For unskilled labor, that sort of money just isn't available.

A NEW "FUNCTION"

Given that the older central cities have lost their capacity to serve as effective staging areas for newcomers, the question inevitably poses itself: What *is* the function of these cities? Permit me to suggest that it has become essentially that of a sandbox.

A sandbox is a place where adults park their children in order to converse, play, or work with a minimum of interference. The adults, having found a distraction for the children, can get on with the serious things of life. There is some reward for the children in all this. The sandbox is given to them as their own turf. Occasionally, fresh sand or toys are put in the sandbox, along with an implicit admonition that these things are furnished to minimize the level of noise and nuisance. If the children do become noisy and distract their parents, fresh toys may be brought. If the occupants of the sandbox choose up sides and start bashing each other over the head, the adults will come running, smack the juniors more or less indiscriminately, calm things down, and then, perhaps, in an act of semicontrition, bring fresh sand and fresh toys, pat the occupants of the sandbox on the head, and disappear once again into their adult involvements and pursuits.

That is what the city has become—a sandbox. Government programs in the core city have increasingly taken on this cast. A glance at Sar Levitan's *The Great Society's Poor Law,* or the Marris and Rein work, or for that matter Tom Wolfe's *Mau-Mauing the Flack Catchers* is enough to make clear the lack of effective flow of much poverty money to its ostensible targets. Instead, this money has been used to create a growing bureaucracy which is sustained by the plight of the poor, the threat of the poor, the misery of the poor, but which yields little in the way of loaves and fishes to the poor. This is the height of sandboxism. When old programs begin to lose their credibility or become unfashionable, they are given new names—therefore, they are new programs. The act of repackaging or relabelling is equated with creativity.

This is not to belittle the importance of government programs. They do have trickle-down effects; they are creating, if not efficiently then certainly in bulk, some measure of leadership, and this leadership is highly cynical about the nature of the faucet from whence all goodies flow and, possibly as a result, is increasingly effective. Perhaps most significantly, these programs have become forms of symbolic action. In their ritualistic aspects they are of particular value. They give psychic satisfaction to the patrons of the poor, convince outsiders—especially the media—that "something is being done," and indicate to the urban poor that some one up there really cares. In a word, these programs are placebos, and they often produce all the authentic, positive results which placebos can have in medical practice. One of the greatest shortcomings of the present administration in Washington is its failure to recognize the salutary placebo-effects of social programs. The failure has been not so much in what it has done, as in what it has called what it has done—not so much in the substance of its programs, as in its rejection of the gamesmanship which does not merely accompany programs but is central to them.

The fact that so many programs are of only symbolic value is the result, not of Machiavellian scheming, but of simple incapacity. If the 1960s demonstrated anything, it was that the social sciences had not yet arrived at the point of being able to design programs that could be counted on actually to accomplish what they were supposed to accomplish. It is true that social scientists themselves were often quick to recognize the failure of a given program and would attempt to design a better one in light of that failure. But the new programs usually did not arise from any strong theory or experimentation; they were rather the complements of past failure. One simply took apparently salient parameters of the failed program and reversed them. The façade of intellectual rationalization was produced *post hoc*. Schools don't work because classes are too large and lack the personal touch? Make classes smaller. If smaller classes don't work, what is left? Ah! Skin color, the teacher's doesn't match that of the student; change the skin color. That doesn't seem to be working as well as one would have anticipated? It must be the supervisor's color—paint principal black. Principal black doesn't seem to provide the answer? Paint the board of education an appropriate hue. And when this entire mountain of strategems brings forth nothing but mice, bring the parents in. Parents don't want to come in? Pay them, we'll call them paraprofessionals. And so it has gone. The rationalizers of these programs dutifully turn out Ph.D. theses and proposals without end to justify the programs.

In this kind of "social science," anecdotal accounts began to pass as consequential theories and models for the design of new institutions. A typical specimen of the genus is the account of how I, a young draft dodger, full of beans and aware of the fact that I wasn't going to spend my career there, came into a class of young sullens; in six months they loved me. This sort of recital became dignified both as an indictment of the flywheels of our institutions and also possibly as a model for new educational institutions of the future. The former may well have validity, but the latter defies rationality. The wonder is not the existence of a number of these anecdotal descriptions, but rather the childlike acceptance of them as a vision of a future that can be reproduced on a scale commensurate with the number of children and situations involved. The sordid fact that they enjoy such acceptance is but another indication of the extent to which we have begun to escape into fantasy.

THE FUTURE OF THE CENTRAL CITY

Jobs are leaving the central city. Except for insurance companies, banks, and other institutions which juridically find it difficult to leave, business institutions are virtually deserting the central cities. All major department store chains now do the bulk of their business in the suburbs; the efforts of urban renewal to retain major retail facilities in the core areas have died and are mourned by few. Smaller retailers in secondary urban shopping areas on the "trolley car streets" are also leaving or going out of business. The old mom and pop stores, candy stores, grocery stores on every block, fish stores, neighborhood bakeries, and so on are things of the far past. There has also been a flight of professionals. In the last 10 years, Newark has lost half its physicians, and many of those who remain have one foot in the suburbs and are just waiting for their practices to take hold before moving out. As for cultural activities, it is the first-run movie theaters rather than opera houses or symphony halls which have been of especially great economic importance to the vitality of the core city. In Newark, *there is not a single first-run theater left in the entire city of 400,000,* while in the suburbs one of the most desirable pieces of realty available is a site for a movie theater and shopping center. True, the museum and public library still exist downtown, but their wealthy patrons become fewer, galleries must be closed off for lack of money to pay guards, and book acquisition budgets and opening hours must be reduced as the city's budget crisis makes its impact felt.

Meanwhile, the suburbs have achieved critical mass, a scale of population and buying power which permits them to sustain amenities of a type and at a level which once only the central city was capable of sustaining. The shopping center which had at best a single department store branch now has 3 and soon will have 4. The suburban music calendar is evolving from a marginal summer collection of odds and ends to a year-round independent activity. Small suburban hospitals have grown to thousand-bed monsters which can supply all the services and specialists available in the biggest central-city hospitals.

Who is left in the central city? Ride down the Central Avenues and Main Streets of our older cities and you will see that the new tenants are offshoots of the poverty program: pseudo-training programs for the poor, enlarged offices of the Welfare Department, and the like. These are the focal points of the new central-city entrepreneurs, the people who, in the absence of a booming private economy, are trying to make it with government money. The predominance of these public-sector entrepreneurs is an index of the degree to which the central city—its inhabitants' training irrelevant to the needs of the larger society—has become a forgotten back alley in a nation whose principal business still is business.

This process of the "defunctioning" of the central city would have occurred even if there had not been a problem of race. It would have been considerably slower in that case, and the capacity of society to adjust to it would have been greater, for the pace of change in our central cities has unquestionably been speeded up by racial tensions and fears. But serious though that cost has been, perhaps the greatest cost of the race factor is that it has obscured the real nature of what is going on in the central city. Even if there were no racial difference in our society, there would probably still be as many people on welfare and as many under- or unemployed, and they would still be unwelcome among their more affluent fellow citizens.

What, then, of the future? The first point to be made is that there is no going back in time. The city as we have known it, and the forms of economic and social organization which characterized it, are simply irrecoverable. The folkways of our society have changed; they have also become homogeneous and monolithically dominant as no fashion has ever before been. The thin mist of eloquence emanating from upper-middle-class occupants of high-rise apartments cannot hide the fact that the dominant ethos today is a suburban one. It is as pervasive among minority groups as it is in the society as a whole. Thus, if we define the problems of the city as the gap between the reality of the cities as they exist today and a romanticized fantasy of cities as they used to be—as the economic center of the nation, as the font of civility and graciousness, as the source of everything that warms the hearts of social critics—then those problems are simply unsolvable and always will be unsolvable, at least for many of our older central cities.

Yet there is another way of defining the problems of the cities that does permit some real choice: Are they to become sandboxes entirely, or will we permit them to regain some useful economic function? Shall we optimize the machine, maximize capital investment and capital returns at the cost of human involvement, and then take the largesse so provided and redistribute it in the form of welfare or subsidized, irrelevant, unproductive make-work? Or should we reject the sandbox on the ground that useful, productive work is essential to human well-being, and design our policies to insure that everyone has an opportunity for such work, even if this involves cost to overall economic growth and wealth?

The plight of the inhabitants of our central cities, and the strategy we seem to be adopting to meet that plight, indicate that we are opting for the sandbox. What this will mean for our society in the future we do not fully know; but that the consequences are likely to be cruel and disagreeable has become only too clear.

part 4 HOUSING AND URBAN RENEWAL

Housing markets play an important role in the analysis of urban problems. Segregation of minorities, slums, and the suburbanization of the middle class are problems that are related to the distribution of high quality housing in urban areas. In the first selection of this part, Edgar O. Olsen presents an analysis of the housing market in the framework of classical economic theory. The terms that are common to discussions of housing policy are defined in this article and an analysis of public policy is presented. Olsen concludes that urban renewal is not an efficient way for the government to improve the quality of housing and suggests a housing subsidy instead.

The second selection, authored by Marc Fried and Peggy Gleicher, suggests that the eradication of slums may in some cases lower the welfare of the residents even if they are moved to "standard" housing. Housing not only provides shelter for a family; it may also give them a place within a commu-

133

nity. As evidence, Fried and Gleicher suggest that residents of Boston's West End experienced a sense of community identity that was lost when this area was demolished by an urban renewal program. It is not likely that the destruction of this community identification in the West End was offset by the improvement in material housing quality.

Herbert J. Gans is equally critical of urban renewal programs but argues for their reform rather than their abolition. The principal shortcoming of urban renewal, according to Gans, is that the programs have often benefited upper-income groups desiring luxury apartments while the supply of housing available to the poor was reduced. The interests of the poor have been badly represented in most urban renewal projects. Programs that build low-cost housing and relocate residents before dilapidated housing is demolished may be a valuable tool in efforts to improve the socioeconomic status of the poor. In his view, urban renewal can be used to improve the well-being of the poor as well as be a cornerstone for the rebuilding of the central city.

12
A COMPETITIVE THEORY OF THE HOUSING MARKET
Edgar O. Olsen

In his article on the demand for nonfarm housing, Richard Muth [11] rigorously developed a competitive theory of the housing market.[1] Muth used this theory in the statistical estimation of the demand function for housing service and of the speed of adjustment to long-run equilibrium in this market. His theory also makes possible the translation of some of the idiosyncratic concepts used by housing specialists into the familiar terms of microeconomic theory. A secondary purpose of this article is to make these translations. More importantly, this theory has implications for a number of crucial issues in government housing policy. The primary purpose of this article is to derive these implications, and use them to suggest additional tests of the competitive theory of the housing market. In order to achieve these purposes, it is first necessary to explain the crucial simplifying assumption which makes

[1] There are clearly two housing markets. There is a demand for and supply of a consumer good which we shall call housing service. There is also a derived demand for and supply of an investment good which we shall call housing stock. These two markets are integrally related. Indeed, Muth [11, p. 32] defines one unit of housing service to be that quantity of service yielded by one unit of housing stock per unit of time. Thus, he assumes that housing stock is the only input in the production of housing service. Although all buyers of housing stock are also sellers of housing service, there are many people who participate in one market but not in the other. Consumers who occupy rental housing are not typically in the market for housing stock. They are not buyers or sellers of this capital asset. Builders who construct housing for sale are sellers of housing stock but not of housing service. This paper will focus primarily on the market for housing service. Finally, it must be emphasized at the outset that this paper abstracts from consideration of the land on which dwelling units stand.

Reprinted by permission from the *American Economic Review,* September 1969.

it possible to view the market for housing service as a competitive market in which a homogeneous good is sold.

I. THE ASSUMPTIONS

Let us assume that the following conditions are satisfied in markets for housing service: (1) both buyers and sellers of housing service are numerous, (2) the sales or purchases of each individual unit are small in relation to the aggregate volume of transactions, (3) neither buyers nor sellers collude, (4) entry into and exit from the market are free for both producers and consumers, (5) both producers and consumers possess perfect knowledge about the prevailing price and current bids, and they take advantage of every opportunity to increase profits and utility respectively, (6) no artificial restrictions are placed on demands for, supplies of, and prices of housing service and the resources used to produce housing service, and (7) housing service is a homogeneous commodity.

This set of conditions is nothing other than a conventional statement of one set of conditions sufficient for a perfectly competitive market.[2] While objections to all of these assumptions can be found in the housing literature, most scholars would probably find (7) to be the least plausible assumption. Noting the great variations among residential structures as to size, type of construction, and other characteristics to which consumers attach value, many presume that a very heterogeneous good is traded in the housing market. This paper presents a theory with a very different view of the good being traded. An understanding of this theory of the housing market requires an elaboration on its conception of housing. Therefore, we will now focus our attention on this crucial simplifying assumption.

In order to view the housing market as one in which a homogeneous commodity is bought and sold, an unobservable theoretical entity called housing service is introduced.[3] Each dwelling (or housing) unit is presumed to yield some quantity of this good during each time period. It is assumed to be the only thing in a dwelling unit to which consumers attach value. Consequently, in this theory there is no distinction between the quantity and quality of a dwelling unit as these terms are customarily used.

---

[2] This set is a composite taken from three standard price theory textbooks. See Leftwich [7, pp. 23–25], Stigler [14, pp. 87–89], and Henderson and Quandt [6, pp. 86–89]. As Stigler clearly explains, this is by no means the weakest set of assumptions sufficient for perfect competition. A strong set of assumptions is used in order to obtain clear-cut implications of the competitive theory.

[3] Hempel [5, pp. 70–84] gives an elementary but lucid explanation of the role of unobservable theoretical entities in scientific theories.

This conception of housing is bound to raise objections. It will be argued that housing is a complex bundle of technically independent attributes. However, since housing service is not observable directly, it is not possible to argue for or against this assumption directly.[4] Hence, it is not possible to test this theory other than by reference to its implications. The competitive theory of the housing market does contain bridge principles which relate housing service to observable phenomena and it does have testable implications in terms of these phenomena. Muth [11] has already tested some of these implications. Other implications will be derived in this paper. Eyesight is not a satisfactory judge of the question of homogeneity. The assumption of a homogeneous good called housing service can only be rejected if theories of the housing market without this assumption have greater explanatory power.

II. THE TRANSLATION OF CONCEPTS

Based on the assumptions of the preceding section, four concepts—dwelling unit, slum, filtering, and shortage—traditionally used in housing market analysis, can be translated into the jargon of conventional microeconomic theory.

What is a dwelling unit? A *dwelling unit* is a package composed of a certain quantity of a capital asset called housing stock. Some dwelling units will contain 10 units of housing stock, other dwelling units will contain 20 units of housing stock. By definition, these dwelling units will be said to yield 10 and 20 units of housing service per time period respectively.[5] In long run competitive equilibrium only one price per unit applies to all units of housing stock and another price to all units of housing service regardless of the size of the package in which these goods come. Hence, if we observe that one dwelling unit sells for twice the amount of another dwelling unit in the same market, then we say that the more expensive unit contains twice the quantity of housing stock and, hence, involves twice the total expenditure. This distinction between price, quantity, and total expenditure is not usually made in housing market analysis where it is simply said that the price of the one dwelling unit is twice that of the other dwelling unit. Similarly, if we

[4] Intuitively, it does seem more reasonable to conceive of the difference between an apartment renting for $50 and one renting for $100 in the same city as more akin to the difference between $50 and $100 worth of oranges than to the difference between $50 worth of oranges and $100 worth of golf balls. However, arguments of this sort are not scientific.

[5] Dwelling unit means the same thing as housing unit. Therefore, a housing unit is quite different from a unit of housing stock or housing service. The term dwelling unit is used throughout this paper to avoid this natural confusion.

observe that one dwelling unit rents for twice the amount of another dwelling unit, then we say that the more expensive dwelling unit yields twice the quantity of housing service per time period and, hence, involves twice the total expenditure per time period. Here again, traditional housing market analysis uses a price theory concept, in this case "rent," in a way far removed from its original meaning. Despite the fact that housing service and housing stock are not directly observable, the competitive theory of the housing market contains bridge principles which permit us to compare the relative amounts of housing service yielded by different dwelling units.

What is a slum dwelling unit? A *slum dwelling unit* is one which yields less than some arbitrary quantity of housing service per time period. Using the relationship established between total expenditure and quantity, we might decide to call all dwelling units in a particular locality renting for less than $60 per month slum dwelling units. What is a slum area? A *slum area* is a contiguous area which contains a high (but arbitrary) percentage of slum dwelling units.

It would be possible to give the word "slum" a welfare economics definition in which a slum dwelling unit would necessarily represent suboptimal resource allocation. Otto Davis and Andrew Whinston [3, pp. 111–112] have provided such a definition. At least one other distinctly different definition of this sort is possible.[6] However, the definition provided above is more in keeping with the use of this word in both popular and scholarly writings.

What is a housing shortage? The most frequently used unit of quantity for housing market analysis has been the dwelling unit. As a result, a housing shortage has usually been defined as a situation in which everyone who is willing to pay the market price for a separate dwelling unit is not able to obtain a separate dwelling unit. This is an unnecessarily narrow definition of a shortage which results from the acceptance of the dwelling unit as the unit of quantity. The unit of quantity introduced by Muth allows us to take a broader view of a housing shortage. To be precise, a *short-run housing shortage* is said to exist if, and only if, the quantity of housing service demanded at the existing market price is greater than the quantity of housing service supplied. Short-run shortages will be eliminated by a rise in the price of housing service for bundles of the size which are in excess demand initially. A *long-run housing shortage* is said to exist if, and only if, the quantity of housing

---

[6] Some people care about the housing occupied by low-income families for altruistic and more selfish reasons. The market will not properly account for these preferences and, hence, low-income families may consume too little housing service by the criterion of efficiency. We might call the dwelling units occupied by these low-income families slum dwelling units. Clearly, with this definition slumness is not a characteristic of the housing alone.

service demanded at the long-run equilibrium price is greater than the quantity of housing service supplied. Long-run shortages are eliminated by maintenance, repairs, alterations, and additions as well as by new construction. Clearly, a housing shortage can exist by these definitions even if everyone who wants to occupy a separate dwelling unit at the relevant price is doing so because everyone may want to occupy better housing (that is, to consume a greater quantity of housing service) at this price than they presently occupy and none may be available.

Although the concept of filtering has been used in housing economics for many years, a rigorous definition of this term has only recently been proposed. Ira Lowry [8, p. 363] defines filtering as ". . . a change in the real value (price in constant dollars) of an existing dwelling unit." Lowry uses this definition together with a theory of the housing market to demonstrate that filtering is not a process which necessarily results in all families occupying housing above certain minimum standards. With the competitive theory of the housing market, it is possible to define filtering slightly more rigorously and in a manner which significantly clarifies the meaning of the concept and the method of detecting the process. Using this new definition and a competitive theory of the housing market, it is easy to demonstrate the result which Lowry showed with great difficulty.

A dwelling unit has *filtered* if, and only if the quantity of housing stock contained in this unit has changed. A dwelling unit has *filtered up* if, and only if the quantity of housing stock contained in this unit has increased. A dwelling unit has *filtered down* if, and only if the quantity of housing stock contained in this unit has decreased.[7] Within the theory presented in this paper, Lowry's definition is the same as the new definition if he intended to deflate money values by the cost of construction. This is true because in a perfectly competitive housing market in long-run equilibrium the price per unit of housing stock equals the minimum long-run average cost of production and, hence, the quantity of housing stock contained in a particular dwelling unit is equal to the market value of this dwelling unit divided by the cost of production.[8] For example, if the cost-of-construction index was 100 in 1960 and 110 in 1962 and if a particular dwelling unit sold for $6000 in 1960 and $6050 in 1962, then we would say that this particular unit has filtered down between 1960 and 1962 because our index of quantity of housing stock fell from 60 to 55.[9]

[7] In these definitions, "housing stock contained in" could be replaced by "housing service yielded per time period by." These definitions are stated in stock terms to facilitate the comparison with Lowry's definition.

[8] Lowry does not say what he intends to use as a deflator.

[9] This method abstracts from changes in the price paid for a particular structure attributable to changes in the relative desirability of its location. Since I do not want to include these changes in

To determine whether particular dwelling units have filtered is of far less importance than understanding the function of filtering in the operation of the housing market. In essence, Lowry set out to demonstrate that filtering is not a process that insures that all consumers will purchase greater than an arbitrarily chosen quantity of housing service per time period. If the housing market is perfectly competitive, then this result is trivial since there is nothing in the operation of such a market which insures that all individuals will consume greater than an arbitrary quantity of the good.[10] As will be shown in the next section, filtering is a process by which the quantity of housing service yielded by particular dwelling units is adjusted to conform to the pattern of consumer demand. The profit incentive leads producers to make these adjustments.

None of the definitions in this section corresponds exactly with previous usage of the terms. No simple definitions could. These definitions have been offered in order to bring housing market analysis within the realm of standard microeconomic theory where advantage can be taken of the accumulated knowledge in this field. The value of this transformation should be strongly emphasized. Even as eminent a price theorist as Milton Friedman [4, pp. 178–180] reaches an undoubtedly fallacious conclusion about public housing simply because he did not apply the conventional distinction between the very short run and the long run to the housing market.[11]

---

my concept of filtering, the market value of the land must be subtracted from the total price of structure and land in determining whether a dwelling unit has filtered. Practically, this might be done by observing the sale price per square foot of nearby vacant land and assuming that the land containing the structure of interest has the same market value per square foot.

[10] For any given positive quantity, there exists a set of admissible indifference curves, relative prices, and income such that the consumer associated with these will choose less than the given quantity.

[11] Friedman [4, p. 179] concludes that ". . . far from improving the housing of the poor, as its proponents expected, public housing has done just the reverse. The number of dwelling units destroyed in the course of erecting public housing projects has been far larger than the number of new units constructed." Aside from the factual question of whether far more units have been destroyed than constructed and aside from Friedman's use of numbers of gainers, and losers rather than the values of gains and losses, Friedman ignores the fact that the displaced families will lose over a few years while housed families will gain over the much longer physical life of the project. As will be demonstrated in Section V, in long-run equilibrium the displaced families will occupy the same type of housing and pay the same rent as prior to the public housing project. According to Muth [11, pp. 49–52], the market for housing service adjusts at a rate of one-third of the difference between the present situation and long run equilibrium each year. Hence, there is a 90 percent adjustment in six years. By comparison, the physical life of public housing projects is likely to be far in excess of 50 years. From Olsen's calculations [12, pp. 83–87] it can be estimated that the average public housing tenant received benefits from public housing which he valued at $263 in 1965. This benefit would be received each year by some poor family during the entire physical life of the project.

III. THE WORKINGS OF THE MARKET

The workings of the market for housing service under the set of assumptions introduced in Section I can best be illustrated by beginning from a situation in which the price per unit of housing service for bundles of all sizes but one is equal to the long-run average cost of production. For the one bundle size, the price is assumed to be greater than the long-run average cost. In this situation, producers will be making profits (that is, they will be making more than a normal rate of return on capital) only on this one size bundle of housing service.

Owners of housing stock can change the quantity of housing stock contained in and, hence, the quantity of housing service yielded by their dwelling units through maintenance, repair, alteration, and addition.[12] In the absence of maintenance, dwelling units deteriorate with use and over time which means that they yield smaller and smaller quantities of housing service per time period. Normally, producers of housing service find it profitable to invest in maintenance (although not enough to halt deterioration completely). If bundles of some particular size become more profitable than bundles of other sizes, then some producers with larger bundles of housing service will allow their housing units to deteriorate more than they would otherwise. That is, they will allow their dwelling units to filter down to the bundle size which is most profitable. This is accomplished by following a lower maintenance policy than would have been followed had all bundle sizes been equally profitable. By the same token, some producers of smaller bundles of housing service will follow a higher maintenance policy than otherwise resulting in a filtering up of their dwelling units.

The supply of the most profitable size bundle having increased, the price per unit of housing service for bundles of this size will decrease. Since initially there were zero profits for bundles of housing service slightly greater and slightly less than the profitable size bundle, the filtering down of larger bundles and the filtering up of smaller bundles will create short-run shortages, higher prices, and profits for bundles of these sizes. This will result in filtering down of still larger bundles and filtering up of smaller bundles. Eventually the process will reach bundles of sizes which can be provided by the construction of new dwelling units. This new construction will continue until there are no profits to be made on bundles of any size. This requires the price per unit of housing service for bundles of all sizes to be the same.

---

[12] In the remainder of this paper, the word "maintenance" will be used to denote all 4 of these phenomena.

IV. THE POOR-PAY-MORE HYPOTHESIS

A popular claim in current policy discussions is that the poor pay more for many goods including housing. If the housing markets are perfectly competitive and if it is neither more costly to provide small quantities of housing service nor to provide housing service to low-income families, then the poor will not pay more for housing service. It is instructive of the workings of a perfectly competitive housing market to demonstrate this result.

We begin by interpreting the poor-pay-more hypothesis in terms of the theory presented in this article. For some reason the price per unit of housing service is greater for dwelling units yielding small quantities of housing service than for dwelling units yielding large quantities. This price difference is not attributable to differences in cost.[13] For large bundles of housing service, the market works efficiently. The price of housing service tends towards the minimum long-run average cost of production of housing service. Consequently, the price per unit of housing service for small bundles exceeds the minimum average cost. As a result, owners of dwelling units yielding small quantities of housing service make economic profits. For some reason, these profits do not stimulate an increase in the supply of these small bundles of housing service. As a result, the consumers of these small bundles (that is, primarily the poor) consume a smaller quantity of housing service than required for efficient resource allocation.

Participants in a competitive housing market would not allow this situation to persist. Suppose that owners of bundles of housing stock yielding quantities of housing service less than x received a higher price per unit for their production than owners of bundles which yield greater than x units of housing service. These slum landlords would be making higher profits per dollar invested than other landlords. In this case, some owners of dwelling units yielding slightly more than x units will follow a lower maintenance policy than otherwise, allowing the quantity of housing service yielded by their units per time period to fall below x. The supply of dwelling units yielding less than x units of housing service per time period will increase and the price per unit for these small bundles will fall. Eventually, new construction will be induced. Only when the price per unit of housing service for bundles of all sizes is equal to the minimum long-run average cost of production will there be no incentive for change.

---

[13] If the price difference is solely attributable to differences in cost, then no market imperfection is involved and government action on grounds of efficiency is not required. A recent study by the U.S. Bureau of Labor Statistics [15] has shown that the poor do pay more for food, but that this difference is fully explained by difference in cost. The poor tend to shop in small stores where merchandising cost per unit is high.

If we actually observe that the poor consistently pay more per unit of housing service than the rich and that it is not more expensive per unit to provide small packages of housing service or to provide housing service to low-income families, then we have evidence contrary to the assumption that the housing market is competitive. This is one of the testable implications of the competitive theory.[14]

V. WILL SLUM CLEARANCE AND URBAN RENEWAL RESULT IN A NET REDUCTION IN SLUMS?

Slum clearance is the destruction of slum dwelling units by government with or without compensation to the owner. It is required by the Housing Act of 1937 as part of the public housing program. It is undertaken independently by many local governments. Finally, slum clearance is the first stage of urban renewal. Slum clearance and urban renewal have been premised in large part on the naive belief that the physical destruction of slum dwelling units results in a net reduction in the number of families occupying such units. Many writers have questioned this presumption and have suggested that slum clearance merely results in the transfer of slums from one location to another.[15] Indeed, this argument should suggest itself to all economists since slum clearance does not increase the incomes of or decrease the prices of any goods to the former residents of the cleared areas. If the market for housing service is perfectly competitive, then this argument can be made completely rigorous.

We have defined a slum dwelling unit as a dwelling unit yielding a flow of less than x units of housing service. Starting from a situation of long-run equilibrium in the housing market with normal vacancy rates, the immediate effect of slum clearance is to decrease the supply of slum dwelling units. Some of the former residents of the destroyed dwelling units will move into vacant dwelling units providing the same quantity of housing service. Others will have to move into dwelling units

---

[14] A recent study by the *BLS*[16] has shown that the quality of housing occupied by richer families is superior to that occupied by poorer people in the same rent range. Unfortunately, it is almost certainly true that within each rent range the higher the income range, the higher the average rent. The higher rent may completely explain the differences in quality. This author is trying to obtain the *BLS* data to check this possibility with regression analysis. Finally, the *BLS* study does not consider the possibility that it is more costly per unit of housing service either to provide small bundles or to sell to low-income families. For example, it is reputed to be much more difficult to collect rents from low-income tenants. This involves extra costs in time and nonpayment. Furthermore, the existence and enforcement of building and occupancy codes with penalties for violations increase the long-run equilibrium price of low-quantity housing in a competitive market because there exist some producers and consumers who will have an incentive to violate the code. (I owe this point to Richard Muth.)

[15] For example, see Bailey [2, p. 291], Davis and Whinston [3, p. 112] and Anderson [1, pp. 8–9].

which provide slightly more or slightly less housing service than they prefer to buy at the long-run equilibrium price. The owners of slum dwelling units will realize that they can both charge higher prices and have lower vacancy rates than before slum clearance. They will take advantage of the short-run shortage to raise prices in order to increase their profits. This, however, is only the very short-run impact of slum clearance.

In the long run, the owners of slightly better than slum dwelling units will allow their dwelling units to filter down to the level of slum dwelling units in order to take advantage of the profits to be made on such units. This adjustment will continue until the rate of return on capital invested in bundles of housing stock of all sizes is the same. In long-run equilibrium the price per unit of housing service must be the same for bundles of all sizes. Since neither slum clearance nor urban renewal subsidizes housing consumption by low-income families, and since neither results in a lower cost of production of housing service, therefore, neither results in a lower price of housing service to the former residents of slum clearance or urban renewal sites in the long run. Neither slum clearance nor urban renewal results in change in the incomes of, or the prices paid for nonhousing goods by the former residents. Consequently, the former residents of the cleared area will, in long-run equilibrium, consume exactly the same quantity of housing service as before slum clearance or urban renewal. Slum clearance and urban renewal do not result in a net reduction in the occupancy of slums in the long run.

This implication of the competitive theory is testable. To conduct this test, we might observe the characteristics of the housing occupied by former residents of slum clearance sites and their incomes just prior to slum clearance and for 6 years afterwards. With respect to each characteristic, we shall probably observe that the percentage of families occupying housing with that characteristic is different immediately after slum clearance from what it was immediately before. For example, the percentage of families in dilapidated dwelling units might have been 90 percent before slum clearance and 50 percent afterwards. The competitive theory suggests that in long-run equilibrium, we will again find 90 percent of these families in dilapidated dwelling units if these families experience no change in real income. Therefore, if we determine the percentage of families occupying dwelling units with each particular characteristic by income groups, then we should observe that within each income group the percentage of families occupying housing having the particular characteristic should, over time, approach the before-slum-clearance percentage. This convergence provides a weak test of the competitive hypothesis. As mentioned before, Muth [11, pp.

49–52] estimates that we get a 90 percent adjustment in the housing market in 6 years.[16] Consequently, we expect that the difference between the percentage at the end of 6 years and the percentage immediately after slum clearance will be roughly 90 percent of the difference between the percentage immediately before slum clearance and the percentage immediately afterwards. A test of the statistical significance of the difference between these 2 variables is a strong test of the competitive theory.[17]

There have been, and continue to be, many instances of slum clearance, especially associated with urban renewal. It is quite feasible to conduct studies of displaced families at least partly for the purpose of testing this implication of the competitive theory of the housing market. Since the nature of the housing market is very relevant to the choice of government housing policies, these data might reasonably be collected by the U.S. Department of Housing and Urban Development in conjunction with urban renewal and public housing.

If the housing market is perfectly competitive, then slum clearance and urban renewal result only in a shift in the location of slums rather than in a net reduction in slums. Consequently, we should expect neither urban renewal nor slum clearance to lead to a reduction in the social costs of slum living or to net beneficial spillover effects for properties not on the slum clearance site. Cost-benefit analyses of urban renewal typically find that measured benefits are far less than measured costs.[18] The authors of these studies usually do not attempt to calculate the alleged benefits from these two sources, but they claim that the benefits from the reduction in social costs of slums and the net beneficial spillover effects on neighboring properties might well overcome the excess of measured costs over measured benefits.[19] If the housing market were perfectly competitive, then the expected value of these alleged benefits would be zero and, hence, almost all slum clearance and urban renewal projects would be extremely wasteful.

---

[16] Specifically, Muth's estimates indicate that individuals seek to add about one-third of the difference between desired and actual stock during a year, which implies that for the adjustment of the actual housing stock to be 90 percent completed, 6 years are required.

[17] If there is much variation in the speed of adjustment among the housing markets in the United States, then it would be desirable to estimate Muth's equation with data from the particular local housing market to obtain the speed of adjustment for that market and to use this estimate for our test.

[18] For example, see Rothenberg [13, p. 341, Table 4] and Messner [9, p. 78, Table 13]. In each study, costs and benefits for 3 projects were calculated. Total benefits for the 6 projects were only 27 percent of total costs. The highest benefit-cost ratio was 0.37 and the lowest was 0.05. Rothenberg's calculations were intended to be illustrative only, but Messner's calculations based on Rothenberg's framework are very careful and detailed.

[19] See Rothenberg [13, p. 340]. Messner [9, p. 78] takes a much more guarded view of the likelihood of significant benefits from these two sources.

VI. THE EFFECT OF RENT CERTIFICATES ON
THE HOUSING OCCUPIED BY THEIR RECIPIENTS

If it is desired either to decrease the number of occupied slum dwelling units or to improve the housing occupied by low-income families and if the housing market is competitive, then slum clearance and urban renewal are not the answers. They would have neither of these effects. The most direct ways of obtaining these results are to tax (or prohibit) the occupation of slum dwelling units or to subsidize the housing of low-income families. The former method would make the occupants of slum dwelling units worse off as they judge their own well-being. Consequently, to the extent that the desire to decrease the amount of slum housing and to increase the housing consumption of low-income families is motivated by a desire to help these people, to that extent the tax (or prohibition) alternative can be dropped from consideration.

Probably the most efficient method of subsidizing the housing of low-income families is to allow these families to buy certificates which they could use to pay the rent or make mortgage payments up to an amount equal to the face value of the certificate.[20] The low-income family would purchase this certificate for an amount less than the face value.[21] These certificates would be redeemed by the government from sellers of housing service. It would be illegal to exchange these certificates for other than housing service.

Given the amount of public money likely to be spent for such a program and the amount that might be reasonably charged for these certificates, the face values of rent certificates will not be large enough to induce many low-income families to move to newly produced housing because new housing typically comes in relatively large bundles of housing stock. Since a rent certificate plan does not directly increase the supply of newly constructed housing and since few of the recipients are likely to demand new housing, many people wonder how a rent certificate plan could result in an increase in the total quantity of housing stock. They suggest that since there will be no increase in housing stock, the only result of the increase in demand stemming from the rent certificate plan will be higher prices for housing service purchased by the low-income families who use rent certificates.[22]

By now it should be clear that if the market for housing service is

[20] Olsen [12, pp. 69–116] has made estimates which strongly suggest the rent certificate plan to be significantly more efficient than public housing.

[21] Under the principle of benefit taxation, each recipient should be charged an amount equal to average expenditure on housing service prior to the program by families of the same size and with the same income. See Olsen [12, pp. 110–116]. This result follows primarily from Muth's finding [11] that the price elasticity of demand for housing service is roughly constant and unitary.

[22] For a lucid statement of this position taken by many housing specialists, see Meyerson, Terrett, and Wheaton [10, pp. 71–72].

perfectly competitive, then this is only the very short run effect of a rent certificate plan.[23] In the long run, the owners of the smallest bundles of housing stock will either increase their maintenance expenditures (and thereby increase the quantity of housing service yielded by their units) or convert their buildings to other uses. There would no longer be any demand for dwelling units which provide less housing service than can be purchased with rent certificates of the smallest face values.

Some owners of dwelling units presently providing bundles of housing service larger than could be purchased with rent certificates of the highest face value will allow their units to filter down to the relatively more profitable sectors initially affected by rent certificates. As a result, there will be shortages and, hence, economic profits for these larger bundles of housing service. Owners of dwelling units yielding still larger quantities of housing service will allow their units to filter down. Eventually shortages will result for bundles of housing stock which can be provided by new construction. Construction of new dwelling units will continue until there are no more excess profits in the market for housing service. In long run competitive equilibrium all consumers must pay the same price per unit of housing service. Consequently, purchasers of rent certificates with a face value of x dollars per month should be able to consume the same quantity of housing service as individuals who spent this much per month for housing service prior to the program.

This result leads to yet another testable implication of the competitive theory of the housing market. If the competitive theory is correct, then we should observe that the buyers of rent certificates with a face value of x dollars will occupy housing as good as the housing which rented for x dollars prior to the rent certificate plan.[24] This is the long run equilibrium situation. The adjustment of this equilibrium will take several years. As already pointed out, Muth's evidence suggests a 90 percent adjustment in 6 years. Hence, we should observe that the characteristics of the housing occupied by recipients (for example, whether the dwelling unit has hot and cold running water) should approach the characteristics of the housing occupied by individuals who spent the same amount on housing prior to the program.

It should not be necessary to wait until a national rent certificate plan

[23] Indeed, since a rent certificate plan would undoubtedly be discussed by Congress for some time before passage, it would be anticipated by sellers of housing service who would find it profitable to adjust their maintenance policy in advance of passage. Consequently, there might be little price inflation immediately after implementation.

[24] It would be necessary to correct for changes in the general price level, but we should not expect the relative price of housing to rise in the long run because of the increase in the total demand for housing service which is a result of the rent certificate plan. Muth [11, pp. 42–46] finds the supply curve to be perfectly elastic.

is adopted to test this implication. According to Meyerson, Terrett, and Wheaton [10, p. 71], ". . . welfare agencies in many states in this country do issue rent certificates to families on relief. During the Depression, millions of families received such payments." There may already be data from these experiences to test this implication of the competitive theory of the housing market. Given the demonstrated inefficiency of urban renewal and public housing, it would also seem reasonable for a city to propose and the Federal Government to accept a rent certificate plan in place of the two other programs on a demonstration basis. The experience of the buyers of rent certificates in this city could be used to test the competitive theory.

VII. CONCLUSION

In this article, the assumptions of Muth's competitive theory of the housing market are stated and the nature of the good called housing service is elaborated upon. This theory is used to translate 4 familiar terms of housing market analysis—dwelling unit, slum, shortage, and filtering—into the standard concepts of microeconomic theory. If the housing market is perfectly competitive and if it is not more costly per unit to provide housing to low-income families or to provide small packages of housing service, then (1) the poor would not pay more per unit for housing, (2) slum clearance and urban renewal would not result in a net reduction in the number of occupied substandard units, and (3) the recipients of rent certificates would enjoy housing just as good as the housing occupied by others who spent as much on housing as the face value of the certificates. These results and their implications for government policy are deduced. In each of the three cases, testable implications of the assumptions are derived and the nature of the test made explicit. It is hoped that this article will serve to bring housing market analysis within the realm of conventional economic theory and to suggest additional tests of one particular conventional economic theory of markets.

REFERENCES

1. M. ANDERSON, *The Federal Bulldozer* (Cambridge, Mass.: MIT Press, 1964).
2. M. J. BAILEY, "Note on the Economics of Residential Zoning and Urban Renewal," *Land Econ.*, 35 (August 1959), pp. 288–292.
3. O. A. DAVIS and A. B. WHINSTON. "Economics of Urban Renewal," *Law and Contemp. Prob.*, 26 (Winter 1961), pp. 105–117.

4. M. FRIEDMAN, *Capitalism and Freedom* (Chicago: University of Chicago Press, 1964).
5. C. G. HEMPEL, *Philosophy of Natural Science* (Englewood Cliffs, N.J.: Prentice-Hall, 1966).
6. J. M. HENDERSON and R. E. QUANDT, *Microeconomic Theory* (New York: McGraw-Hill, 1958).
7. R. H. LEFTWICH, *The Price System and Resource Allocation* (New York: Holt, Rinehart & Winston, 1961).
8. I. S. LOWRY, "Filtering and Housing Standards: A Conceptual Analysis," *Land Econ.*, 36 (Nov. 1960), pp. 362–370.
9. S. D. MESSNER, *A Benefit Cost Analysis of Urban Redevelopment*, Bureau of Business Research (Bloomington: Indiana University, 1967).
10. M. MEYERSON, B. TERRETT, and W. L. C. WHEATON, *Housing, People, and Cities* (New York: McGraw-Hill, 1962).
11. R. F. MUTH, "The Demand for Non-Farm Housing," in A. C. Harberger, ed., *The Demand for Durable Goods* (Chicago: University of Chicago Press, 1960), pp. 29–96.
12. E. O. OLSEN, "A Welfare Economic Evaluation of Public Housing," unpublished Ph.D. dissertation, Rice University, 1968.
13. J. ROTHENBERG, "Urban Renewal Programs," in R. Dorfman, ed., *Measuring Benefits of Government Investments* (Washington, D.C.: Brookings, 1966), pp. 292–341.
14. G. J. STIGLER, *The Theory of Price* (New York: Macmillan, 1966).
15. U.S. BUREAU OF LABOR STATISTICS, "A Study of Prices Charged in Food Stores Located in Low and High Income Areas of Six Large Cities, February 1966," mimeographed, June 12, 1966.
16. U.S. BUREAU OF LABOR STATISTICS, "Differences in the Characteristics of Rental Housing Occupied by Families in Three Income Ranges Paying Approximately the Same Rent in Six Cities," mimeographed, Sept. 1966.

13
SOME SOURCES OF RESIDENTIAL SATISFACTION IN AN URBAN SLUM
Marc Fried
and Peggy Gleicher

The gradual deterioration of older urban dwellings and the belief that such areas provide a locus for considerable social pathology have stimulated concern with altering the physical habitat of the slum. Yet the technical difficulties, the practical inadequacies, and the moral problems of such planned revisions of the human environment are also forcing themselves upon our attention most strikingly.[1] While a full evaluation of the advantages and disadvantages of urban renewal must await studies which derive from various disciplines, there is little likelihood that the vast sums currently available will be withheld until there is a more systematic basis for rational decisions. Thus it is of the utmost importance that we discuss all aspects of the issue as thoroughly as possible and make available even the more fragmentary findings which begin to clarify the many unsolved problems.

Since the most common foci of urban renewal are areas which have been designated as slums, it is particularly important to obtain a clearer

* Authors' Note: This report is part of a study entitled "Relocation and Mental Health: Adaptation Under Stress," conducted by the Center for Community Studies in the Department of Psychiatry of the Massachusetts General Hospital and the Harvard Medical School. The research is supported by the National Institute of Mental Health, Grant No. 3M 9137-C3. We are grateful to Erich Lindemann, the Principal Investigator, and to Leonard Duhl of the Professional Services Branch, NIMH, for their continued help and encouragement. Edward Ryan has contributed in many ways to the final formulations of this paper, and Chester Hartman and Joan Levin have given helpful criticism and advice.
1 Herbert Gans, "The Human Implications of Current Redevelopment and Relocation Planning," *Journal of the American Institute of Planners,* 25, No. 1 (February 1959), pp. 15–25.

Reprinted by permission of the *Journal of the American Institute of Planners,* 27, No. 4, November 1961.

picture of so-called slum areas and their populations. Slum areas undoubtedly show much variation, both variation from one slum to another and heterogeneity within urban slum areas. However, certain consistencies from one slum area to another have begun to show up in the growing body of literature. It is quite notable that the available systematic studies of slum areas indicate a very broad working-class composition in slums, ranging from highly skilled workers to the non-working and sporadically working members of the "working" class. Moreover, even in our worst residential slums it is likely that only a minority of the inhabitants (although sometimes a fairly large and visible minority) are afflicted with one or another form of social pathology. Certainly the idea that social pathology in any form is decreased by slum clearance finds little support in the available data. The belief that poverty, delinquency, prostitution, and alcoholism magically inhere in the buildings of slums and will die with the demolition of the slum has a curious persistence but can hardly provide adequate justification for the vast enterprise of renewal planning.

In a larger social sense, beyond the political and economic issues involved, planning for uban renewal has important human objectives. Through such planning we wish to make available to a larger proportion of the population some of the advantages of modern urban facilities, ranging from better plumbing and decreased fire hazards to improved utilization of local space and better neighborhood resources. These values are all on the side of the greater good for the greatest number. Yet it is all too apparent that we know little enough about the meaning and consequences of differences in physical environment either generally or for specific groups. Urban renewal may lead, directly and indirectly, to improved housing for slum residents. But we cannot evaluate the larger effects of relocation or its appropriateness without a more basic understanding than we now have of the meaning of the slum's physical and social environment. This report is an initial essay toward understanding the issue. We shall consider some of the factors that give meaning to the residential environment of the slum dweller. Although the meaning of the environment to the resident of a slum touches only one part of the larger problem, it is critical that we understand this if we are to achieve a more effectively planned and designed urban environment.[2]

---

[2] This is one of a series of reports on the meaning and significance of various aspects of working-class life. This group of studies will provide a basis for a subsequent analysis of the impact of relocation through a comparison of the pre-relocation and the post-relocation situation. The population of the original area was predominantly white, of mixed ethnic composition (mainly Italian, Polish, and Jewish). The many ethnic differences do not vitiate the larger generalizations of this study.

THE SIGNIFICANCE OF THE SLUM ENVIRONMENT

People do not like to be dispossessed from their dwellings, and every renewal project that involves relocation can anticipate considerable resistance, despite the best efforts to insure community support.[3] It is never quite clear whether most people object mainly to being forced to do something they have not voluntarily elected to do; or whether they simply object to relocation, voluntary or involuntary. There is, of course, considerable evidence for the commitment of slum residents to their habitat. Why this should be so is less clear and quite incomprehensible in the face of all middle-class residential values. In order to evaluate the issue more closely we shall consider the problem of the meaning and functional significance of residence in a slum area. Although we are primarily concerned with a few broadly applicable generalizations, a complete analysis will take better account of the diversities in the composition of slum populations.

The fact that more than half the respondents in our sample[4] have a long-standing experience of familiarity with the area in which they lived before relocation suggests a very basic residential stability. Fifty-five percent of the sample first moved to or were born in the West End approximately 20 years ago or more. Almost one-fourth of the entire sample was born in the West End. Not only is there marked residential stability within the larger area of the West End, but the total rate of movement from one dwelling unit to another has been exceedingly low. Table 1 gives the distribution of movement from one dwelling unit to

TABLE 1. Number of moves in previous 10 years

Moves	Number	Percent
Totals	473	100
None	162	34
One	146	31
Two	73	15
Three or more	86	19
No answer	6	1

[3] This does not seem limited to contemporary relocation situations. Firey reports a similar phenomenon in Boston during the nineteenth century. Walter Firey, *Land Use in Central Boston* (Cambridge, Mass.: Harvard University Press, 1947).

[4] These data are based on a probability sample of residents from the West End of Boston interviewed during 1958–1959. The sampling criteria included only households in which there was a female household member between the ages of 20 and 65. The present analysis is based on the prerelocation data from the female respondents. Less systematic prerelocation data on the husbands are also available, as well as systematic postrelocation data for both wives and husbands and women without husbands.

another within the 10 years prior to the interview. It is readily evident that the largest proportion of the sample has made very few moves indeed. In fact, a disproportionate share of the frequent moves is made by a small group of relatively high-status people, largely professional and semiprofessional people who were living in the West End only temporarily. Regardless of which criterion we use, these data indicate that we cannot readily accept those impressions of a slum which suggest a highly transient population. An extremely large proportion shows unusual residential stability, and this is quite evenly distributed among the several levels of working-class occupational groups.

The slum environment as home

What are the sources of this residential stability? Undoubtedly they are many and variable, and we could not hope to extricate the precise contribution of each factor. Rents were certainly low. If we add individually expended heating costs to the rental figures reported we find that 25 percent were paying $34 a month or less, and 85 percent paying $54 a month or less. But though this undoubtedly played a role as a background factor, it can hardly account for the larger findings. Low rental costs are rarely mentioned in discussing aspects of the West End or of the apartment that were sources of satisfaction. And references to the low West End rents are infrequent in discussing the sources of difficulty which people expected in the course of moving. In giving reasons for having moved to the last apartment they occupied before relocation, only 12 percent gave any type of economic reason (including decreased transportation costs as well as low rents). Thus, regardless of the practical importance that low rents must have had for a relatively low income population, they were not among the most salient aspects of the perceived issues in living in the West End.

On the other hand, there is considerable evidence to indicate that living in the West End had particular meaning for a vast majority of West End residents. Table 2 shows the distribution in response to the question, "How do you feel about living in the West End?", clearly indicating how the West End was a focus for very positive sentiments.

That the majority of West Enders do not remain in or come back to the West End simply because it is practical (inexpensive, close to facilities) is further documented by the responses of the question, "Which neighborhood, this one or any other place, do you think of as your real home, that is where you feel you really belong?" It is quite striking that fully 71 percent of the people named the West End as their real home, only slightly less than the proportion who specify liking the West End or liking it very much. Although there is a strong relationship between

TABLE 2. Feelings about the West End

Feelings	Number	Percent	
Totals	473	100	
Like very well	174	37 }	75
Like	183	38 }	
Mixed like-dislike	47	10 }	14
Indifferent	18	4 }	
Dislike	25	5 }	10
Dislike very much	23	5 }	
No answer	3	1	

liking the West End and viewing it as home, 14 percent of those who view the West End as home have moderately or markedly negative feelings about the area. On the other hand, 50 percent of those who do not regard the West End as home have moderately or markedly positive feelings about the area. Thus, liking the West End is not contingent on experiencing the area as that place in which one most belongs. However, the responses to this item give us an even more basic and global sense of the meaning the West End had for a very large proportion of its inhabitants.

These responses merely summarize a group of sentiments that pervade the interviews, and they form the essential context for understanding more discrete meanings and functions of the area. There are clearly differences in the details, but the common core lies in a widespread feeling of belonging someplace, of being "at home" in a region that extends out from but well beyond the dwelling unit. Nor is this only because of familiarity, since a very large proportion of the more recent residents (64 percent of those who moved into the West End during 1950 or after) also showed clearly positive feelings about the area. And 30 percent of those who moved in during 1950 or after regard the West End as their real home.[5]

Types of residential "belonging"

Finer distinctions in the quality and substance of positive feelings about the West End reveal a number of variations. In categorizing the qualita-

---

[5] It is possible, of course, that we have obtained an exaggerated report of positive feelings about the area because of the threat of relocation. Not only does the consistency of the replies and their internal relationships lead us to believe that this has not caused a major shift in response, but, bearing in mind the relative lack of verbal facility of many of the respondents and their frequent tendencies to give brief replies, we suspect that the interview data often lead to underestimating the strength of sentiment.

tive aspects of responses to two questions which were analyzed together ("How do you feel about living in the West End?" and "What will you miss most about the West End?"), we distinguished three broad differences of emphasis among the positive replies. The three large categories are: (1) *integral belonging:* sense of *exclusive* commitment, taking West End for granted as home, thorough familiarity and security; (2) *global commitment:* sense of profound gratification (rather than familiarity), pleasure in West End and enjoyment; and (3) *discrete satisfaction:* specific satisfying or pleasurable opportunities or atmosphere involving no special commitment to *this* place.

Only a small proportion (13 percent) express their positive feelings in terms of logically irreplaceable ties to people and places. They do so in often stark and fundamental ways: this is my home; it's all I know; everyone I know is here; I won't leave. A larger group (38 percent) are less embedded and take the West End less for granted but, nonetheless, express an all-encompassing involvement with the area which few areas are likely to provide them again. Their replies point up a less global but poignant sense of loss: it's one big happy family; I'll be sad; we were happy here; it's so friendly; it's handy to everything and everyone is congenial and friendly. The largest group (40 percent) are yet further removed from a total commitment but, in spite of the focused and discrete nature of their satisfaction with the interpersonal atmosphere or the convenience of the area, remain largely positive in feeling.

Differences in foci of positive feelings

Thus, there is considerable variability in the depth and type of feeling implied by liking the West End; and the West End as home had different connotations for different people. For a large group, the West End as home seems to have implied a comfortable and satisfying base for moving out into the world and back. Among this group, in fact, the largest proportion were more concerned with accessibility to other places than with the locality itself. But for more than half the people, their West End homes formed a far more central feature of their total life space.

There is a difference within this larger group between a small number for whom the West End seems to have been the place *to* which they belonged and a larger number for whom it seems rather to have been the place *in* which they belonged. But for the larger group as a whole the West End occupied a unique status, beyond any of the specific attributes one could list and point to concretely. This sense of uniqueness, of home, was not simply a function of social relationships, for the place in itself was the object of strong positive feelings. Most people

(42 percent) specify both people and places or offer a global, encompassing reason for their positive feelings. But almost an equally small proportion (13 percent and 10 percent, respectively) select out people or places as the primary objects of positive experience.

With respect to the discrete foci for positive feelings, similar conclusions can be drawn from another question: "Which places do you mostly expect to miss when you leave the West End?" In spite of the place-orientation of the question, 16 percent specify some aspect of interpersonal loss as the most prominent issue. But 40 percent expect to miss one of the places which is completely identified with the area or, minimally, carries a specific local identity. The sense of the West End as a local region, as an area with a spatial identity going beyond (although it may include) the social relationships involved, is a common perception. In response to the question: "Do you think of your home in the West End as part of a local neighborhood?"[6] 81 percent replied affirmatively. It is this sense of localism as a basic feature of lower-class life and the functional significance of local interpersonal relationships and of local places which have been stressed by a number of studies of the working class[7] and are documented by many aspects of our data.

In summary, then, we observe that a number of factors contribute to the special importance that the West End seemed to bear for the large majority of its inhabitants.

1. Residence in the West End was highly stable, with relatively little movement from one dwelling unit to another and with minimal transience into and out of the area. Although residential stability is a fact of importance in itself, it does not wholly account for commitment to the area.

2. For the great majority of the people, the local area was a focus for strongly positive sentiments and was perceived, probably in its multiple meanings, as home. The critical significance of belonging in or to an area has been one of the most consistent findings in working-class communities both in the United States and in England.

3. The importance of localism in the West End, as well as in other working-class areas, can hardly be emphasized enough. This sense of a local spatial identity includes both local social relationships and local places. Although oriented around a common conception of the area as "home," there are a number of specific factors dominating the concrete meaning of the area for different people.

---

[6] This question is from the interview designed by Leo Srole and his associates for the Yorkville study in New York.

[7] The importance of localism in working-class areas has been most cogently described by Richard Hoggart, *The Uses of Literacy* (London: Chatto & Windus, 1857), and by Michael Young and Peter Wilmott, *Family and Kinship in East London* (New York: Free Press, 1957). In our own data, the perception of the area as a local neighborhood is largely independent of the individual's own commitment to the area.

The aims of urban renewal and the sources of pressure for renewal are manifold: Among the objectives we may include more rational and efficient use of land, the elimination of dilapidated buildings, increase in the municipal tax base, and the improvement of living conditions for slum dwellers. Although the social benefit to the slum dweller has received maximum public attention, it is always unclear how the life situation (or even the housing situation) of the working-class resident of a slum is supposed to be improved by slum clearance or even slum improvement. Public housing has not proved to be an adequate answer to this problem for many reasons. Yet public housing is the only feature of renewal programs that has even attempted to deal seriously with this issue.

In recent years, a number of reports have suggested that concern about slum conditions has been used to maneuver public opinion in order to justify use of eminent domain powers and demolition, largely for the benefit of middle- and upper-status groups. Although we cannot evaluate this political and economic issue, we do hope to understand the ways in which dislocation from a slum and relocation to new residential areas has, in fact, benefited or damaged the working-class residents involved. It is all too apparent, however, that the currently available data are inadequate for clarifying some of the most critical issues concerning the effects of residential relocation upon the subject populations.

We know very little about slums and the personal and social consequences of living in a slum. We know even less about the effects of forced dislocation from residential areas on people in general and on working-class people specifically. But national urban planning which, under these circumstances, becomes urban *social* planning, requires considerable knowledge and understanding of people and places affected by the plans. It is incumbent upon us to know both what is wrong with the slum and with slum life and what is right about slums and living in slums.[8] It is essentially this question, formulated as the meaning and consequences of living in a slum, that has motivated our inquiry into the sources of residential satisfaction in an urban slum. In turn, this study provides one of the bases for understanding the ways in which dislocation and relocation affect the patterns of personal and social adaptation of former residents of a slum.

In studying the reasons for satisfaction that the majority of slum residents experience, two major components have emerged. On the one hand, the residential area is the region in which a vast and interlock-

[8] There is, of course, the evident danger of considering a social pattern on the basis of "right" and "wrong" which, inevitably, merely reproduce our own transitory values. A careful and thorough analysis, however, provides its own correctives to our all-too-human biases.

ing set of social networks is localized. And, on the other, the physical area has considerable meaning as an extension of home, in which various parts are delineated and structured on the basis of a sense of belonging. These two components provide the context in which the residential area may so easily be invested with considerable, multiply determined meaning. Certainly, there are variations both in the importance of various factors for different people and in the total sense which people have of the local area. But the greatest proportion of this working-class group (like other working-class slum residents who have been described) shows a fairly common experience and usage of the residential area. This common experience and usage is dominated by a conception of the local area beyond the dwelling unit as an integral part of home. This view of an area as home and the significance of local people and local places are so profoundly at variance with typical middle-class orientations that it is difficult to appreciate the intensity of meaning, the basic sense of identity involved in living in the particular area. Yet it seems to form the core of the extensive social integration that characterizes this (and other) working-class slum populations.

These observations lead us to question the extent to which, through urban renewal, we relieve a situation of stress or create further damage. If the local spatial area and an orientation toward localism provide the core of social organization and integration for a large proportion of the working class, and if, as current behavioral theories would suggest, social organization and integration are primary factors in providing a base for effective social functioning, what are the consequences of dislocating people from their local areas? Or, assuming that the potentialities of people for adaptation to crisis are great, what deeper damage occurs in the process? And, if there are deleterious effects, are these widespread or do they selectively affect certain predictable parts of the population? We emphasize the negative possibilities because these are closest to the expectations of the population involved and because, so frequently in the past, vague positive effects on slum populations have been arbitrarily assumed. But it is clear that, in lieu of or along with negative consequences, there may be considerable social benefit.

The potential social benefits also require careful, systematic evaluation, since they may manifest themselves in various and sometimes subtle ways. Through a variety of direct and intervening factors, the forced residential shift may lead to changes in orientations toward work, leading to increased satisfaction in the occupational sphere; or, changes may occur in the marital and total familial relationship to compensate for decreased kinship and friendship contacts and, in turn, lead to an alternative (and culturally more syntonic) form of interpersonal satisfaction; or, there may be either widespread or selective decreases in problems such as delinquency, mental illness, and physical malfunctioning.

A realistic understanding of the effects, beneficial and/or deleterious, of dislocation and relocation from an urban slum clearly requires further study and analysis. Our consideration of some of the factors involved in working-class residential satisfaction in the slum provides one basis for evaluating the significance of the changes that take place with a transition to a new geographic and social environment. Only the careful comparison of prerelocation and postrelocation data can begin to answer these more fundamental questions and, in this way, provide a sound basis for planning urban social change.

14
THE FAILURE OF URBAN RENEWAL: A Critique and Some Proposals
Herbert J. Gans

Suppose that the government decided that jalopies were a menace to public safety and a blight on the beauty of our highways, and therefore took them away from their drivers. Suppose, then, that to replenish the supply of automobiles, it gave these drivers a hundred dollars each to buy a good used car and also made special grants to General Motors, Ford, and Chrysler to lower the cost—although not necessarily the price—of Cadillacs, Lincolns, and Imperials by a few hundred dollars. Absurd as this may sound, change the jalopies to slum housing, and I have described, with only slight poetic license, the first fifteen years of a federal program called urban renewal.

Since 1949, this program has provided local renewal agencies with federal funds and the power of eminent domain to condemn slum neighborhoods, tear down the buildings, and resell the cleared land to private developers at a reduced price. In addition to relocating the slum dwellers in "decent, safe, and sanitary" housing, the program was intended to stimulate large-scale private rebuilding, add new tax revenues to the dwindling coffers of the cities, revitalize their downtown areas, and halt the exodus of middle-class whites to the suburbs.

For some time now, a few city planners and housing experts have been pointing out that urban renewal was not achieving its general aims, and social scientists have produced a number of critical studies of individual renewal projects. These critiques, however, have mostly appeared in academic books and journals; otherwise there has been remarkably little public discussion of the federal program. Slum dwellers whose homes were to be torn down have indeed protested bitterly, but their outcries have been limited to particular projects; and because such outcries have rarely been supported by the local press, they have been easily brushed aside by the political power of the supporters of the projects in question. In the last few years, the civil rights movement has backed protesting slum dwellers, though again only at the local level, while rightists have opposed the use of eminent domain to take private property from one owner in order to give it to another (especially when the new one is likely to be from out-of-town and financed by New York capital).

Slum clearance has also come under fire from several prominent architectural and social critics, led by Jane Jacobs, who have been struggling to preserve neighborhoods like Greenwich Village, with their brownstones, lofts, and small apartment houses, against the encroachment of the large, high-rise projects built for the luxury market and the poor alike. But these efforts have been directed mainly at private clearance outside the federal program, and their intent has been to save the city for people (intellectuals and artists, for example) who, like tourists, want jumbled diversity, antique "charm," and narrow streets for visual adventure and aesthetic pleasure. (Norman Mailer carried such thinking to its farthest point in his recent attack in the *New York Times Magazine* on the physical and social sterility of high-rise housing; Mailer's attack was also accompanied by an entirely reasonable suggestion—in fact the only viable one that could be made in this context—that the advantages of brownstone living be incorporated into skyscraper projects.)

But if criticism of the urban renewal program has in the past been spotty and sporadic, there are signs that the program as a whole is now beginning to be seriously and tellingly evaluated. At least two comprehensive studies, by Charles Abrams and Scott Greer, are nearing publication, and one highly negative analysis—by an ultraconservative economist and often irresponsible polemicist—has already appeared: Martin Anderson's *The Federal Bulldozer.*[1] Ironically enough, Anderson's data are based largely on statistics collected by the Urban Renewal Administration. What, according to these and other data, has the program accomplished? It has cleared slums to make room for many luxury-housing and a few middle-income projects, and it has also provided inexpensive land for the expansion of colleges, hospitals, libraries, shopping areas, and other such institutions located in slum areas. As of March 1961, 126,000 dwelling units had been demolished and about 28,000 new ones built. The median monthly rental of all those

[1] (Cambridge, Mass.: MIT Press, 1964).

erected during 1960 came to $158, and in 1962, to $192—a stagger-ing figure for any area outside of Manhattan.

Needless to say, none of the slum dwellers who were dispossessed in the process could afford to move into these new apartments. Local renewal agencies were supposed to relocate the dispossessed tenants in "standard" housing within their means before demolition began, but such vacant housing is scarce in most cities, and altogether unavailable in some. And since the agencies were under strong pressure to clear the land and get renewal projects going, the relocation of the tenants was impatiently, if not ruthlessly, handled. Thus, a 1961 study of renewal projects in 41 cities showed that 60 percent of the dispos-sessed tenants were merely relocated in other slums; and in big cities, the proportion was even higher (over 70 percent in Philadelphia, ac-cording to a 1958 study). Renewal sometimes even created new slums by pushing relocatees into areas and buildings which then became overcrowded and deteriorated rapidly. This has principally been the case with Negroes who, both for economic and racial reasons, have been forced to double up in other ghettos. Indeed, because almost two-thirds of the cleared slum units have been occupied by Negroes, the urban renewal program has often been characterized as Negro clearance, and in too many cities, this has been its intent.

Moreover, those dispossessed tenants who found better housing usu-ally had to pay more rent than they could afford. In his careful study of relocation in Boston's heavily Italian West End,[2] Chester Hartman shows that 41 percent of the West Enders lived in good housing in this so-called slum (thus suggesting that much of it should not have been torn down) and that 73 percent were relocated in good housing— thanks in part to the fact that the West Enders were white. This im-provement was achieved at a heavy price, however, for median rents rose from $41 to $71 per month after the move.

According to renewal officials, 80 percent of all persons relocated now live in good housing, and rent increases were justified because many had been paying unduly low rent before. Hartman's study was the first to compare these official statistics with housing realities, and his figure of 73 percent challenges the official claim that 97 percent of the Boston West Enders were properly rehoused. This discrepancy may arise from the fact that renewal officials collected their data after the poorest of the uprooted tenants had fled in panic to other slums, and that officials also tended toward a rather lenient evaluation of the relocation housing of those actually studied in order to make a good record for their agency. (On the other hand, when they were certifying

[2] See the November 1964 issue of the *Journal of the American Institute of Planners.* The article also reviews all other relocation research and is a more reliable study of the consequences of renewal than Anderson's.

areas for clearance, these officials often exaggerated the degree of "blight" in order to prove their case.)

As for the substandard rents paid by slum dwellers, this is true in only a small proportion of cases, and then mostly among whites. Real-estate economists argue that families should pay at least 20 percent of their income for housing, but what is manageable for middle-income people is a burden to those with low incomes who pay a higher share of their earnings for food and other necessities. Yet even so, Negroes generally have to devote about 30 percent of their income to housing, and a Chicago study cited by Hartman reports that among nonwhite families earning less than $3000 a year, median rent rose from 35 percent of income before relocation to 46 percent afterward.

To compound the failure of urban renewal to help the poor, many clearance areas (Boston's West End is an example) were chosen, as Anderson points out, not because they had the worst slums, but because they offered the best sites for luxury housing—housing which would have been built whether the urban renewal program existed or not. Since public funds were used to clear the slums and to make the land available to private builders at reduced costs, the low-income population was in effect subsidizing its own removal for the benefit of the wealthy. What was done for the slum dwellers in return is starkly suggested by the following statistic: *only one-half of one percent* of all federal expenditures for urban renewal between 1949 and 1964 was spent on relocation of families and individuals; and 2 percent if payments are included.

Finally, because the policy has been to clear a district of all slums at once in order to assemble large sites to attract private developers, entire neighborhoods have frequently been destroyed, uprooting people who had lived there for decades, closing down their institutions, ruining small businesses by the hundreds, and scattering families and friends all over the city. By removing the structure of social and emotional support provided by the neighborhood, and by forcing people to rebuild their lives separately and amid strangers elsewhere, slum clearance has often come at a serious psychological as well as financial cost to its supposed beneficiaries. Marc Fried, a clinical psychologist who studied the West Enders after relocation, reported that 46 percent of the women and 38 percent of the men "give evidence of a fairly severe grief reaction or worse" in response to questions about leaving their tight-knit community. Far from "adjusting" eventually to this trauma, 26 percent of the women remained sad or depressed even two years after they had been pushed out of the West End.[3]

[3] See "Grieving for a Lost Home," in Leonard Duhl, ed., *The Urban Condition* (New York: Basic Books, 1963).

People like the Italians or the Puerto Ricans who live in an intensely group-centered way among three-generation "extended families" and ethnic peers have naturally suffered greatly from the clearance of entire neighborhoods. It may well be, however, that slum clearance has inflicted yet graver emotional burdens on Negroes, despite the fact that they generally live in less cohesive and often disorganized neighborhoods. In fact, I suspect that Negroes who lack a stable family life and have trouble finding neighbors, shopkeepers, and institutions they can trust may have been hurt even more by forcible removal to new areas. This suspicion is supported by another of Fried's findings—that the socially marginal West Enders were more injured by relocation than those who had been integral members of the old neighborhood. Admittedly, some Negroes move very often on their own, but then they at least do so voluntarily, and not in consequence of a public policy which is supposed to help them in the first place. Admittedly also, relocation has made it possible for social workers to help slum dwellers whom they could not reach until renewal brought them out in the open, so to speak. But then only a few cities have so far used social workers to make relocation a more humane process.

These high financial, social, and emotional costs paid by the slum dwellers have generally been written off as an unavoidable by-product of "progress," the price of helping cities to collect more taxes, bring back the middle class, make better use of downtown land, stimulate private investment, and restore civic pride. But as Anderson shows, urban renewal has hardly justified these claims either. (For one thing, urban renewal is a slow process: the average project has taken twelve years to complete.) Moreover, while the few areas suitable for luxury housing were quickly rebuilt, less desirable cleared land might lie vacant for many years because developers were—and are—unwilling to risk putting up high- and middle-income housing in areas still surrounded by slums. Frequently, they can be attracted only by promises of tax write-offs, which absorb the increased revenues that renewal is supposed to create for the city. Anderson reports that, instead of the anticipated 4 dollars for every public dollar, private investments have only just matched the public subsidies, and even the money for luxury housing has come forth largely because of federal subsidies. Thus, all too few of the new projects have produced tax gains and returned suburbanites, or generated the magic rebuilding boom.

Anderson goes on to argue that during the fifteen years of the federal urban renewal program, the private housing market has achieved what urban renewal has failed to do. Between 1950 and 1960, 12 million new dwelling units were built, and fully 6 million substandard ones disappeared—all without government action. The proportion of substandard housing in the total housing supply was reduced from 37 to 19 percent, and even among the dwelling units occupied by nonwhites, the proportion of substandard units has dropped from 72 to 44 percent. This comparison leads Anderson to the conclusion that the private market is much more effective than government action in removing slums and supplying new housing, and that the urban renewal program ought to be repealed.

It would appear that Anderson's findings and those of the other studies I have cited make an excellent case for doing so. However, a less biased analysis of the figures and a less tendentious mode of evaluating them than Anderson's leads to a different conclusion. To begin with, Anderson's use of nationwide statistics misses the few good renewal projects, those which have helped both the slum dwellers and the cities, or those which brought in enough new taxes to finance other city services for the poor. Such projects can be found in small cities and especially in those where high vacancy rates assured sufficient relocation housing of standard quality. More important, all the studies I have mentioned deal with projects carried out during the 1950s, and fail to take account of the improvements in urban renewal practice under the Kennedy and Johnson administrations. Although Anderson's study supposedly covers the period up to 1963, much of his data go no further than 1960. Since then, the federal bulldozer has moved into fewer neighborhoods, and the concept of rehabilitating rather than clearing blighted neighborhoods is more and more being underwritten by subsidized loans. A new housing subsidy program—known as 221(d) (3)—for families above the income ceiling for public housing has also been launched, and in 1964, Congress passed legislation for assistance to relocatees who cannot afford their new rents.

None of this is to say that Anderson would have had to revise his findings drastically if he had taken the pains to update them. These recent innovations have so far been small in scope—only 13,000 units were financed under 211 (d) (3) in the first two years—and they still do not provide subsidies sufficient to bring better housing within the price range of the slum residents. In addition, rehabilitation unaccompanied by new construction is nearly useless because it does not eliminate overcrowding. And finally, some cities are still scheduling projects to clear away the nonwhite poor who stand in the path of the progress of private enterprise. Unfortunately, many cities pay little attention to federal pleas to improve the program, using the local initiative granted them by urban renewal legislation to perpetuate the practices of the 1950s. Yet even with the legislation of the 1960s, the basic error in the original design of urban renewal remains: It is still a method for eliminating the slums in order to "renew" the city, rather than a program for properly rehousing slum dwellers.

Before going into this crucial distinction, we first need to be clear that private housing is not going to solve our slum problems. In the first place, Anderson conveniently ignores the fact that if urban renewal has benefited anyone, it is private enterprise. Bending to the pressure of the real-estate lobby, the legislation that launched urban renewal in effect required that private developers do the rebuilding, and most projects could therefore get off the drawing board only if they appeared to be financially attractive to a developer. Thus, his choice of a site and his rebuilding plans inevitably took priority over the needs of the slum dwellers.

It is true that Anderson is not defending private enterprise per se but the free market, although he forgets that it only exists today as a concept in reactionary minds and dated economics texts. The costs of land, capital, and construction have long since made it impossible for private developers to build for anyone but the rich, and some form of subsidy is needed to house everyone else. The building boom of the 1950s which Anderson credits to the free market was subsidized by income-tax deductions to homeowners and by F.H.A. 2nd V.A. mortgage insurance, not to mention the federal highway programs that have made the suburbs possible.

To be sure, these supports enabled private builders to put up a great deal of housing for middle-class whites. This in turn permitted well-employed workers, including some nonwhites, to improve their own situation by moving into the vacated neighborhoods. Anderson is quite right in arguing that if people earn good wages, they can obtain better housing more easily and cheaply in the not-quite-private market than through urban renewal. But this market is of little help to those employed at low or even factory wages, or the unemployed, or most Negroes who, whatever their earnings, cannot live in the suburbs. In consequence, 44 percent of all housing occupied by nonwhites in 1960 was still substandard, and even with present subsidies, private enterprise can do nothing for these people. As for laissez faire, it played a major role in creating the slums in the first place.

The solution, then, is not to repeal urban renewal, but to transform it from a program of slum clearance and rehabilitation into a program of urban rehousing. This means, first, building low- and moderate-cost housing on vacant land in cities, suburbs, and new towns beyond the suburbs, and also helping slum dwellers to move into existing housing outside the slums; and then, *after* a portion of the urban low-income population has left the slums, clearing and rehabilitating them through urban renewal. This approach is commonplace in many European countries, which have long since realized that private enterprise can no more house the population and eliminate slums than it can run the post office.

Of course, governments in Europe have a much easier task than ours in developing decent low-income projects. Because they take it for granted that housing is a national rather than a local responsibility, the government agencies are not hampered by the kind of real-estate and construction lobbies which can defeat or subvert American programs by charges of socialism. Moreover, their municipalities own a great deal of the vacant land, and have greater control over the use of private land than do American cities. But pehaps their main advantage is the lack of popular opposition to moving the poor out of the slums and into the midst of the more affluent residents. Not only is housing desperately short for all income groups, but the European class structure, even in Western socialist countries, is still rigid enough so that low- and middle-income groups can live near each other if not next to each other, and still "know their place."

In America, on the other hand, one's house and address are major signs of social status, and no one who has any say in the matter wants people of lower income or status in his neighborhood. Middle-class homeowners use zoning as a way of keeping out cheaper or less prestigious housing, while working-class communities employ less subtle forms of exclusion. Consequently, low-income groups, whatever their creed or color, have been forced to live in slums or near-slums, and to wait until they could acquire the means to move as a group, taking over better neighborhoods when the older occupants were ready to move on themselves.

part 5 URBAN TRANSPORTATION

Transportation systems facilitate the contact between people and their places of employment, thereby making urban agglomeration economies possible. The quality of transportation services is therefore an important factor in the effective operation of the urban economy. Transportation is also a major commodity purchased by most people, accounting for about 10 percent of all outlays for consumption. Automobile congestion and poor quality public transit service increase the monetary and time costs of mobility within cities, lowering the welfare of the population. An effective transportation policy improves the welfare of area residents indirectly by improving communication among socioeconomic units and directly by lowering the costs associated with a major item in the typical consumer's budget.

A characteristic of modern urban life in America is the deterioration of public transportation systems. Roger Sherman argues that the average cost pricing of public transportation makes the automobile a cheaper alternative for most people. Declining patronage of public transportation systems may be a result of the different methods of pricing automobiles and public transit. Sherman proposes pricing of public transportation facilities more like that of the private automobile, hence eliminating the bias in favor of the automobile.

William S. Vickrey agrees that pricing is at the root of the urban transportation problem. In contrast to Sherman, he argues that the congestion and other negative external effects from the use of the private automobile should be controlled by making the price of automobile use higher. Vickrey would have the users of automobiles pay the social as well as the private costs of their transportation. Various mechanisms for pricing illustrate that price can be an effective method of controlling the use of the private automobile.

As it is often alleged that the dominant position of the private automobile in America is a major reason for the decay of the central cities, controlling the private automobile might give the central core of metropolitan areas a new lease on life. John R. Meyer argues that most urban problems are not likely to be solved by the resurgence of public transit in our major cities. Consumers must choose between inferior mass transit or expensive private transportation. Meyer argues that cities should be able to generate more attractive alternatives.

170

15
A PRIVATE OWNERSHIP BIAS IN TRANSIT CHOICE
Roger Sherman

The continuing defection of public transit riders in big cities suggests that eventual dominance by private automobiles may be inevitable [7, pp. 267–269]. A Chicago survey has indicated that only a very large subsidy would persuade a significant number of auto travelers to switch to public modes [8]. There remains a question, however, whether the private auto is gaining ascendancy by genuine consumer choice or because private costs differ sufficiently from social costs to produce a misallocation of resources in favor of autos. A. A. Walters attempted the difficult analysis of auto travel's social cost using data from several studios and concluded: "In order to make private costs approach social cost we suggest that a *minimum* fuel tax of 33 cents a gallon must be raised" [9, p. 67].[1] C. O. Meiburg raised another allocation issue by pointing out tendencies toward overinvestment in highways through our political decision process, which builds highways to relieve congestion but also distributes them free so that congestion is inevitable [5].

* Assistant professor of economics, University of Virginia. This research was begun under a Graduate School of Industrial Administration Fellowship at Carnegie Institute of Technology. I am grateful to Professors James M. Buchanan, Kalman J. Cohen, Otto A. Davis, and Allan H. Meltzer for criticism and advice. Any remaining errors are mine.

[1] Walters argues further that railroad fares are greater than the marginal cost of the service they purchase (except for peak periods on commuter services). This argument, combined with evidence that private auto costs are less than their marginal social cost, makes the allocation bias complete. Johnson calls for more precise pricing, after reaching similar conclusions regarding private and social costs [3]. Vickrey has long advocated more precise pricing and has proposed several practical means for achieving it [10].

Reprinted by permission from the *American Economic Review*, December 1967.

Such studies suggest that present institutional arrangements may not enable consumers to choose the allocation of transit resources they prefer.

On the reasonable assumption that costs decrease for each transit mode, we demonstrate in Section I a bias in consumer choice that favors private autos over public transit. The bias arises as a result of an auto traveler's commitment to auto ownership, which forces a choice between auto and other modes and also makes the average price he pays per mile vary with his usage while for public modes it does not. Also, constant prices for decreasing cost public transit modes can prevent optimal allocation among them, thereby making them a less effective substitute for auto travel. Section II describes one way of financing public transit that will avoid this particular allocation bias.

I. PRIVATE CHOICE: AUTOMOBILE, OR PUBLIC TRANSIT?

Broadly, there are 2 alternative travel means, the private automobile and public means, including bus, railroad, taxi, airplane, or rental vehicles. We should expect a consumer to choose either automobile or public transit, not both, because auto ownership carries with it a substantial commitment to the automobile as a means of travel. If used-car markets were perfect this might not be so, for a consumer could then buy a car for 1 trip and sell it afterward. But transaction costs in automobile markets are high. Not only does the purchase of an automobile require time and effort, its sudden sale at an inopportune time will result in financial sacrifice. A tendency of persons to travel either by auto or public transit is evident in data from a Chicago study of commuters [6, pp. 138–141]. Of those who owned cars (85 percent owned cars), 4 out of 5 used the car in traveling to work, 3 out of 4 traveling all the way into the city by car. Of those who did not own cars, 85 percent traveled to work via public transit.

Over a short period, the marginal cost of auto travel will be very low for an auto owner while for a nonowner, transaction costs make short-period marginal cost very high. Thus, the short-run choice between public and private transit will depend on whether the chooser already owns an automobile. Analysis of choice must extend over a time period long enough to permit an effective choice, enough time for a consumer to purchase or sell an automobile and satisfactorily amortize his transaction costs. The average period of automobile ownership in the United States is a little more than three years [11], and we shall assume that the auto-traveling consumer bases his choice on an estimate of his auto travel costs over that period. To avail himself of such long-run costs, however, he must commit himself to auto travel for the period. Failing such commitment, he will have to confine his travel primarily to the public mode.

Some costs of auto travel vary with time (for example, insurance, licensing, garaging, some depreciation) and others vary with miles traveled, so traveling more miles over a given time period will lead to a lower average cost per mile. Notice that the cost per auto mile, or consumer price per mile, will therefore be different for different consumers, depending on how many miles they travel. The effect of miles traveled on price per mile will, in turn, affect the consumer's decision regarding the number of miles he travels. By thus affecting planned travel miles, marginal cost exerts an influence on the eventual average price per auto mile, making the average cost lower for consumers who travel more. Average cost per mile also decreases with more miles traveled via public transit. In the public transit case, however, there can exist one average cost per mile, when fixed costs are allocated over the total number of passenger miles traveled. As a consequence of such cost allocation a single, constant price per mile can be charged users of public transit and related to the cost per passenger mile.[2] Since we wish to examine allocation in the absence of subsidies, and because we consider a combination of public modes some of which are not subsidized, we shall assume that cost and price per mile are equal. In the public transit case, then, one consumer's price is not affected by his usage. To see the difficulties this arrangement causes for resource allocation among transportation modes, consider the consumer's utility-maximizing problem.

Well-known conditions for the consumer to maximize his utility require that his marginal utility from each good divided by its marginal price be equal for all goods and services consumed, this ratio of marginal utility to marginal price being the consumer's marginal utility of income. In planning his possible auto travel over a 3-year period, the consumer must first reduce income available for all goods by making fixed payments associated with auto ownership. Consumption of all goods (ignoring inferior goods) is reduced as a result. At the same time, a lower marginal price is used to evaluate auto miles traveled, and this invites the consumer to travel more than he would if he paid a constant average price per mile. In planning possible public transit travel, in contrast, the consumer bases his usage on a constant average price which equals average cost but is greater than marginal cost. The private auto arrangement has an advantage for utility maximizing that can be

---

[2] The charge may only approximate a price equal to cost per passenger mile because of administrative problems in fare collection, but we regard the pricing of public transit as on a fee-per-mile basis.

illustrated easily. Regard as private transit an automobile, privately purchased. Consider as a public transit alternative an automobile that can be rented, the rental rate per mile for one person being regulated at an average price equal to average cost. If a person is given a private or public choice in these terms, he will always prefer the private alternative, for he can reach the same consumption goods mix that is available to him under the public arrangement and because of a lower effective marginal price can reach a preferred position as well (assuming only that the marginal rate of substitution between travel and other goods diminishes).

When this example is extended to a genuine public transit service, there will be only one average price for all public transit consumers rather than a different one for each consumer. That single average price is affected not by one's own usage of the service, but by the usage of all other consumers combined. Those whose marginal utility from travel diminishes rapidly are then likely to prefer public transit because the price per public transit mile is lower than they can achieve privately. Those who travel much, however, will face a lower cost per mile via auto travel. It is this effect that is troublesome in decreasing cost industries, where long-run average cost can be lowered by higher rates of usage. The commitment that will enable an individual to achieve the benefits of his own higher usage is a commitment to automobile ownership, which will simultaneously reduce the usage of public transit services. It does so because the auto owner enjoys a low marginal price per mile by auto once he commits himself to ownership, and is therefore less likely to seek public transportation at a price equal to its average cost. Thus, if benefits of higher usage are available only through the private auto transportation mode, that mode will be made more attractive, while passenger miles lost to it from public modes will raise the average cost of service via those modes.

The allocation problem is further aggravated by the presence of many separate public transit modes. From the utility-maximizing model we know that in choosing among public transit modes, a consumer's marginal utility from each mode divided by its marginal price must be equal for every mode that is used. If marginal costs of public transit modes are not proportional to average costs,[3] consumers who face prices equal to average cost are sure to reach an equilibrium that is nonoptimal. Exchanges among the consumers, at marginal costs, could improve their welfare. Thus, the coordination of different public modes

---

[3] We are not suggesting that proportionality to marginal cost is a satisfactory price criterion. It is surely not satisfied by public transit modes.

through single, fixed prices is imperfect. And failure to achieve an optimal combination of the different modes reduces the effectiveness of public transit as a substitute for auto travel.

II. AVOIDING OWNERSHIP BIAS

One way to achieve an efficient combination of public transit services, and at the same time offset the advantage of marginal cost influence in private auto choice, is to subsidize all public transit modes so that they may price at marginal cost. Unfortunately, this will not solve the problem completely, for it makes inefficiencies necessary elsewhere in order to finance the subsidy. More important, it implicitly raises the question: Should an automobile be given to every family as well, so that only short-run marginal costs will influence the choice between public and private transit? The costly duplication that would result from such a scheme reveals the importance, shown clearly by R. H. Coase [2], of affording long-run as well as short-run choice; consumers must take into account all costs when expressing their preference, not just short-run marginal costs. But to cover all costs, the fees would have to be in two parts: one for short-run marginal costs, and another for fixed costs which depend on time rather than usage.[4]

Since coordination of public transit modes is needed to make public transit effective as an alternative to the private automobile, a collective institution such as a public transit club would offer genuine advantages. Membership fees could correspond to fixed costs of the modes chosen by the member. Nonmembers could still have access to the public modes but at higher prices per mile than members, who would pay only marginal costs. The club could of course serve as a credit institution as well, for it would be a billing and collection agency. Fixed fees could be distributed among the modes by the club, dividing the fee among different firms within each mode in proportion to the direct services provided by the firms. To be sure, allocating investment risks and fixed costs of the modes among members in the form of fixed fees is not easy. The degree of commitment to an automobile is evident to any owner; he makes an investment in an auto and he assumes risks of ownership. Unlike the automobile case, public transit investment does not occur in separate parts that are identified with each user. Nevertheless, the fixed costs of a public transit mode, for example, vehicles, roadbed, and

[4] According to Lewis [4] a "two-part tariff" was first proposed by Dr. John Hopkinson in 1892 in a recommendation for fixed and variable prices of electric power in England.

structures, will depend on the number of passengers it must be capable of carrying, not just on passenger miles. Indeed, the number of rush-hour passengers has repeatedly been revealed to be a crucial determinant of costs for different public transit modes.[5] And if members can influence their average price per public transit mile by making a fixed payment and then paying a marginal price equal to marginal cost, the bias in favor of automobiles will be eliminated.[6]

It would be possible to accommodate many variations in a membership institution. When several agencies offer service by the same mode, differences in variable fees are possible and would enforce competition *within* those modes. Classes of service could also be distinguished, in fixed or variable fees or in both. Where different services share fixed costs jointly it might be desirable to grant access to both services, at appropriate prices per mile, for only one fixed fee. Peak load pricing can be accommodated, too. For example, limited memberships which deny rush-hour access might be offered at lower fees.[7] Our purpose is only to register feasibility, and so we shall not elaborate further on these possibilities. Fortunately, large, established public transportation institutions already exist. Thus, the major problems would be those that accompany transition to an institutional form which would unify pricing, not problems associated with the initiation of new transit agencies or modes.

Organizing such an institution is not a simple matter, to be sure. Especially difficult is the question of its geographic scope. It seems most appropriate for individual cities, yet one of its advantages is coordination of all transit modes into an effective consumer service including intercity railroads and airlines, which would suggest national scope. The most practical form might be a federation of metropolitan Riders' Clubs, each serving major urban centers in the country. Whether the Riders' Clubs be public or private enterprises is an interesting issue we cannot open here. Our objective is only to sketch an alternative institu-

---

[5] See, for example, [6] and [10].

[6] This proposal does not guarantee ideal resource allocation beyond the transportation sector. In particular, it may favor transportation generally, for it lets consumers evaluate their own effect on the price they pay per transportation unit, while prices for nontransportation goods and services are held constant (see [1]). If these other goods and services are produced by perfectly competitive industries, however, their marginal costs should equal their prices and so no misallocation need arise. Alternative goods supplied by public utilities such as telephone and electricity are often priced in a manner that reflects usage, and this proposal only offsets their former advantage.

It should be noted that two-part price arrangements, often called incentive prices, have been applied to transit in a number of places with varying degrees of success. Some communities forbid their use. While such prices would tend to reduce the bias examined here, they have not been broad enough in scope to significantly offset it.

[7] A family could possess one membership with rush-hour privileges and limited membership for all other family members. Occasional rush-hour travel could still be made, of course, but at higher nonmember prices.

tion which might enhance the effectiveness of consumer choice and of the competitive process among those who provide transportation services.

III. SUMMARY

A resource allocation bias can favor private autos when an ownership commitment encourages an either/or choice between private and public modes, assuming that all transit is characterized by decreasing costs, and that public transit must cover its costs and uses single, constant prices to do so. Possible misallocation among the public transit modes was also demonstrated. To compensate for these allocative biases, we proposed a collective institution to implement fixed and variable fees. The proposed institution would enable each consumer to plan his transit usage, taking account of approximate marginal social costs, and on that basis make a forward commitment either to private or public transit means. In this way investment in transit resources, as well as short-run usage, can be coordinated. The rise in alternative transit modes makes this approach more appropriate than the traditional regulation of separate monopolies. The argument is relevant primarily for urban areas, where substitution possibilities are greatest, where necessary organizing is most feasible, and where transit resource allocation problems are most urgent.

REFERENCES

1. J. M. BUCHANAN, "The Theory of Monopolistic Quantity Discounts," *Rev. Econ. Stud.,* 20 (3), 1953, 199–208.
2. R. H. COASE, "The Marginal Cost Controversy," *Economica,* 13 (Aug. 1946) 169–182.
3. M. B. JOHNSON, "The Economics of Highway Congestion," *Econometrica,* 32 (April 1964), 137–150.
4. W. A. LEWIS, *Overhead Costs* (Clifton, N.J.: Kelley, repr. 1970).
5. C. O. MEIBURG, "An Economic Analysis of Highway Services," *Quart. Jour. Econ.,* 77 (Nov. 1963), 648–656.
6. J. R. MEYER, J. F. KAIN, AND M. WOHL, *The Urban Transportation Problem* (Cambridge, Mass.: Harvard University Press, 1965).
7. J. R. MEYER, M. J. PECK. J. P. STENASON, AND C. J. ZWICK, *Competition in the Transportation Industries* (Cambridge, Mass.: Harvard University Press, 1960).
8. L. N. MOSES AND H. F. WILLIAMSON, JR., "Value of Time, Choice of Mode,

and the Subsidy Issue in Urban Transportation," *Jour. Pol. Econ.*, 71 (June 1963), 247–264.

9. A. A. WALTERS, "The Theory and Measurement of Private and Social Cost of Highway Congestion," *Econometrica*, 29 (Oct. 1961), 676–699.

10. W. S. VICKREY, *The Revision of the Rapid Transit Fare Structure of the City of New York*, Mayor's Committee on Management Survey of the City of New York, Tech. Monogr. No. 3, New York, 1952.

11. AUTOMOBILE MANUFACTURERS' ASSOCIATION, *Automobile Facts and Figures*. Detroit, 1964.

16
PRICING IN URBAN
AND SUBURBAN TRANSPORT
William S. Vickrey

I will begin with the proposition that in no other major area are pricing practices so irrational, so out of date, and so conducive to waste as in urban transportation. Two aspects are particularly deficient: the absence of adequate peak-off differentials and the gross underpricing of some modes relative to others.

In nearly all other operations characterized by peak load problems, at least some attempt is made to differentiate between the rates charged for peak and for off-peak service. Where competition exists, this pattern is enforced by competition: resort hotels have off-season rates; theaters charge more on weekends and less for matinees. Telephone calls are cheaper at night, though I suspect not sufficiently so to promote a fully efficient utilization of the plant. Power rates are varied to a considerable extent according to the measured or the imputed load factor of the consumer, and in some cases, usually for special-purpose uses such as water heating, according to the time of use. In France, this practice is carried out logically by charging according to season and time of day for all consumption but that of the smallest domestic consumers; rate changes at the consumers' meters are triggered by a special frequency signal actuating a tuned relay which connects or disconnects auxiliary registers. But in transportation, such differentiation as exists is usually perverse. Off-peak concessions are virtually unknown in transit. Such concessions as are made in suburban service for "shoppers tickets" and the like are usually relatively

Reprinted by permission from the *American Economic Review*, May 1963.

small, indeed are often no greater than those available in multitrip tickets not restricted to off-peak riding, and usually result in fares still far above those enjoyed by regular commuters who are predominantly peak-hour passengers.

In the case of suburban railroad fares, the existing pattern is even contrary to what would be most profitable in terms of the relative elasticities of demand. Both on a priori grounds and on the basis of the analysis of the historical experience recently made by Elbert Segelhorat in a forthcoming Columbia dissertation, it is clear that the price elasticity of the off-peak traffic, at current fare levels at least, is substantially higher than that of peak-hour traffic. If, for example, the average suburban family spends $300 per year for commuting and peak-hour trips and $50 per year for occasional off-peak trips and the commutation fares were increased by 5 percent, causing a 1 percent drop in this traffic, while off-peak fares were reduced 40 percent, with a 30 percent increase in traffic, gross revenues per commuting family would go up from $350.00 to $350.85, with operating costs if anything reduced slightly, since nearly all costs are determined by the peak traffic level. The riding public would on the average be substantially better off: The above typical family, if it maintained the same pattern of usage, would pay only $315 + $30 = $345 instead of $350 as formerly, and any adaptation that it chose to make to the new rates would represent a further benefit, since the alternative of no change would still be open to it if it preferred. Things may not work out quite this neatly in practice, but the potential for substantial gains from even more drastic revisions in the rate structure is certainly there.

Fare collection procedures are sometimes urged as an excuse for not going to a more rational fare structure, but here there has been a deplorable lag behind what a little ingenuity or modern technology makes possible. There would be relatively little difficulty in devising apparatus for collecting subway fares on as elaborate an origin, destination, and time basis as might be desired, simply by dispensing a coded check at the entrance turnstile against the deposit of an interim fare, this check being deposited in an exit turnstile which will then either refund any excess or release only on the deposit of the remainder of the fare. Bus fares represent a problem that has yet to be satisfactorily solved, but considering the vast waste of the time of operators and passengers through delays caused by present fare collection methods, a concerted attack on this problem should yield high dividends. For commuter railroads, the possibility exists of issuing machine-readable subscriber's cards, with passengers making a record of their trips by inserting the card in a register at the origin and destination of the trips actually made by the subscriber, his family, and guests. Something like this seems to be in the offing for the new San Francisco system, which in many respects is more of a commuter service than an urban transit system. Actually, it is not even necessary to enclose the stations in order to use such a system: Proper registering at the stations can be enforced by dispensing a dated seat check to be displayed during the trip and deposited in registering out at the destination.

Even short of such mechanization, existing ticketing arrangements are needlessly clumsy, involving in many cases a duplication of effort between station agent and conductor and fairly elaborate accounting and auditing procedures. The New York Central has recently taken a step forward in this respect by arranging to mail monthly commutation tickets to patrons and receive payment by mail. Gross delinquency appears to be running appreciably less than the saving in ticket agents' time, and the net credit loss is undoubtedly much less than this, since many who fail to return or pay for their tickets in fact do not use them, as when they die or move away. Another wrinkle worth trying would be the use of a universal form of multiride ticket, to be sold by ticket agents or conductors at a flat price of $5.00 or $10.00, validated for bearer and those accompanying him, with a liberal time limit, for a number of rides or trip units depending on the stations between which it is designated to be used by appropriate punches at time of sale. An off-peak differential could be provided in conjunction with this type of ticket by providing that two units would be charged for an off-peak ride as against three units for a peak-hour ride. The ticket itself, for a typical suburban route, need be no larger than an ordinary playing card. Accounting would be greatly simplified, conductor's cash fare transactions would be both simplified and greatly reduced in number, and the use of the service would become much more convenient for passengers. Such a ticket would provide a more effective off-peak differential than the shoppers' type of ticket, since those who are either going or returning during the peak or are returning at a later date cannot usually avail themselves of such tickets.

But while suburban and transit fare structures are seriously deficient, the pricing of the use of urban streets is all but nonexistent. Superficially, it is often thought that since reported highway expenditures by the state and federal government are roughly balanced by highway tax and license revenues, the motorist is on the whole paying his way. But what is true on the average is far from true of users of the more congested urban streets. Much of the expenditure on such streets is borne by city budgets supported slightly if at all by explicit contributions from highway sources, in most states. More important, much of the real economic cost of providing the space for city streets and highways does not appear in the accounts at all, being concealed by the fact that this space has usually been "dedicated" to the public use at some time in the past. It is extremely difficult to make close evaluations from the scanty and scattered data available, but very roughly it appears to me that if we take the burden of all the gasoline and other vehicular taxes borne by motorists by reason of their use of city streets, this amounts to only about a third of the real economic cost of the facilities they use. In current terms, the high marginal cost of increased street space becomes painfully apparent whenever a street widening scheme is evaluated. Even in terms of long-range planning, urban expressways cost many times as much as expressways in rural areas built to comparable specifications, and while the flow of traffic may be greater, this is not enough to come anywhere near amortizing the cost out of the taxes paid by the traffic flowing over the urban expressways. Even when tolls are charged in conjunction with special features such as bridges or tunnels, these seldom cover the cost of the connecting expressways and city streets. And except where the street layout is exceptionally favorable, such tolls usually have an unfavorable effect on the routing of traffic.

The perversity of present pricing practices is at its height, perhaps, for the East River crossings to Long Island and Brooklyn. Here the peculiar political logic is that the older bridges are in some sense "paid for," and hence must be free, while tolls must be charged on the newer facilities. The result is that considerable traffic is diverted from the newer facilities that have relatively adequate and less congested approaches to the older bridges such as the Manhattan and the Queensboro bridges, which dump their traffic right in the middle of some of the worst congestion in New York. The construction of the proposed expressway across lower Manhattan from the Holland Tunnel to the Manhattan and Williamsburg bridges would be at least less urgent, if not actually unwarranted, in view of its enormous cost, if, as would seem possible, traffic could be diverted from the Manhattan Bridge to the Brooklyn-Battery tunnel by imposing tolls on the Manhattan and other East River bridges and reducing or removing the toll on the tunnel. The delusion still persists that the primary role of pricing should always be that of financing the service rather than that of promoting economy in its use. In practice there are many alternative ways of financing; but no device can function quite as effectively and smoothly as a properly designed price structure in controlling use and providing a guide to the efficient deployment of capital.

The underpricing of highway services is even more strongly pronounced during peak hours. Even if urban motorists on the average paid the full cost of the urban facilities, rush-hour use would still be seriously underpriced; moreover, this underpricing would be relatively more severe than for transit or commutation service. This is because off-peak traffic on the highways and streets is a much larger percentage of the total than is the case for either transit or commutation traffic; and therefore in the process of averaging out the costs, much more of the costs properly attributable to the peak can be shifted to the shoulders of the off-peak traffic than can be thus shifted in the case of transit or commutation service. The effect of this is that while the commutation fare problem is chiefly one of the overpricing of off-peak travel, and to a minor extent if at all one of underpricing of peak travel, the problem of the pricing of automobile travel is chiefly that of remedying the underpricing of peak travel, and to a relatively minor extent if at all of the overpricing of off-peak travel. These 2 relationships combine to give the result that even if motor traffic and commuter train traffic each on the whole fully paid their way on the basis of a uniform charge per trip, the proportion by which the peak-hour motorist would be subsidized by the off-peak motorists would be far greater than the proportion by which the peak-hour commuter is subsidized by the off-peak commuter.

A quantitative indication of the seriousness of the problem of peak-hour automobile traffic is derivable from some projections made for Washington, D.C. Two alternative programs were developed for taking care of traffic predicted under 2 alternative conditions, differing chiefly as to the extent to which express transit service would be provided. The additional traffic lanes required for the larger of the 2 volumes of traffic would be needed almost solely to provide for this added rush-hour traffic, the less extensive road system being adequate for the off-peak traffic even at the higher over-all traffic level. Dividing the extra cost by the extra rush-hour traffic, it turned out that for each additional car making a daily trip that contributes to the dominant flow, during the peak hour, an additional investment of $23,000 was projected. In other words, a man who bought a $3,000 car for the purpose of driving downtown to work every day would be asking the community, in effect, to match his $3000 investment with $23,000 from general highway funds. Or if the wage earners in a development were all to drive downtown to work, the investment in highways that this development would require would be of the same order of magnitude as the entire investment in a moderate-sized house for each family. It may be that the affluent society will be able to shoulder such a cost, but even if it could there would seem to be many much more profitable and urgent uses to which sums of this magnitude could be put. And even if we assume that staggering of working hours could spread the peak traffic more or less evenly over three hours, this would still mean $8000 per daily trip, even though achievement of such staggering would represent an achievement second only to the highway construction itself. At 250 round trips per year, allowing 10 percent as the gross return which a comparable investment in the private sector would have to earn to cover interest, amortization, and property and corporate income taxes, this amounts to over $3.00 per round trip, or, on a one-hour peak basis, to $9.00 per round trip, if staggering is ruled out. This is over and above costs of maintenance or of provision for parking. When costs threaten to reach such levels, it is high time to think seriously about controlling the use through pricing.

It is sometimes thought that pricing of roadway use would apply chiefly to arterial streets and highways and that it would have no application to streets used mainly for access, which should allegedly be paid for by property taxes on the abutting property to which access is given. But the relevant criterion is not the function performed, but the degree of congestion that would obtain in the absence of pricing. To be sure, there would be little point in levying a specific charge for the use of suburban residential side streets or lightly traveled rural roads, since the congestion added by an increment in traffic is virtually nil in such circumstances and the wear and tear usually negligible. In effect, at these levels of traffic the economics of scale are such that marginal cost is only a small fraction of the average cost. But this does not hold for roadways used for access at the center of a city. A truck making a delivery on a narrow side street may cause as much congestion and delay to others as it would in many miles of running on an arterial highway. Even in the case of a cul-de-sac that is used exclusively for access and carries no through traffic, a firm with frequent deliveries will make access more difficult for his neighbors; only by specific pricing of such use can the firm requiring much access be differentiated from firms requiring relatively little, and encouraged to locate where its activities will be less burdensome to the remainder of the community; or to receive and ship goods at times when less congestion is generated. Some of the worst traffic congestion in New York occurs as a result of the way access is had to firms in the garment district; restrictions on truck size and exhortations have produced only minor improvement. It seems likely that a suitable charge for such use of road space would be more acceptable than an arbitrary and drastic ban, and that with a definite financial incentive methods might be found to avoid the creation of congestion.

But talk of direct and specific charges for roadway use conjures up visions of a clutter of toll booths, an army of toll collectors, and traffic endlessly tangled up in queues. Conventional methods of toll collection are, to be sure, costly in manpower, space, and interference with the smooth flow of traffic. Furthermore, unless the street configuration is exceptionally favorable, tools often contribute to congestion over parallel routes. However, with a little ingenuity, it is possible to devise methods of charging for the use of the city streets that are relatively inexpensive, produce no interference with the free flow of traffic, and are capable of adjusting the charge in close conformity with variations in costs and traffic conditions. My own fairly elaborate scheme involves equipping all cars with an electronic identifier which hopefully can be produced on a large-scale basis for about $20 each. These blocks would be scanned by roadside equipment at a fairly dense network of cordon points, making a record of the identity of the car; these records would then be taken to a central processing plant once a month and the records assembled on electronic digital computers and bills sent out. Preliminary estimates indicate a total cost of the equipment on a moderately large scale of about $35 per vehicle, including the identifier; the operating cost would be approximately that involved in sending out telephone bills. Bills could be itemized to whatever extent is desired to furnish the owner with a record that would guide him in the further use of his car. In addition, roadside signals could be installed to indicate the current level of charge and enable drivers to shift to less costly routes where these are available.

Other methods have been devised in England, where the country can less well afford the vast outlays demanded by our rubber-tired sacred cow, and where street layouts are such as to make provision for large volumes of vehicular traffic both more costly and more destructive of civic amenities. One scheme suggested for use in a pilot scheme for the town of Cambridge involves the use of identifiers to actuate a tallying register, the rate of tallying being governed by impulses the frequency of which would vary according to the degree of traffic congestion existing in the zone in which the car is reported to be. Another extremely simple and low-cost but less automatic device would consist of a meter installed in each car so as to be visible from outside, which could be wound up by the insertion of a token sold at an appropriate price—the token being subject to inspection through a window and being destroyed when the subsequent token is brought into place. The driver can control the rate at which the meter runs down by a lever or switch which simultaneously displays a signal which will indicate to outside observers the rate currently being charged. The driver is then required to keep this signal set to correspond with the rate in effect in the zone in which he is driving as indicated by appropriate wayside signals. Extremely simple methods of varying the rate at which the meter runs down have been devised in England, which for the time being I must treat as confidential. The rate can appropriately be a time rate rather than a distance rate, since the greater the congestion the greater is the appropriate charge, so that no connection to the wheels is needed and the whole meter can be extremely compact, rugged, and cheap. The chief difficulty with this method is the likelihood that drivers will "forget" to turn the rate of the meter up promptly on entering a higher rate zone, but given a reasonable amount of policing this difficulty might be overcome after an initial period of habituation.

A slightly more elaborate version of this method would call for the changes in the meter rate to be actuated automatically in response to signals emitted from wayside equipment at the boundaries of the various zones. This would probably raise the cost to something above the level of the response block method. On the other hand, both this and the previous method are somewhat better adapted to serving to assess charges for parking as well as for moving about within an area, so that the cost of servicing and installing parking meters could be properly credited against the cost of the new system.

Another version would call for the meter to be run down by pulses emitted from cables laid along the roadway, with the pulse rate varied according to traffic density and other factors. Alternatively, the cables could be arranged to emit continuously and located across the roadway—the number of cables turned on at any one time being varied according to traffic conditions. Reliability of operation can be assured by using two alternative frequencies in alternate cables successively. The cables need not be spaced evenly, but for economy in operation may be placed in groups so that they can be energized from a single source. With either of these methods, any failure of the meter to operate could be checked by requiring the meter to be placed in plain view and arranging for a visible signal to be changed cyclically as the meter is actuated.

Adequate methods for enforcement of each of the schemes seem available which are reasonably simple, with the possible exception of the manual system, where minor negligence might be difficult to check and lead to major negligence. With identifier methods, the registering of the proper vehicle number could be checked by having a few of the detector stations equipped with apparatus to display the number being registered, which could be compared with the license plate by observers. Errors due to malfunction, as well as most fraudulent tampering, would show up as a matter of course during the processing of the records, as each record showing a car entering a zone must match the immediately succeeding record for that car leaving that zone. Cameras can also be arranged at some locations to take pictures of cars not producing a valid response signal. With meters, arrangements can be made to hold used and mutilated tokens in a sealed box; these could be inspected and their number compared with a nonresettable counter with a capacity not likely to be exceeded during the life of the car, as a part of an annual safety inspection program.

Ultimately, one would expect that all cars in an entire country would be equipped with meters or electronic identifiers. Initially, however, it would be necessary to make some provision for cars from other areas. Cars in transit or making infrequent visits to the congested area could be given the freedom of the city in a spirit of hospitality. Cars making a longer stay or more frequent visits would be required to equip themselves—say at cordon points established along the major arteries entering the controlled area. Unequipped cars would be prohibited from using the minor streets crossing the boundary of the controlled area. Such provisions would be particularly easy to enforce with electronic identifier methods: unequipped cars passing major control points would set off a camera; unequipped cars using routes prohibited to them would set off an alarm signal, facilitating their apprehension. With a meter system, checking on unequipped cars would have to be largely a manual operation and would probably be considerably less rigorous. Actually a similar problem occurs at present in enforcing provisions against the use of out-of-state license plates in a given state for longer than a limited period.

Such charging for street use could have a far-reaching impact on the pattern of urban transportation and even on the patterns of land use, by promoting a more economical distribution of traffic between various modes, the various modes being used in accordance with their suitability for the particular trip in the light of the costs involved, instead of, as at present, being chosen to suit the preferences and whims of the individual regardless of the impact on others. Motorists will no longer be maneuvered into the position of being forced to pay for a luxury that they can ill-afford. Mass transportation will have an opportunity to develop in line with its inherent characteristics, eventually developing a quality and frequency of service that will in many cases be preferred even to the spuriously low-priced private car transportation that might be provided in the absence of a system of specific charges. Traffic-generating activities will tend to be located more rationally in relation to real transportation costs. For example, appropriate transportation charges might have been sufficient to have inhibited the construction of the Pan-American subway-jammer over Grand Central. Rapid vehicular transportation within congested areas, not now available at any price, will be generally available for meeting emergency and high priority needs where the cost is justified. Traffic will be routed more efficiently, so as to provide a smoother functioning of the roadway system as a whole. The levels of charge required to balance marginal cost and marginal benefit in the short run will provide a much more definite and reliable guide than is now available as to where and to what extent the provision of additional facilities can be justified. One can cite, for example, the extra half hour that the airlines have to allow during rush hours for the trip from East 38th Street to JFK International, in spite of the fact that this route is almost entirely over grade-separated expressways.

One effect of such charging would be to change the relative attractiveness of different forms of mass transportation. Under present conditions, buses are involved in the same traffic tangle as the private car and are often further handicapped by their inferior maneuverability. It is then difficult to make a bus service sufficiently attractive relative to use of a private car to attract a sufficient volume of traffic to make the frequency of service satisfactory. In order to give the transit facility a chance to compete with the private automobile, it becomes necessary to provide some sort of reserved right of way. With buses this in theory takes the form of a lane reserved for them, but in practice this faces formidable problems in dealing with intersections and pickup points, and at best means that the lanes thus provided are likely to be underutilized, since it is seldom desirable to schedule just enough bus service to fully utilize a whole lane of capacity. These difficulties provide a strong argument for going to the very substantial expense of a rail rapid transit system.

With street use controlled by pricing, however, it is possible to insure that the level of congestion is kept down to the point at which buses will provide a satisfactory level of service, and rail rapid transit systems will be required only where a volume of traffic arises that will warrant their high cost on the basis of superior service and operating economies.

But while the most dramatic impact of street use pricing would be to permit the economical allocation of traffic among the various modes, it would be of great importance even in cases where intermodal substitution is not a factor. Even in a community entirely without mass-transit service, street pricing could have an important function to perform. For example, traffic between opposite sides of town often has the choice of going right through the center of town or taking a more circuitous route. Left to itself, this traffic is likely to choose the direct route through the center, unless indeed the center becomes so congested as to make it quicker to go the longer way around. In the absence of pricing, one may be faced with the alternatives of either tolerating the congestion in the center of town, or if it is considered mandatory to provide congestion-free access to the center of town, of providing relatively costly facilities in the center of town adequate to accommodate through traffic as well. With pricing it becomes possible to restrict the use of the center streets to those having no ready alternative and provide for the through traffic on peripheral roadways at much lower cost. Without pricing, bypass routes, though beneficial, often attract only part of the traffic that they should carry for the greatest overall economy of transport.

Pricing of street use can in the long run have significant effects on the whole pattern of development of urban communities and on property values. While on general principles one can hardly imagine this impact to be other than beneficial, it is a little difficult to discern the net direction in which it would tend—for example, whether the concentration of activity at the center would increase or decrease.

17
KNOCKING DOWN
THE STRAW MEN
John R. Meyer

Improving urban transit facilities, despite popular notions to the contrary, is only an indirect and excessively expensive way of solving the
problems of our large cities. In addition, such improvement would
hardly arrest the continuing shift of people, businesses and employment opportunities to the suburbs. John R. Meyer, Professor of Economics at Harvard University, attributes the change in the nation's
population pattern to more fundamental forces at work within our rapidly changing industrial society. The views expressed, which are solely
the author's, grew out of research done for the RAND Corporation's
Urban Transportation Study under a grant from the Ford Foundation.

It has become quite fashionable to worry about the present state and
future possibilities of American cities which are allegedly sick and
decaying. These developments, so the argument runs, are a cause for
deep concern because Americans are increasingly an urban people,
and large urban concentrations are essential to the maintenance of our
cultural and aesthetic values. And finally, say the critics, the condition
of our urban centers is in sharp contrast to the vitality and growth of
low-density suburbs filled with single-family, mass-produced dwellings
—deprecatingly referred to as "urban sprawl."

The sources of these "urban anxieties" are many. They have a hard,
substantial basis in the fact that populations within the incorporated

Reprinted by permission from *Challenge*, December 1962, published by the International Arts and
Sciences Press, Inc., White Plains, N.Y.

limits of most large cities have either declined or just remained stable in the past decade while populations just outside of these limits, in suburbia and exurbia, have often grown phenomenally. There has also been a tendency for the wealthier segments of society to migrate outward to a greater degree than the poor.

This out-migration has been followed by a dispersal of retailing with the result that the older central business districts have become relatively and often absolutely less important as commercial centers. Less obviously, but just as surely, industry has also been relocating from central to suburban locations.

Loss of both higher-income groups and commerce and industry usually means, of course, an erosion of city tax bases. This is occurring, moreover, at a time when city responsibilities as centers of urban regions may be rising since the rapidly growing suburbs contribute to a heavy increase in the total population and urban amenity requirements of most metropolitan areas. These population and income shifts also often increase, quite inequitably, central city shares of total welfare burdens in metropolitan areas. Obviously, many of these inequities are a result of archaic political institutions and boundaries that do not reflect present-day realities.

Unfavorable patterns of urban change are often blamed on the prevalence of the private automobile. In some city planning circles the automobile has almost become an emotional symbol of all that is wrong with American cities. Not only is the automobile seen as the cause of much of the deplored decentralization, but it ostensibly has been aided and abetted in its wayward ways by unfortunate government policies that implicitly or explicitly subsidize overuse of automobiles. Among the many unfortunate results attributed to this "folly" is a decline in public transit services, often to the point of bankruptcy and abandonment.

At best, public transit reputedly is reduced to such a precarious financial state that it cannot find the money needed to develop new services in the areas of heavy population growth, thus giving residents in such areas no other option than traveling by car. The resulting rush of cars into downtown areas is said to be "strangling our cities," subjecting the public to a great health hazard by poisoning the air with noxious fumes, gobbling up precious urban land for "unproductive" automobile use and, in general, ruining and debilitating our cities.

The usual proposal for correcting this ostensible mess into which urban transportation has fallen is to grant subsidies to public transit to compensate for the subsidies allegedly being given to urban auto users. These subsidies would be used to restore services and otherwise improve the quality of public transit to the point where automobile users would find it attractive to abandon their cars. It is often suggested that this subsidy money could be put to the best use by developing and extending rail rapid transit because this type of transportation can attain higher maximum operating speeds more quickly than any alternative and because it is "obviously cheaper" than other forms of urban transit.

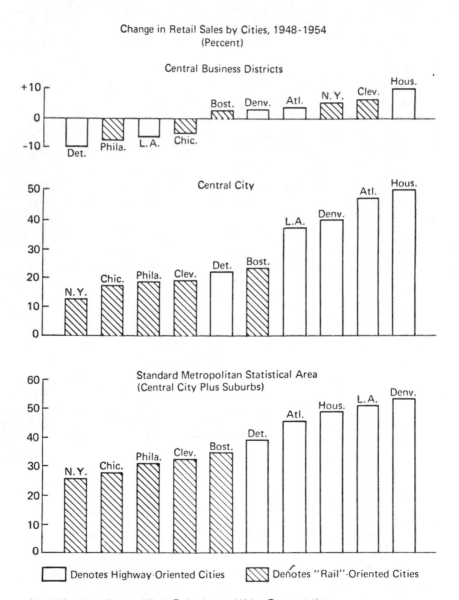

Change in Retail Sales by Cities, 1948-1954
(Percent)

Central Business Districts

Central City

Standard Metropolitan Statistical Area
(Central City Plus Suburbs)

☐ Denotes Highway-Oriented Cities   ▨ Denotes "Rail"-Oriented Cities

SOURCE: Meyer, Kain, and Wohl, *Technology and Urban Transportation.*

Thus, at the moment, new rail rapid transit systems or extensions of existing systems are either being proposed or are under consideration in, among other places, Los Angeles, San Francisco, Atlanta, Cleveland, Washington, Boston, Philadelphia.

It is also often alleged that the revival of good public transit, especially of a rail variety, will have many favorable side effects. It will help arrest urban decentralization, maintain downtown property values, and create higher property values along its right of way. In general, the availability or unavailability of rapid transit is often pictured as a prime determinant of urban land use and development patterns.

Sorting fact from fiction in all of this is very difficult, mainly because the two are so evenly balanced and thoroughly intermingled. There is no denying, for example, that some relative decentralization has apparently taken place in urban areas, but it is difficult to define and quantitatively assess the importance of the various factors contributing to this development.

It is clear, though, that the availability of public transit is just one of many factors contributing to decentralization. For example, many industries moved to less centralized locations because they needed large tracts of unencumbered land to properly set up efficient one-story manufacturing layouts. Also, the development of trucking, piggybacking and other new techniques of moving freight from city to city no longer makes a location near a railroad marshaling yard necessary to receive either low-cost or high-quality freight service. The extremely low freight transport requirements of several important modern industries such as electronics, aircraft and motion picture manufacture, to cite only a few, have further contributed to decentralization.

Furthermore, the increasing substitution of trucks for railroad freight cars as well as the increasing use of airlines instead of railroads for passenger transportation have moved employment opportunities in intercity transportation away from the central city.

In addition, bookkeeping industries like insurance are no longer as dependent on central locations and access to public transportation as a means of recruiting a low-salaried, unskilled female labor force. The existence of both cheap private transportation and electronic computers has made location far less important for these activities.

Similarly, a move to a suburban shopping center may not only provide a retailer with an opportunity "to get closer to his customers." It may, in addition, give him a chance to redesign his store structure from the ground up and thus enable him to incorporate a number of economies, particularly in freight handling and warehousing, that are impossible or difficult to introduce in an older building with a more constricted downtown location. Indeed, some suburban shopping centers have been created in advance of local residential demand in their vicinity.

A decentralization of employment opportunities is crucial because it permits a decentralizing of residences without incurring any increase in commuter travel time or costs. As a consequence, a diffusion of employment locations can be enough to reduce urban population densities in and of itself. Reinforced by and interacting with increased ownership of private automobiles and higher personal incomes that permit wider ownership of single-family dwellings, the pressures for decentralization can be very nearly undeniable, regardless of what form of public transit may be available.

In the same vein, there is very little evidence that the presence of rail rapid transit tends to centralize employment opportunities or retailing, or that a dependence on highways leads to decentralization. As shown in the chart on page 192, central business districts and central cities have both prospered and languished with and without rapid transit. Furthermore, the presence of rapid transit provides no major barrier to the general tendency toward decentralization of employment opportunities in American cities.

The dispersion of employment opportunities also has a significant impact on the pattern of urban travel. One simple way of describing this change is to say that the pattern becomes characterized more by a large number of relatively uniform, low-level and crisscrossing trip densities than by very high concentrations in a few corridors emanating like spokes from the center of the city, as was previously the case.

Among other things, the emergence of this crisscross travel pattern and its accompanying reduction in the density of trip demands makes it harder to design a satisfactory public transit system and alters the cost comparisons between different modes of public transit, as well as between public and private transport.

In general, an efficient public transit system is easier to design for a high density of demand than for a low density. This basic truth is strongly illustrated by the fact that even most existing or proposed rapid transit systems depend on automobiles and buses to conduce feeder operations from residential areas where population densities are low.

In fact, an integral part of most new transit proposals is the provision of extensive parking facilities at transfer points in the suburbs. A similar reliance on surface vehicles, usually buses, also characterizes most sensible plans for performing the collection and distribution function in central business districts. It is usually very inefficient to use high performance line haul vehicles, whether trains or buses, to perform downtown feeder functions because of the number of stops required.

It is often said that the chief advantage of railroad transit, particularly on highly traveled lines, is its low cost. The usual assertions of cost superiority for rail are based on the simple notion that rail can move 40,000 or more people per hour over a given stretch of right of way for less money than any alternative form of transport. Even granting that this is true, which it very well may not be, such an assertion is essentially irrelevant because rarely are demands of 40,000 persons per hour ever encountered in public transit operations, New York City being the one notable exception.

Additional perspective on the crucial demand density problem can be obtained by looking at figures on the approximate number of persons leaving the central business districts of major United States cities during the evening peak hours. These are shown in the table that follows. The evening peak is particularly relevant because it usually exceeds the morning peak and represents the maximum demand placed on an urban transportation system.

The outstanding feature of these figures is the magnitude of New York's peak volume over the 2 next largest cities and the relatively modest level of peak hour volumes in most United States cities.

Translated into capacity requirements, 250,000 persons per hour can be accommodated easily in buses using only 10 lanes of street or highway and 150,000 by using 6 lanes. Private autos with only an average of 1.5 people in each car would require about 40 lanes to handle 100,000 per hour, 20 lanes for 50,000, and so on. Assuming only 2 lanes of usable outgoing capacity to a street, 5 highways would be required to handle a 250,000 volume level in buses and 20 exit streets and highways would be needed for 100,000 persons in private autos.

Of course, traffic would rarely move by only one mode. Assuming for illustrative purposes that half of the commuters could be induced to travel by transit bus while the rest went by auto, approximately 9 or 10 lanes would be required to move 50,000 people per hour, 20 lanes for 100,000, etc. While 20 lanes is a considerable highway capacity, it is not beyond that presently or about to be available in most United States cities. The only cities, moreover, with a peak rush hour demand over 100,000 that are not *already* equipped with rail rapid transit are San Francisco and Los Angeles, which also happen to have 2 of the more extensive systems of limited access urban highways.

Finally, it should be noted that the fragmentary data that are available on recent changes in peak hour levels suggests that these are declining slightly, reflecting the tendencies toward decentralization mentioned earlier. In general, the aggregate level of demand for urban transportation, even during peak periods, would seem to be within manageable proportions in all but the largest cities and should become more manageable in the future.

For travel purposes other than commuting, both cost and service considerations have led to an increasing substitution of the private automobile for public transit. The auto's relatively low off-peak marginal cost, schedule flexibility, privacy, comfort, and cargo-carrying capacity have all combined to make it the dominant mode of transportation for shopping, personal business, social, and recreational trips. Since these trips tend to occur mainly in noncommuter hours, loss of this business has tended to intensify the off-peak excess capacity problem of public transit systems and created a loss in revenue unaccompanied by any significant cost reduction.

Indeed, the increased specialization of public transit in trips to and from work is a major source of many a transit system's financial problems. One possible solution to these problems, of course, would be to

Peak Rush Hour Volume
Leaving Central Business
District

(Cities with Over 500,000 Population)

Number of Commuters	City
More than 800,000	New York
250,000–800,000	None
200,000–250,000	Chicago
150,000–200,000	Philadelphia
100,000–150,000	Boston Los Angeles San Francisco
75,000-100,000	Atlanta Baltimore Cleveland Detroit New Orleans Pittsburgh St. Louis
50,000–75,000	Dallas Ft. Worth Milwaukee Minneapolis Providence St. Paul
Less than 50,000	Cincinnati Kansas City Miami Rochester Seattle

SOURCE: Meyer, Kain, and Wohl, *Technology and Urban Transportation.*

increase sharply prices charged to peak-hour users. Such a policy, however, is usually considered "politically impossible," and since public transit is usually either government-owned or regulated, these political considerations normally prevail.

Much the same conflict between economic and political reality also occurs in the pricing of highway facilities. For example, while there is little evidence that urban highway users are subsidized in the aggregate (in fact, urban contributions to highway and fuel taxes usually exceed expenditure), it seems highly probable that vehicles using high-cost central arteries and streets during peak periods are not paying their full costs. Again, rather than granting compensating subsidies to competing forms of transport, the economically rational solution would be to charge more for the use of these special facilities during rush hours; but such a solution is also considered politically impossible.

Because of the political obstacles, various alternatives to raising the cost of using these facilities have been suggested or actually put into use on urban highways. The search for an effective rationing device for urban highways during peak hours is highly important since, if it is granted that urban highways must be constructed to meet off-peak social, recreational and shopping trip demands, then the least expensive solution to the urban transportation problem is to find a way to make these same highways serve commuter needs. A fairly common suggestion has been to reserve lanes on freeways and streets for exclusive bus use during peak hours. Highways built exclusively for bus use also have been recommended.

Both of these plans, however, involve at least some probable under-utilization of capacity since the lanes reserved exclusively for buses would either be inadequate for meeting peak demands or would be in excess supply during all other periods. Such excess capacity could be costly, moreover, if it occurred on limited access facilities.

A preferable alternative, therefore, would be to combine priority access for buses with metering and control of access to high performance urban expressways. Highway use would be limited to levels that permitted operation at high speeds and prevented traffic jams. Giving buses priority of access to these superior facilities would permit bus operations at high speeds without reserving lanes for exclusive bus use. The automobile commuter might also benefit since the elimination of traffic jams should increase the effective peak hour carrying capacity of expressways for all purposes.

This metered-flow, priority access idea is not only inexpensive to implement, but, like reserved lanes and special busways, does not involve a large investment in facilities that have no major alternative use, a weakness of rail transit investments.

A number of other policies might be instituted to effectuate relatively quick improvements in the availability of urban highway capacity during rush hours. Greater use of reversible lanes is one of the more obvious. Early completion of inner belt and other circumferential highways often would prove helpful since a very high percentage of downtown rush hour traffic is commonly attributable to through traffic.

The development of more efficient urban transport also would be facilitated by the elimination of many archaic franchise regulations that restrict entry into taxi and bus operations. Most of these regulations serve no useful public purpose under modern conditions, their main effect being to create artificial property values for existing franchise holders. These controls inhibit experimentation with new forms of urban transport and thereby create a rigidity that is most undesirable during a time of rapid change.

At present, the urban commuter usually has little range of consumer choice since he is essentially restricted to either using a rather inferior mass transit or an expensive and reasonably high-quality private auto service. It would seem highly probable that considerable potential exists for other services between these two extremes.

In sum, a number of simple, inexpensive policies exist which could eliminate much of the so-called urban transportation problem in most United States cities. Only New York, with its very special scale and complexity, might require drastic action. At a minimum, the available simpler remedies should be tested before large investments are made in expensive rail transit systems, the reputed advantages of which are doubtful at best.

Indeed, all transportation solutions to urban problems must be recognized as rather indirect attacks on the basic difficulties of poor land use patterns, declining populations and tax bases, and unequal sharing of public burdens. By contrast, federally aided urban renewal, metropolitan governments and more state aid to urban areas are all more direct ways of meeting these problems.

Since, the resources available for meeting urgent urban problems are scarce, it seems foolish to undertake highly expensive, quixotic transportation programs of unproven effectiveness.

part 6 THE URBAN PUBLIC SECTOR

It has long been recognized that one function of the public sector is to correct failures in the market system. In the first selection Burton A. Weisbrod argues that the private market will often undervalue many commodities that are usually thought to be "individual consumption goods." If consumers are benefited by having more effective options, an important and neglected role of the public sector is to foster consumer choice. This suggests that government should attempt to maintain diversity within metropolitan areas. For example, the high density central city should be saved so residents have an alternative to low density suburban living. Similarly, automobile ownership should not be thrust upon people because there is no adequate public transportation system.

The remaining articles analyze some of the causes of the urban fiscal crisis and the efficacy of revenue sharing, one of the more popular remedies for the financial condition of local governments. In a classic article, William J. Baumol argues

199

that the slow rate of technological advance in the production of public goods is responsibile for the rising costs in the public sector. Although his model suggests that the public sector will continue to absorb an increasing proportion of our resources, Baumol looks to revenue sharing as a possible antidote to the crisis. In the following selection one of the nation's leading economic figures, former Presidential Advisor Walter W. Heller, presents a program under which the federal government shares its revenue with state and local governments.

Naïve faith in revenue sharing is inappropriate, according to an editorial which appeared in *Fortune* magazine, since a dynamic federalist system requires that each level of government perform the functions it does best. If the federal government took responsibility for all programs related to the distribution of income, local governments could be relieved of a large portion of its outlays. Since Washington regulates such expenditures, a realignment of responsibility may be preferred to revenue sharing. In the concluding article, Norton E. Long suggests that revenue sharing cannot guarantee the salvation of the central city from a fate of poverty and degradation. Government must make a dramatic commitment to save the city if such a fate is to be avoided.

18
COLLECTIVE CONSUMPTION ASPECTS OF INDIVIDUAL CONSUMPTION GOODS
Burton A. Weisbrod

It is customary to distinguish individual-consumption (private) goods from collective-consumption (public) goods. To be sure these are polar cases; but to distinguish between them is to imply that a particular commodity cannot be at both poles. The principal objectives of this paper are: (1) to point out that a number of significant commodities exist which are apparently of a pure individual-consumption variety, but which also possess characteristics of a pure collective-consumption good; and (2) to discuss some implications of this observation, in particular showing that even if some apparently individual-consumption goods cannot profitably be provided by private enterprise it may serve the social welfare to subsidize their production.

The main point to be made below involves (a) the infrequency and uncertainty of purchase of particular commodities, and (b) the cost (in time or resources) of expanding production once it has been curtailed. Thus, I begin by considering an extreme case of a commodity the purchase of which is infrequent and uncertain, and production of which cannot be reinitiated at any cost once it has been halted and the inputs devoted to other uses. The commodity is a visit to a particular national park, such as Sequoia. Other illustrations will be discussed later and generalizations will be developed.

Let us assume that the location of the park and its means of access are such that it is easy to charge an admission fee of all consumers (users, viewers). Assume further that the park is privately owned, at

Reprinted by permission from the *Quarterly Journal of Economics,* August 1964.

least to begin with. (This assumption is useful for the following exposition, but it is not essential to the argument.) Next assume that the entrepreneur practices price discrimination among all park visitors, but that even so, total costs cannot be covered. There are no external economies of either production or consumption, at least in the usual forms. Finally, the commodity (service) is not storable; it cannot be purchased prior to consumption. Under these circumstances, allocative-efficiency considerations would dictate "closing" the park, assuming that private and social rates of discount are equal. Total benefits (revenue) falling short of costs, the "firm" should close down in the interest of efficiency, and its resources (trees, minerals) should be devoted to alternative uses.[1] Needless to say, this recommendation disregards income distribution considerations and other social goals except allocative efficiency.[2]

Such may seem to be the result of the usual Marshallian analysis. It is certainly true that a profit-maximizing entrepreneur would cease operating if all costs could not be covered—that is, if the present value of future costs exceeded the present value of future revenue. But it may be unsound socially for him to do so. To see why, the reader need recognize the existence of people who anticipate purchasing the commodity (visiting the park) at some time in the future, but who, in fact, never will purchase (visit) it. Nevertheless, if these consumers behave as "economic men" they will be willing to pay something for the option to consume the commodity in the future. This "option value" should influence the decision of whether or not to close the park and turn it to an alternative use. But it probably will not exert any influence if the private market is allocating resources, because there may be no practical mechanism by which the entrepreneur can charge nonusers for this option. Schemes to charge them can be imagined, but noncoercive devices may be extremely difficult to implement.[3] In any event, the

---

[1] This view, with specific respect to national parks, is held by Milton Friedman. See his *Capitalism and Freedom* (Chicago: University of Chicago Press, 1962), p. 31. While the discussion here is in terms of current costs and revenues, it should be clear that, in principle, what is relevant to the closing-down decision is the present value of expected future costs and revenues.

[2] Strictly speaking, another requirement, generally unfulfilled, for recommending closing is that prices equal marginal costs throughout the economy.

[3] Since the option demand is automatically satisfied when the park operates, it will pay every potential user to mask his preferences in order to minimize his private cost. This, of course, is the usual problem of getting consumers to reveal their preferences for pure public goods (such as the option).

Against this background of "uncooperative" consumers, the inability of a private entrepreneur to enforce payment by nonusers is likely to be a serious problem. An entrepreneur could conceivably tell people each year that they must pay a fee for the option of consuming in the future (at the sale price effective then); thus admission would be denied anyone who did not have option-tickets for *each* year prior to the time of purchase of the commodity (visit to the park). Such a scheme would surely be costly and cumbersome because of the large number of persons and undoubtedly very small per capita annual fees, the need to make collections throughout the country (not merely at the park), and the problem of lost receipts or expensive record-keeping.

point to be emphasized is that user charges (admission fees) are an inadequate (understated) guide to the total value of the park. And of course, if revenue is insufficient, so that the park is closed and its trees cut down, the option demands of potential future users would not be satisfied.

Nor is the issue simply one of short period versus long period demand. A potential consumer may have an option demand throughout his lifetime, and yet he may die without ever having purchased the commodity.[4]

If actual users were willing to pay enough to provide adequate profit, the park would remain in business, and the option demand of persons who were *not* current consumers would be satisfied at zero marginal cost. That is, as long as the park operates, provision of the option is a pure collective good of standard type: it (the option to consume in the future) may be "consumed" (enjoyed) by all persons simultaneously, and the consumption by one person does not subtract from the consumption opportunities for others. But when the park is on the verge of closing down (or reducing its scale), the option to consume in the future ceases being a costless by-product of the park's operations; the option demand would not be met at all if the firm closed (or would be met less satisfactorily if the firm reduced its scale) assuming that it could not reverse its action—for example, because its giant trees had been cut down. In the interest of economic efficiency it would be desirable to keep the firm in business if the total of fees potentially collectable from current consumers *and* fees potentially collectable from prospective future consumers—including those who, in fact, will not become consumers—are adequate to cover costs.[5]

The collective-good aspect of the commodity—in satisfying the option demand—may be viewed as an external economy from current production; that is, current production enters positively into the utility functions of *prospective* users. Or the park may be thought of as producing two outputs: services of an individual-consumption sort to actual users, and standby, or option, services of a collective-consumption sort to nonusers. The latter is difficult to sell especially if some of its "consumers" do not become actual users.

Infrequency and uncertainty of purchase are not the only conditions bringing about a potential deviation of optimal private from optimal social behavior. In the present context there is another requirement:

---

[4] The analogy with insurance may be drawn. Loss (purchase) is infrequent, and a person may, as in the case of property insurance, never have a loss though he pays annual premiums for the protection for many years. The insurance was providing a service, protection against a large financial loss, though the protection was only of a stand-by nature and was, in fact, never "used."

[5] Of course, the latter might equal zero if the consumption of park services went out of fashion permanently, for then the option value would be zero. At the same time there might be no demand for current use of the park, and yet the option value could be positive.

expansion or recommencement of production at the time any occasional-purchasers wish to make a purchase must be difficult (in time or resources) or impossible; this implies that storage of the commodity (service) must be expensive—at the limit, impossible. In the case of a natural phenomenon such as Sequoia National Forest, if the trees were destroyed (allocated to alternative use), centuries would be required to restore them.

But a national park is an extreme case both in terms of the infrequent purchase of its services by most consumers, and the high cost of restarting production once its inputs have been redirected. Less extreme, but more numerous, examples would be hospitals. A hospital is utilized infrequently by most persons and not at all by some; yet, like the national park, it provides a valuable standby service, so that its value cannot be measured by the number of its users or the fees collectable from them alone. This standby or option value may be sizable enough to justify the existence of the hospital on efficiency grounds, but the private entrepreneur without the power of taxation may have great difficulty in charging nonusers, and so may find the hospital to be continuously unprofitable. Again, the issue is more than one of the time horizon. The option will have value even for persons who never become patients, as it also will for former patients in the years between their last hospital admission and death. Of course, it must be reiterated that the option value is important for resource allocation only to the extent that when added to user demand it would affect the level of supply—that is, would make the difference to a firm between remaining open and closing, or between opening in the first place and not doing so, or between providing a given increment of service or not.

A third example may suffice to indicate the frequency with which the option demand concept is relevant. Urban transit firms have come to recognize that persons who normally walk or use private automobiles will occasionally use public transportation—for example, when weather is bad, or when the auto breaks down. These and other occasional users may patronize the transit system once or twice a year, or even less often. Yet an option demand will exist for the standby facilities. A structure of user charges which differentiates between classes of users can perhaps be developed, though cases in which they have been used successfully are difficult to find. In any case, such a structure would still not catch persons who never use the system, but who value its availability.[6]

---

[6] It may be socially profitable to maintain a currently unprofitable transit system because of the possibility that highway congestion in the future may produce a greater demand for it. However, this is beside the point being made here. Private entrepreneurs may be expected to take this future demand into account insofar as it is translated into sales. But insofar as that demand reflects the

A system of user charges designed to capture *some* of the option demand would charge the occasional rider more per ride than the regular rider, *ceteris paribus.* Tokens sold in large quantity lots at rates below the cash fare are sometimes used, but differentials are usually minor. If the differential grew, it would be increasingly circumvented by resales from regular to occasional patrons. Thus, the tokens, tickets, and so on would have to be made nontransferable. And so the administrative problems would grow.

It is interesting to note that the argument for levying greater user fees on occasional users (as a means of tapping their option demand) may conflict with the argument for levying greater fees on rush-hour users (as a means of indicating the high marginal cost of the service they consume).[7] Rush-hour users are frequently regular users. Thus, on balance it may be sensible to have lower fees for regular, rush-hour users than for occasional, nonrush-hour users.

Actually, four classes of users may be distinguished: (1) regular non-rush-hour, (2) regular rush-hour, (3) occasional nonrush-hour, (4) occasional rush-hour. Class (1) users would qualify for low charges on both cost and option-demand grounds; at the opposite extreme, class (4) users would be subjected to high charges on both grounds. Between these limits would be the charges to class (3) and class (2) users. Class (2) would be charged less than class (3) with respect to the option demand, but *more* with respect to costs. Thus, depending on the relative weights attached to each factor, a group of rush-hour users might be charged less than a group of nonrush-hour users.

Now to generalize. The fact that the revenue of a private operator is limited, as a practical matter, to user charges prevents his capturing the option demand of nonusers. It follows that the inability of the operator to make a profit does not necessarily imply the economic inefficiency of the firm. If he had the power to tax he could supplement user charges with charges for the option services being generated.

The range of frequency of purchase for various commodities is a wide one, from once-in-a-lifetime attendance at a national park to daily purchase of tap water. "Infrequent purchase" is a matter of degree. Similarly, costs of expanding production to meet the demand of occasional purchasers exist for all commodities, although in varying degrees. It seems, therefore, that in principle the option demand exists for all

---

(option) demand of persons who, *ex post*, do not purchase the service, it will, presumably, not affect the decisions of private producers regarding the level of services.

[7] A strenuous advocate of lower charges for off-peak users of urban transport service in particular is William Vickrey; see, for example, his "Pricing in Urban and Suburban Transport," presented to a session of the American Economic Association, December 28, 1962, mimeographed, p. 4.

commodities. The more frequently the commodity is purchased (the smaller the ratio of "occasional" to "regular" purchasers), and the less costly the expansion of output, the smaller will be the significance of the option demand—the easier it will be for sellers to rely on a system of user charges.

Even for those commodities purchased infrequently, the option demand is of no significance so long as production is sufficiently profitable to insure that output can be provided at a level adequate to meet the demand of the infrequent purchaser. The all-night drug store, for example, presumably makes sufficient sales at night, at regular or specially high prices, to cover its added costs, and so it remains open and provides a standby service for many noncustomers. Under these conditions the option demand is satisfied as a costless by-product of production for current purchasers. But the option demand becomes important with respect to resource-allocation decisions when user charges (current and discounted future) begin to fall short of costs at the margin of service, so that private entrepreneurs will cease or curtail operations. Recognition of the option demand may dictate continued operation in the social interest, with "losses" made up from charges (taxes) on "occasional" purchasers. This is simply an extension of the well-known proposition that achievement of an optimal level of output in an industry generating external economies (in this case, fulfilling the option demand) requires subsidization. Consequently there appears to be an a priori case for at least consideration of public operation or subsidy when a producer of an infrequently purchased, nonstorable commodity with sharply rising short-period marginal costs contemplates closing or cutting service because of unprofitable operations. Of course, if the sum of user charges and the value of the option demand falls short of costs (on a present-value basis), then efficient resource allocation would require that operations be halted or curtailed and resources shifted to alternative uses.

Although it is only at the margin of closing down or, in general, of curtailing supply, that the option demand is relevant, these are precisely the points at which the question is likely to arise: Should the private firm be subsidized or possibly operated publicly rather than permit its services to be cut? The argument presented above does not imply an affirmative answer in all cases. It does imply that a negative answer is not necessarily justified, even on the grounds of allocative efficiency.

19
MACROECONOMICS OF UNBALANCED GROWTH:
The Anatomy of Urban Crisis
William J. Baumol

There are some economic forces so powerful that they constantly break through all barriers erected for their suppression. Such, for example, are the forces of supply and demand which have resisted alike medieval efforts to abolish usury and contemporary attempts to control prices. In this paper I discuss what I believe to be another such mechanism which has colored the past and seems likely to stamp its character on the future. It helps us to understand the prospective roles of a wide variety of economic services: municipal government, education, the performing arts, restaurants, and leisure time activity. I will argue that inherent in the technological structure of each of these activities are forces working almost unavoidably for progressive and cumulative increases in the real costs incurred in supplying them. As a consequence, efforts to offset these cost increases, while they may succeed temporarily, in the long run are merely palliatives which can have no significant effect on the underlying trends.

The justification of a macroeconomic model should reside primarily in its ability to provide insights into the workings of observed phenomena. Its aggregation of diverse variables usually deny it the elegance and the rigor that are provided by microeconomic analysis at its best. Yet macro models have succeeded in explaining the structure of practical problems and in offering guidance for policy to a degree that has so far eluded the more painstaking modes of economic analysis. This article hopes to follow in the tradition—the structure of its basic model

Reprinted by permission from the *American Economic Review*, June 1967.

is rudimentary. Yet it can perhaps shed some light on a variety of economic problems of our generation.

1. PREMISES

Our model will proceed on several assumptions, only one of which is really essential. This basic premise asserts that economic activities can, not entirely arbitrarily, be grouped into two types: technologically progressive activities in which innovations, capital accumulation, and economies of large scale all make for a cumulative rise in output per man-hour and activities which, by their very nature, permit only sporadic increases in productivity.

Of course, one would expect that productivity would not grow at a uniform rate throughout the economy so it is hardly surprising that, given any arbitrarily chosen dividing line, one can fit all goods and services into one or the other of two such categories in whatever way the dividing line is drawn. I am, however, making a much stronger assertion: that the place of any particular activity in this classification is not primarily a fortuitous matter determined by the particulars of its history, but rather that it is a manifestation of the activity's technological structure, which determines quite definitely whether the productivity of its labor inputs will grow slowly or rapidly.

The basic source of differentiation resides in the role played by labor in the activity. In some cases labor is primarily an instrument—an incidental requisite for the attainment of the final product, while in other fields of endeavor, for all practical purposes the labor is itself the end product. Manufacturing encompasses the most obvious examples of the former type of activity. When someone purchases an air conditioner he neither knows nor cares how much labor went into it. He is not concerned one way or the other with an innovation that reduces the manpower requirements for the production of his purchase by 10 percent if the price and the quality of the product are unaffected. Thus it has been possible, as it were, behind the scenes, to effect successive and cumulative decreases in the labor input coefficient for most manufactured goods, often along with some degree of improvement in the quality of the product.

On the other hand there are a number of services in which the labor is an end in itself, in which quality is judged directly in terms of amount of labor. Teaching is a clearcut example, where class size (number of teaching hours expended per student) is often taken as a critical index of quality. Here, despite the invention of teaching machines and the use of closed circuit television and a variety of other innovations, there still seem to be fairly firm limits to class size. We are deeply concerned when elementary school classes grow to 50 pupils and are disquieted by the idea of college lectures attended by 2000 underclassmen. Without a complete revolution in our approach to teaching there is no prospect that we can ever go beyond these levels (or even up to them) with any degree of equanimity. An even more extreme example is one I have offered in another context: live performance. A half-hour horn quintet calls for the expenditure of $2^{1}/2$ man-hours in its performance, and any attempt to increase productivity here is likely to be viewed with concern by critics and audience alike.

The difference between the two types of activity in the flexibility of their productivity levels should not be exaggerated. It is a matter of degree rather than an absolute dichotomy. The jet airplane has increased the productivity per man-hour of a faculty member who is going from New York to California to give a lecture. Certainly the mass media have created what may be considered a new set of products that are close substitutes for live performance and by which productivity was increased spectacularly. In addition, there are, as the reader will recognize, all sorts of intermediate activities which fall between the two more extreme varieties. Yet, the distinction between the relatively constant productivity industries and those in which productivity can and does rise is a very real one, and one which, we shall see, is of considerable practical importance.

In addition to the separability of activities into our two basic categories I shall utilize three other assumptions, two of them primarily for ease of exposition. The reader will recognize, as we proceed, that neither is essential to the argument. The first of the incidental premises consists simply in the assertion that all outlays other than labor costs can be ignored. This assertion is patently unrealistic but it simplifies greatly our mathematical model. A second, far more important, and more realistic assumption is that wages in the two sectors of the economy go up and down together. In the long run there is some degree of mobility in all labor markets and consequently, while wages in one activity can lag behind those in another, unless the former is in process of disappearing altogether we cannot expect the disparity to continue indefinitely. For simplicity I will in the next section take hourly wages to be precisely the same in both sectors, but the model is easily complicated to allow for some diversity in wage levels and their movements.

A final inessential assumption which is, however, not altogether unrealistic, asserts that money wages will rise as rapidly as output per man hour in the sector where productivity is increasing. Since organized labor is not slow to learn of increases in its productivity it is likely to adjust its wage demands accordingly. This assumption affects only the magnitude of the absolute price level in our model, and does not influence the relative costs and prices that are the critical elements in the analysis.

The logic of the entire analysis can be restated rather simply in intuitive terms. If productivity per man-hour rises cumulatively in one sector relative to its rate of growth elsewhere in the economy, while wages rise commensurately in all areas, then relative costs in the nonprogressive sectors must inevitably rise, *and these costs will rise cumulatively and without limit.* For while in the progressive sector productivity increases will serve as an offset to rising wages, this offset must be smaller in the nonprogressive sectors. For example (ignoring nonwage cost) if wages and productivity in the progressive sector both go up 2 percent per year, costs there will not rise at all. On the other hand, if in the nonprogressive sector productivity is constant, every rise in wages must yield a corresponding addition to costs—a 2 percent cumulative rise in wages means that, year in year out, costs must be 2 percent above those of the preceding year. Thus, the very progress of the technologically progressive sectors inevitably adds to the costs of the technologically unchanging sectors of the economy, unless somehow the labor markets in these areas can be sealed off and wages held absolutely constant, a most unlikely possibility.

We see then that costs in many sectors of the economy will rise relentlessly, and will do so for reasons that are for all practical purposes beyond the control of those involved. The consequence is that the outputs of these sectors may in some cases tend to be driven from the market. If their relative outputs are maintained, an ever increasing proportion of the labor force must be channeled into these activities and the rate of growth of the economy must be slowed correspondingly.

These observations can be used at once to explain a number of observed phenomena.[1] For example, there is evidence that an ever increasing portion of the nation's labor force has been going into retailing and that a rising portion of the cost of commodities is accounted for by outlays on marketing. Now there have been several pronounced changes in the technology of marketing in recent decades: self service, the supermarket, and prewrapping have all increased the productivity per man-hour of the retailing personnel. But ultimately, the activity involved is in the nature of a service and it does not allow for constant and cumulative increases in productivity through capital accumulation, innovation, or economics of large-scale operation. Hence it is neither mismanagement nor lack of ingenuity that accounts for the relatively

[1] Some of the ideas in this section arose out of discussions with Eugene Beem of Sperry and Hutchinson.

constant productivity of this sector. Since some sort of marketing effort is an inescapable element in economic activity, demand for this service is quite income elastic. Our model tells us what to expect in this case—cumulatively increasing costs relative to those of other economic activities, and the absorption of an ever growing proportion of society's resources by this sector—precisely what seems to have been observed.

Higher education is another activity the demand for whose product seems to be relatively income elastic and price inelastic. Higher tuition charges undoubtedly impose serious hardships on lower-income students. But, because a college degree seems increasingly to be a necessary condition for employment in a variety of attractive occupations, most families have apparently been prepared to pay the ever larger fees instituted in recent years. As a result higher education has been absorbing a constantly increasing proportion of per capita income. And the relatively constant productivity of college teaching leads our model to predict that rising educational costs are no temporary phenomenon—that they are not a resultant of wartime inflation which will vanish once faculty salaries are restored to their prewar levels. Rather, it suggests that, as productivity in the remainder of the economy continues to increase, costs of running the educational organizations will mount correspondingly, so that whatever the magnitude of the funds they need today, we can be reasonably certain that they will require more tomorrow, and even more on the day after that.

But not all services in the relatively constant productivity sector of the economy face inelastic demands. Many of them are more readily dispensable than retailing and education as far as individual consumers are concerned. As their costs increase, their utilization tends therefore to decrease and they retreat into the category of luxury goods with very limited markets or disappear almost completely. Fine pottery and glassware produced by the careful labor of skilled craftsmen sell at astronomical prices, though I am told the firms that produce them earn relatively little profit from these product lines which they turn out primarily for prestige and publicity, obtaining the bulk of their earnings from their mass production activities. Fine restaurants and theaters are forced to keep raising their prices, and at least in the case of the latter we know that volume is dwindling while it becomes ever more difficult for suppliers (the producers) to make ends meet.

An extreme example of an activity that has virtually disappeared is the construction (and, indeed, the utilization) of the large and stately houses whose operation even more than their construction allows for little in the way of enhanced productivity, and whose rising costs of operation have apparently decreased their salability even to the wealthy.

These observations suggest something about the likely shape of our economy in the future. Our model tells us that manufactures are likely to continue to decline in relative cost and, unless the income elasticity of demand for manufactured goods is very large, they may absorb an ever smaller proportion of the labor force, which, if it transpires, may make it more difficult for our economy to maintain its overall rate of output growth.

The analysis also suggests that real cost in the "nonprogressive" sectors of the economy may be expected to go on increasing. Some of the services involved—those whose demands are inelastic—may continue viable on the free market. Some, like the theater, may be forced to leave this market and may have to depend on voluntary public support for their survival. Our hospitals, our institutions of private education and a variety of other nonprofit organizations have already long survived on this basis, and can continue to do so if the magnitude of contributions keeps up with costs. Some activities will either disappear or retreat to a small scale of operation catering primariy to a luxury trade. This fate may be in store for restaurants offering true *haute cuisine* and it is already the case for fine hand-worked furniture and for clothes made to measure. Some activities, perhaps many of the preceding among them, will fall increasingly into the hands of the amateurs who already play a considerable role in theatrical and orchestral performances, in gastronomy, in crafts such as woodworking and pottery. Finally, there is a considerable segment of nonprogressive activity that is dependent on tax support. Some of the problems that go with this position will be considered in the remainder of this paper.

In all the observations of this section there is one implicit underlying danger that should not escape the reader: the inherent threat to quality. Amateur activity has its virtues, as an educational device, as a good use for leisure time and so forth. But in a variety of fields it offers a highly imperfect substitute for the highly polished product that can be supplied by the professional. Unbalanced productivity growth, then, threatens to destroy many of the activities that do so much to enrich our existence, and to give others over into the hands of the amateurs. These are dangers which many of us may feel should not be ignored or taken lightly.

One of the major economic problems of our times is the crisis of the larger cities. Together with their suburban periphery the cities are attracting ever greater segments of our population. Yet at least the core of the metropolis is plagued by a variety of ills including spreading blight as entire neighborhoods deteriorate, increasing pollution of its atmosphere, worsening traffic, critical educational problems, and, above all, mounting fiscal pressures. The financial troubles are perhaps central to the entire issue because without adequate funds one cannot hope to mount an effective attack on the other difficulties. More than one reform mayor has taken office determined to undertake a radical program to deal with the city's difficulties and found himself baffled and stymied by the monstrous deficit which he discovered to be hanging over him, a deficit whose source appeared to have no reasonable explanation. There seems in these cases to be no way to account for the growth in the city's financial needs—for the fact that a municipal budget far above that which was roughly adequate a decade earlier threatens to disrupt seriously the city's most vital services today. Where the political process is involved it is easy to blame growing costs on inefficiency and corruption but when they take office, reform administrations seem consistently puzzled by their inability to wring out the funds they require through the elimination of these abuses.

A critical element in the explanation becomes clear when we recognize how large a proportion of the services provided by the city are activities falling in the relatively nonprogressive sector of the economy. The bulk of our municipal expenditures is devoted to education which, as we have already seen, offers very limited scope for cumulative increases in productivity. The same is true of police, of hospitals, of social services, and of a variety of inspection services. Despite the use of the computer in medicine and in traffic planning, despite the use of closed circuit television and a variety of other devices, there is no substitute for the personal attention of a physician or the presence of a police patrol in a crime-ridden neighborhood. The bulk of municipal services is, in fact, of this general stamp and our model tells us clearly what can be expected as a result. Since there is no reason to anticipate a cessation of capital accumulation or innovation in the progressive sectors of the economy, the upward trend in the real costs of municipal services cannot be expected to halt: inexorably and cumulatively, whether or not there is inflation, administrative mismanagement or malfeasance, municipal budgets will almost certainly continue to mount in the future, just as they have been doing in the past. This is a trend for which no man and no group should be blamed, for there is nothing that can be done to stop it.

Though these may be troubles enough for the municipal administrator, there are other compelling forces that plague him simultaneously. Among them are the general class of externality problems which have so long been the welfare economist's stock in trade.

Since the appearance of Marshall's and Pigou's basic writing in the area a most significant development has been the growing impact of external costs on urban living. No longer are road crowding and smoke nuisance only quaint cases serving primarily as textbook illustrations.

Rather, they have become pressing issues of public concern—matters discussed heatedly in the daily press and accorded serious attention by practical politicians. Newspapers devote headlines to an engineer's prediction that the human race is more likely to succumb to its own pollutants than through a nuclear holocaust, and report with glee the quip that Los Angeles is the city in which one is wakened by the sound of birds coughing.

Now there are undoubtedly many reasons for the explosion in external costs but there is a pertinent observation about the relationship between population size in a given area and the cost of externalities that seems not to be obvious. It is easy to assume that these costs will rise roughly in proportion with population but I shall argue now that a much more natural premise is that they will rise more rapidly—perhaps roughly as the square of the number of inhabitants. For example, consider the amount of dirt that falls into the house of a typical urban resident as a result of air pollution, and suppose that this is equal to kn where n is the number of residents in the area. Since the number of homes in the area, an, is also roughly proportionate to population size, total domestic soot-fall will be equal to soot per home times number of homes $= kn \cdot an = akn^2$ Similarly, if delays on a crowded road are roughly proportionate to n, the number of vehicles traversing it, the total number of man-hours lost thereby will increase roughly as n^2, since the number of passengers also grows roughly as the number of cars. The logic of the argument is simple and perhaps rather general: if each inhabitant in an area imposes external costs on every other, and if the magnitude of the costs borne by each individual is roughly proportionate to population size (density), then since these costs are borne by each of the n persons involved, the total external costs will vary not in proportion with n but with n^2. Of course I do not maintain that such a relationship is universal or even that it is ever satisfied more than approximately. Rather I am suggesting that, typically, increases in population size may plausibly be expected to produce disproportionate increases in external costs—thus pressures on the municipality to do something about these costs may then grow correspondingly.

Economic theory indicates yet another source of mounting urban problems. These are the processes of cumulative urban decay which once set in motion induce matters to go from bad to worse. Since I have discussed these elsewhere I can illustrate the central proposition rather briefly. Public transportation is an important example. In many urban areas with declining utilization, frequency of service has been sharply reduced and fares have been increased. But these price rises have only served to produce a further decline in traffic, leading in turn to yet another deterioration in schedules and another fare increase and so on, apparently ad infinitum. More important, perhaps, is the logic of the continued flight to the suburbs in which many persons who apparently would otherwise wish to remain in the city are driven out by growing urban deterioration—rising crime rates, a growing number of blighted neighborhoods, and so on. Once again, the individuals' remedy intensifies the community's problems and each feeds upon the other. Those who leave the city are usually the very persons who care and can afford to care—the ones who maintain their houses, who do not commit crimes, and who are most capable of providing the taxes needed to arrest the process of urban decay. Their exodus therefore leads to further deterioration in urban conditions and so induces yet another wave of emigration, and so on.

It is clear that these cumulative processes can greatly increase the financial pressures besetting a municipality and can do so in a variety of ways: they can increase directly municipal costs by adding to the real quantites of inputs required for the upkeep of buildings, to maintain levels of urban sanitation, to preserve the level of education attained by an average resident, and so on; they can reduce the tax base—the exodus of more affluent urban inhabitants cause a decline in the financial resources available to the city; and with the passage of time the magnitude of the resources necessary to arrest and reverse the cumulative processes itself is likely to grow so that the city may find it increasingly difficult to go beyond programs that slow the processes slightly.[2]

The story is perhaps completed if we add to the preceding observations the fact that each city is in competition with others and with its own surrounding areas for industry and for people with the wherewithal to pay taxes. No city government acting alone can afford to raise its tax rates indefinitely. Even if they were politically feasible, mounting tax rates must eventually produce diminishing and perhaps even negative returns as they depress the tax base further.

We can now quickly pull the pieces of our story together. We have just seen that our municipalities are perhaps unavoidably subject to a

[2] I have argued that the cumulative processes involve what may be considered dynamic externalities. Each passenger who uses public transportation less frequently imposes the increased likelihood of poorer schedules not only on himself but on others as well. As a result these processes will yield results that do not maximize social welfare. For the private and social marginal rates of transformation between present and future will then differ from one another. The individual will tend to cut down on his use of public transportation by an amount greater than that which is optimal because he himself does not bear all of the costs of his action. There is a marginal rate of transformation between the utility derived from public transportation today and that obtainable from transportation tomorrow. If relative prices do not equal that marginal rate of transformation a misallocation of resources is likely to result. The consequences may even be what might be called Pareto-nonoptimal. That is, everyone may be harmed. For example, when automobile traffic becomes sufficiently bad it may become clear that everyone will be better off if passenger cars are banned completely from the downtown area in order to make possible a faster, more efficient public transportation system.

variety of growing financial pressures: the limited sources of tax funds, the pressures imposed by several processes of cumulative decay, the costs of externalities which seem to have a built-in tendency to rise more rapidly than the population. These phenomena imply that the activities of the municipality will have to be expanded if standards of city life are to be maintained. But the funds available for the purpose are extremely limited. And over all this hangs the shadow cast by our model of unbalanced growth which has shown that the costs of even a constant level of activity on the part of a municipal government can be expected to grow constantly higher.

The picture that has been painted is bleak. It suggests strongly that self-help offers no way out for our cities. All of this would then appear to offer stronger theoretical support for the Heller-Pechman proposal that the federal government can provide the resources necessary to prevent the serious crisis that threatens our larger urban communities and whose effects on the quality of life in our society may become one of the nation's most serious economic problems.

REFERENCES

1. W. J. BAUMOL and W. G. BOWEN, *Performing Arts: The Economic Dilemma* (Cambridge, Mass.: MIT Press, 1966).
2. JEAN FOURASTIÉ, *The Causes of Wealth* (New York: Free Press, 1960).
3. TIBOR and ANNE SCITOVSKY, "What Price Economic Progress?" *Yale Review*, 49 (Autumn 1959), 95–110.

20
SHOULD THE GOVERNMENT SHARE ITS TAX TAKE?
Walter W. Heller

Washington *must* find a way to put a generous share of the huge federal fiscal dividend (the automatic increase in tax revenue associated with income growth) at the disposal of the states and cities. If it fails to do so, federalism will suffer, services will suffer, and the state-local tax-payer will suffer.

Economic growth creates a glaring fiscal gap; it bestows its revenue bounties on the federal government, whose progressive income tax is particularly responsive to growth, and imposes the major part of its burdens on state and local governments. Closing that gap must take priority over any federal tax cuts other than the removal of the 10 percent surcharge. And even this exception may not be valid. For, as New York Governor Nelson A. Rockefeller has proposed, the revenue generated by the surcharge can easily be segregated from other federal revenue and earmarked for sharing with the states. So perhaps even the taxpayer's "divine right" to get rid of the surcharge may have to give way to the human rights of the poor, the ignorant, the ill, and the black.

For when the state-local taxpayer is beset with—and, indeed, rebelling against—a rising tide of regressive and repressive property, sales, and excise taxes, what sense would it make to weaken or dismantle the progressive and growth-responsive federal income tax? Whether our concern is for justice and efficiency in taxation, or for better balance

Reprinted by permission from *Saturday Review*, March 22, 1969. Copyright 1969, Saturday Review, Inc.

in our federalism, or, most important, for a more rational system of financing our aching social needs, there is no escape from the logic of putting the power of the federal income tax at the disposal of beleaguered state and local governments.

Calling for redress of the fiscal grievances of our federalism is, of course, far from saying that state-local government has reached the end of its fiscal rope. The taxpayer's will to pay taxes may be exhausted, but his capacity is not.

Our overall tax burden—roughly 28 percent of the GNP—falls far short of the 35-to-40 percent levels in Germany, France, the Netherlands, and Scandinavia. Small solace, perhaps, but a strong suggestion that the United States taxpayer has not been squeezed dry.

Untapped and underutilized tax sources still abound in state and local finance. For example, 15 states still have no income tax, and 6 still have no sales tax. If all 50 states had levied income taxes as high as those of the top ten, state income tax collections in 1966 would have been $11 billion instead of $5 billion. The same type of computation for state and local sales taxes shows a $5-billion add-on. As for that sick giant of our tax system, the property tax, the aforementioned top-10 standard adds $9.3 billion to the existing collection of $24.5 billion.

It is only fair to point out, however, that states and localities have not been exactly reticent about tapping these revenue sources. In spite of taxpayer resistance and the frequent political penalties that go with it, the 6 states have been doing a land-office business in new and used

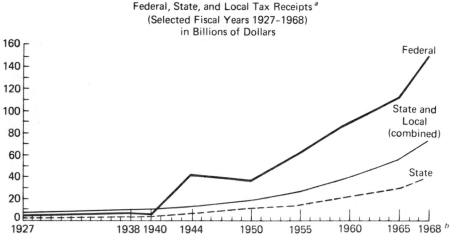

Federal, State, and Local Tax Receipts [a]
(Selected Fiscal Years 1927-1968)
in Billions of Dollars

[a] Includes social insurance taxes
[b] Data for 1968 estimated

SOURCE: Department of Commerce, Bureau of the Census.

taxes. In the past 6 years, the 6 major state taxes (sales, personal and corporate income, gasoline, cigarette, and liquor) were the subject of 309 rate increases and 26 new adoptions. Instead of slowing down, the pace has speeded up; in 1967–1968, the states raised major taxes on 80 occasions and enacted 7 new levies. Meanwhile, property tax burdens have risen faster than anyone thought possible 10 years ago.

Yet, this effort has all the earmarks of a losing battle. Economic growth generates demands for new and better services while leaving a massive problem of water, air, land, and sound pollution in its wake. Population growth, especially the rapid rise of taxeaters relative to taxpayers (the number of Americans in the school-age and over-65 groups is increasing more than twice as rapidly as those in between), is straining state-local budgets. And inflation—which increases the prices of goods and services bought by state-local governments about twice as fast as the average rate of price increase in the economy—also works against state-local budgets.

In trying to meet these spending pressures, state and local governments are inhibited by fears of interstate competition, by limited jurisdiction, by reliance on taxes that respond sluggishly to economic growth, and by fears of taxpayer reprisals at the polls. But it would be a mistake to assume that the case for federal support rests wholly, or even mainly, on these relentless fiscal pressures and handicaps. Far from being just a fiscal problem—a question of meeting fiscal demands from a limited taxable capacity—the issue touches on the very essence of federalism, both in a political and in a socioeconomic sense.

Indeed, it is from the realm of political philosophy—the renewed interest in making state-local government a vital, effective, and reasonably equal partner in a workable federalism—that much of the impetus for more generous levels and new forms of federal assistance has come. The financial plight of state-local government cannot alone explain the introduction of some 100 bills in Congress for various forms of revenue sharing or unconditional block grants since 1954, when my proposal for apportioning taxes was first made public and converted into a detailed plan by the Presidential task force headed by Joseph A. Pechman.

In this connection, I have been amused by how often the following sentences from my *New Dimensions of Political Economy*, published in 1966, have been quoted, especially by surprised conservatives: "The good life will not come, ready made, from some federal assembly line. It has to be custom-built, engaging the effort and imagination and resourcefulness of the community. Whatever fiscal plan is adopted must recognize this need." In expressing similar thoughts publicly for a quarter-century, I have not been alone among liberals. Yet, the statement is now greeted as if the power and the glory of decentralization has just been revealed to us for the first time. May I add that when we are embraced by those "who stand on their states' rights so they can sit on them," we may be forgiven for wincing.

Moving from the political to the economic, one finds strong additional rationale for new and expanded federal support in the economic —or socioeconomic—theory of public expenditures. It is in this theory that our vast programs of federal aid to state and local governments— projected to run at $25 billion in fiscal 1970 (triple the amount in 1960)—are firmly anchored. All too often, they are thought of simply as a piece of political pragmatism growing out of two central fiscal facts: that Washington collects more than two-thirds of the total federal, state, and local tax take; and that nearly two-thirds of government public services (leaving aside defense and social security programs) are provided by state-local government. Throw in the objective of stimulating state-local efforts through matching provisions, and, for many people, the theory of federal grants is complete.

In fact, it is only the beginning. Consider the compelling problems of poverty and race and the related problems of ignorance, disease, squalor, and hardcore unemployment. The roots of these problems are nationwide. And the efforts to overcome them by better education, training, health, welfare, and housing have nationwide effects. Yet, it is precisely these services that we entrust primarily to our circumscribed state and local units.

Clearly, then, many of the problems that the states and localities tackle are not of their own making. And their success or failure in

Federal aid to state and local governments (selected fiscal years 1949–1963) (in millions of dollars)

	1949	1959	1967	1968ᵃ	1969ᵃ
Agriculture	86.6	322.5	448.0	599.4	644.0
Commerce and Transportation	433.6	100.6	226.3	431.7	618.6
Education	36.9	291.3	2298.7	2461.9	2398.2
Health, Labor, Welfare	1231.5	2789.7	6438.0	8207.1	9135.0
Housing, Community Development	8.6	188.4	768.3	1185.2	1812.5
Highway and Unempl. Trust Funds	—	2801.2	4501.7	4773.1	4796.7
Other	5.5	319.7	1120.2	1239.9	1418.0
Total	1802.7	6813.4	15,801.2	18,898.3	20,823.0

ᵃ Data estimated.
SOURCE: Bureau of the Budget.

coping with such problems will have huge spillover effects far transcending state and local lines in our mobile and interdependent society. The increasing controversy over the alleged migration of the poor from state to state in search of higher welfare benefits is only one aspect of this. So, quite apart from any fiscal need to run hat in hand to the national government, states and cities have a dignified and reasonable claim on federal funds with which to carry out national responsibilities. Only the federal government can represent the totality of benefits and strike an efficient balance between benefits and costs. Therein lies the compelling economic case for the existing system of earmarked, conditional grants-in-aid. Such grants will, indeed must, continue to be our major mechanism for transferring funds to the states and localities.

But the interests of a healthy and balanced federalism call for support of the general state-local enterprise as well as specific services. It is hard to argue that the benefits of sanitation, green space, recreation, police and fire protection, street maintenance and lighting in one community have large spillover effects on other communities. Yet, in more or less humdrum services such as these lies much of the difference between a decent environment and a squalid one, between the snug suburb and the grinding ghetto.

Given the limits and inhibitions of state-local taxation and the sharp inequalities in revenue-raising capacity—compounded by the matching requirement in most categorical grants, which pulls funds away from nongrant activities—too many of the states and the cities are forced to strike their fiscal balances at levels of services well below the needs and desires of their citizens. The absence of a system of federal transfers to serve the broad purpose of upgrading the general level of public services, especially in the poorer states, is a serious gap both economic and political—in the fiscal structure of our federalism. Tax sharing could fill it.

The core of a tax-sharing plan is the earmarking of a specified share of the federal individual income tax take for distribution to states and localities, on the basis of population, with next to no strings attached. The so-called Heller-Pechman plan has the following main elements:

The federal government would regularly route into a special trust fund 2 percent of the federal individual income tax base (the amount reported as net taxable income by all individuals). In 1969, for example, this would come to about $7 billion, roughly 10 percent of federal individual income tax revenues. This amount would be channeled to the states at fixed intervals, free from the uncertainties of the annual federal appropriation process.

The basic distribution would be on a straight population formula, so much per capita. Perhaps 10 percent of the proceeds should be set aside each year as an equalization measure—to boost the share of the 17 poorer states (which have 20 percent of the nation's population).

To insure that the fiscal claims of the localities are met, a minimum pass-through—perhaps 50 percent—to local units would be required. In this intrastate allocation, the financial plight of urban areas should be given special emphasis.

The widest possible discretion should be left to the state and local governments in the use of the funds, subject only to the usual accounting and auditing requirements, compliance with the Civil Rights Act, and perhaps a ban on the use of such funds for highways (for which there already is a special federal trust fund).

How well does the tax-sharing plan (also called revenue sharing, unconditional grants, and general assistance grants) measure up to the economic and sociopolitical criteria implicit in the foregoing discussion? Let me rate it briefly, and sympathetically, on six counts.

First, it would significantly relieve the immediate pressures on state-local treasuries and, more important, would make state-local revenues grow more rapidly, in response to economic growth. For example, a 2-percentage-point distribution on a straight per capita basis would provide, in 1969, $650 million each for California and New York, $420 million for Pennsylvania, $375 million for Illinois, $140 million each for Mississippi and Wisconsin, $125 million each for Louisiana and Minnesota, and about $65 million each for Arkansas and Colorado.

The striking growth potential of this source of revenue is evident in two facts: (1) Had the plan been in effect in 1955, the distribution of 2 percent of the $125-billion income-tax base in that year would have yielded a state-local tax share of about $2.5 billion; and (2) by 1972, the base should be about $450 billion, yielding a $9-billion annual share.

Second, tax sharing would serve our federalist interest in state-local vitality and independence by providing new financial elbow room, free of political penalty, for creative state and local officials. Unlike the present grants-in-aid, the tax-shared revenue would yield a dependable flow of federal funds in a form that would enlarge, not restrict, their options.

Third, tax sharing would reverse the present regressive trend in our federal-state-local tax system. It seems politically realistic to assume that the slice of federal income tax revenue put aside for the states and cities would absorb funds otherwise destined to go mainly into federal tax cuts and only partly into spending increases. Given the enormous pressures on state-local budgets, on the other hand, tax shares would go primarily into higher state-local expenditures and only in small part into a slowdown of state-local tax increases. Thus, the combination would produce a more progressive overall fiscal system.

Fourth, tax sharing—especially with the 10 percent equalization feature—would enable the economically weaker states to upgrade the scope and quality of their services without putting crushingly heavier burdens on their citizens. Per capita sharing itself would have a considerable equalizing effect, distributing $35 per person to all of the states, having drawn $47 per person from the ten richest and $24 per person from the ten poorest states. Setting aside an extra 10 percent for equalization would boost the allotments of the seventeen poorest states by one-third to one-half. Thus, the national interest in reducing interstate disparities in the level of services would be well-served.

Fifth, the plan could readily incorporate a direct stimulus to state and local tax efforts. Indeed, the Douglas Commission (the National Commission on Urban Problems), like many other advocates of tax-sharing plans, would adjust the allotments to take account of relative state-local tax efforts. In addition, they propose a bonus for heavy reliance on individual income taxation.

A more direct stimulant to state and local efforts in the income tax field would be to enact credits against the federal income tax for state income taxes paid. For example, if the taxpayer could credit one-third or two-fifths of his state and local income-tax payments directly against his federal tax liability (rather than just treat such taxes as a deduction from taxable income, as at present), it would lead to a far greater use of this fairest and most growth-oriented of all tax sources.

Ideally, income-tax credits should be coupled with income-tax sharing and federal aid in a balanced program of federal support. But if relentless fiscal facts require a choice, the nod must go to tax sharing because (1) credits provide no interstate income-level equalization; (2) at the outset, at least, much of the federal revenue loss becomes a taxpayer gain rather than state-local gain; and (3) since one-third of the states still lack broad-based income taxes, the credit would touch off cries of "coercion." Nevertheless, it is a splendid device that ought to have clearcut priority over further tax cuts.

Sixth, and finally, per capita revenue sharing would miss its mark if it did not relieve some of the intense fiscal pressures on local, and particularly urban, governments. The principle is easy to state. The formula to carry it out is more difficult to devise. But it can be done. The Douglas Commission has already developed an attractive formula that it describes as "deliberately 'loaded' to favor general purpose governments that are sufficiently large in population to give some prospect of viability as urban units." I would agree with the Commission that it is important not to let "no-strings" federal aid sustain and entrench

thousands of small governmental units that ought to wither away—
though I still prefer to see the tax-sharing funds routed through the 50
state capitals, rather than short-circuiting them by direct distribution to
urban units.

Supported by the foregoing logic, espoused by both Democratic and
Republican platforms and candidates in 1968, and incorporated into
bills by dozens of prestigious Senators and Congressmen, one would
think that tax sharing will have clear sailing as soon as our fiscal dividends permit. Not so. The way is strewn with obstacles and objections.

For example, tax sharing poses threats, or seeming threats, to special
interest groups including all the way from top federal bureaucrats who
see tax sharing's gain as their agencies' and programs' loss; through
the powerful lobbyists for special programs such as housing, medical
care, and pollution control programs, who recoil from the prospect of
going back from the federal gusher to 50 state spigots; to the Senators
and Congressmen who see more political mileage in tax cuts or program
boosts than in getting governors and mayors out of their fiscal jam.

But, of course, opposition goes far beyond crass self-interest. It also
grows out of philosophic differences and concern over the alleged
shortcomings of tax sharing. There is the obvious issue of federalism
versus centralism. A strong contingent in this country feels that the
federal government knows best, and that state and local governments
cannot be trusted. Others fear that revenue sharing or unrestricted
grants will make state-local government more dependent on the federal
government—a fear for which I see little or no justification.

On the issues, some would argue that it is better to relieve state-local
budgets by taking over certain burdens through income-maintenance
programs like the negative income tax; while others feel that too much
of the revenue-sharing proceeds would go down the drain in waste and
corruption. Here, one must answer in terms of a willingness to take the
risks that go with an investment in the renaissance of the states and
the cities. Some costs in wasted and diverted funds will undoubtedly
be incurred. My assumption is that these costs will be far outweighed
by the benefits of greater social stability and a more viable federalism
that will flow from the higher and better levels of government services
and the stimulus to state-local initiative and responsibility.

In sum, I view tax sharing as an instrument that (1) will fill a major
gap in our fiscal federalism; (2) will strengthen the fabric of federalism
by infusing funds *and* strength into the state-local enterprise; and (3)
will increase our total governmental capacity to cope with the social
crisis that confronts us. The sooner Congress gets on with the job of
enacting a system of tax sharing, even if it means postponing the end
of the 10 percent surcharge, the better off we shall be.

21
REVENUE SHARING IS NOT ENOUGH
Editors of <u>Fortune</u>

Budget time has seldom added to the gaiety of nations, or even of families. But this year the budget season for state and local governments is proving exceptionally grim. In state after state, governors have been intoning lugubrious warnings of immense impending deficits. California's deficit could turn out to be over $500 million; Pennsylvania's and New York's, $400 million each; Connecticut's, $200 million. And for many cities the long struggle to make revenues meet ever rising expenditures seems to be ending in surrender. At least one city, Hamtramck, a blue-collar community surrounded by Detroit, has been officially declared insolvent and had its affairs put in the hands of receivers. It is no wonder that New York City's budget director should say, "This may be the year of the wolf."

The pleas for help have been heard in Washington. Revenue sharing has suddenly risen from an academic concept argued over by fiscal experts into one of the leading issues before the Ninety-second Congress and a major thrust of President Nixon's domestic program. If Congress obliges, a few more billion federal tax dollars, with a minimum of strings attached, will be flowing to state capitols and city halls.

But let there be no illusions. Revenue sharing by itself is only a pain-killer that would have to be administered in increasing doses. It does not get at the real trouble, which is that, while we have multiplied the things we expect government to do, we have not made up our minds about which level of government should do what. More than a sharing

Reprinted by permission from *Fortune*, February 1971.

of money, the current sorry situation calls for a redistribution of functions, assigning to the federal government, the states, and the various local authorities the activities each can best manage and finance. Such a realignment would give real meaning to what Nixon calls "the New Federalism." It might even lead to the discovery that our problems are not after all overwhelmingly greater than our resources.

MONEY AND POWER

The United States has had revenue sharing of a sort ever since New Deal days, when the federal government began doling out grants-in-aid in ever increasing quantities and for an ever widening range of purposes—highway building, welfare, housing, and so on. Use of the device has been much amplified in the last decade, and now there are more than 400 grant-in-aid programs through which federal funds— about $28 billion in this fiscal year—are channeled to state and local governments.

The rationale for all this, as for any other form of revenue sharing, is that the federal income-tax system is an incredibly efficient revenue raiser, whose take grows even more rapidly than the national income in a growing economy. It could also be added, of course, that grants-in-aid were a handy way for activists in Washington to induce states and localities to get involved in activities that they could not, or would not, take on by themselves.

Whatever may be said about the efficacy of the various programs, the system has resulted in an administrative mess. The swollen federal bureaucracy has had little real power to assure achievement of its goals, while the state and local authorities charged with carrying out the programs have had little real freedom to exercise initiative, since the rules and standards are set in Washington.

A more damaging consequence derives from the financial strings attached—the requirement that states, cities, and counties match the federal grant, in some proportion or other, in order to qualify for the program. They rarely resist a gift from Washington, even if it puts them under an unwanted obligation. When a budget squeeze sets in, that obligation remains fixed and immutable, as we have seen recently in the case of cities swamped by welfare costs that are beyond their control. The skimping has to be done in routine municipal services, with ultimate sacrifice of the amenities that make urban life livable: public safety, clean streets, attractive parks, frequent and thorough garbage removal.

LIFTING A $15-BILLION BURDEN

As the Advisory Commission on Intergovernmental Relations has observed, "There is no sure-fire formula for fiscal salvation in our federal system." But the commission and others have made sensible proposals, requiring no drastic constitutional overhaul, for rearranging the responsibilities allotted to each level of government. In *Fortune's* view, one step toward a more workable arrangement would be to make the federal government fully responsible for a number of health and welfare programs that are already bound by ground rules set in Washington, and deal with problems that are national in scope. The Nixon family-assistance plan, which offers the best promise of bringing welfare costs under control eventually, can work only if its standards of minimum income apply across the country, and the plan does, in fact, call for a large increase in federal financing. If Washington assumed the entire cost of current social programs such as Medicaid, unemployment insurance, aid for dependent children, old-age assistance, and vocational rehabilitation, as much as $15 billion a year would be lifted from the backs of state and local governments.

The states should then assume primary responsibility for financing elementary and secondary education, relieving the heavy burden now borne by cities and local school districts. To a large extent, states already set the standards local school boards must meet, and local taxpayers, even where they are given the opportunity to vote on annual budgets, have very little leeway in deciding what they pay. In the last school year, state aid covered $14.6 billion of the nation's $38.3-billion bill for primary and secondary public education. If the states took over the whole bill, children in rich and poor localities would have a more nearly equal chance to get equality schooling. Equality among taxpayers would certainly be advanced; no longer, for example, would there be tax benefits to be gained by keeping low-income families out of a school district through restrictive zoning.

Perhaps the most salubrious result of all would be to relieve cities of a crushing cost. If they were no longer required to support schools —or welfare—they would have more than enough revenue to effect a significant improvement in their municipal housekeeping. New York City, for example, will raise about $4.2 billion for its own local taxes this fiscal year. Its expense budget totals $7.7 billion, but only $3.6 billion—less than half—will go for municipal services like police and fire protection, sanitation, and street and park maintenance. Most of the rest will go for health, education, and welfare—$700 million for the last alone. Clearly, it is not as a *city* that New York is now in trouble, but as a purveyor of social services mandated not by City Hall but by Albany and Washington.

A GRACEFUL WAY OF SHARING

A realignment of responsibilities could do wonders for the self-reliance of states and cities, but they also should make better use of their own taxing powers. One reason for the vast agglomeration of federal grants-in-aid was that governors and legislators preferred to accept handouts from Washington rather than to risk voters' displeasure by raising taxes. There is great disparity in state tax loads; half the states still don't levy any significant personal income taxes, and the laggards include Connecticut, Pennsylvania, and New Jersey, whose fiscal affairs are usually described as "crises."

To make it easier for state legislatures to raise taxes, federal revenue sharing should include incentives for states to make full use of their own fiscal resources. Better still, state income taxes should be counted as a tax *credit* against the federal income-tax payments and not simply as a deduction against taxable income, as is now the case. The cost of such a credit to the federal government in the coming fiscal year would be about $6 billion—a graceful and useful form of revenue sharing in itself.

For local governments, the need is not to tax more heavily, but to spread the burden more equitably and in such a way as to encourage, rather than inhibit, healthy urban development. The local property tax, abused though it often is, remains an appropriate way to pay for local services that benefit local property. In many cases, however, it is based on out-of-date assessments, causing serious inequities. It falls too lightly on undeveloped land held for speculating and too heavily on built-up property, thereby contributing to the housing shortage and inner-city decay. A reformed property tax would probably be a more fruitful revenue producer, as well as a more tolerable one.

In a federal system restored to full vigor, some taxpayers would have to pay more taxes to their states and localities than they do now. But they would be getting better government for their money.

22
THE CITY AS RESERVATION
Norton E. Long

Max Weber said that when the city lost its walls, the city ceased to be. With this characteristic exaggeration, Weber pointed to what he took to be the central meaning of the city. It was a bounded association, literally enclosed by walls that clearly marked it off from the outside society. Within these walls it had a life in common and a shared common purpose. Its leaders could command the loyalty of citizens who saw in the city a means of their common defense and sustenance. The medieval and early modern city had liberties that entitled it to a substantial measure of self-government and freedom. *Stadt Luft macht frei* (city air confers liberty). This power of self-direction was at the core of a home rule whose vigorous and public-spirited exercise seems worlds apart from the present anemic meaning of the term.

It was the historic function of the modern nation-state to batter down the city's walls and open it to the free play of the forces of the national market. State and national citizens came to be accorded near equality with local citizens. Whether it was in the pursuit of business, the enjoyment of local amenities, or even the receipt of welfare, local citizenship gave scant or no advantage. The cash surrender value of local citizenship was reduced to nil for all but a few protected trades, professions, and institutions. This raised the question of what point there was to belonging to an organization—the city—that anyone could join but that nobody need join to enjoy its privileges. It was predictable that, save

Reprinted from *Public Interest*, No. 25 (Fall 1971) by permission of the publisher. Copyright © National Affairs, Inc., 1971.

for an occasional sentimentalist and the few still enjoying local protection, local loyalty would be weak at best. Such a loyalty might be enough if the tasks confronting the city exacted little from its citizenry. But if faced by any serious burdens, citizens could be expected to solve their problems individually by voting with their feet rather than collectively and politically through the ballot.

CITIZENSHIP AS A CONSUMER GOOD

The ethos of national market capitalism thus tended to transform local citizenship into a species of real estate consumerism. Citizens transferred their allegiance from one residential subdivision to another, much as they shifted their trade from store to store or motel to motel. In a celebrated article, Vincent Ostrom, Charles Tiebout, and Robert Warren praised the metropolitan area as a richly varied market of land uses in which the citizen consumer could take his pick. Rather than seeing the metropolitan area as a politically fragmented social and economic whole, seriously in need of a common government, they preferred to view the fragmentation as an array of choices beneficently governed by the natural forces of the market.

The economism of this concept has until recently been the prevailing view. From Mill's *Representative Government* to the latest text, local government has been a minor affair of housekeeping services, in which economy, efficiency, and honesty were the main issues. Politics in the major case was an affair for the nation-state; local government was considered a species of business to be run like any other business and to be regulated by the forces of the national market. It was largely taken for granted that the results of the national market would be homeostatic and beneficent. When they ceased to be so, with the Great Depression, it was the macro-Keynesianism of national economic policy that was supposed to correct market failings. As Robert Wood pointed out in his study of the governments in metropolitan New York, local governments adapt to market forces, they do not adapt these forces to purposes of their own.

Students of metropolitan areas have long bemoaned these areas' lack of common governments and their resulting inability to plan to meet common physical problems of transport, sewerage, water, and resource management. Piecemeal improvisation has seemed inelegant and wasteful. Yet as Charles Haar and his associates acknowledge in their study of metropolitan planning, though the absence of such planning may have been an inconvenience, it has not yet occasioned real, serious difficulty. Indeed, students like Morton Grodzins and Edward

Banfield have felt that the necessity to bargain across municipal boundaries has been a positive good in the management of conflict such as that between the races.

A more serious criticism of metropolitan fragmentation is that made by Robert Wood: It segregates resources from needs. For some time, the problems of the central city have been seen in these terms, as the result of suburbanization. When Bryce wrote his *American Commonwealth,* he already spoke of social absenteeism as a cause of America's most notable failure, its cities. Sam Bass Warner has recounted the rise of the streetcar suburb, an early indication of the city's vulnerability to changing transport technology. With the Vernon studies of New York, the revolutionary impact of the truck and auto on land values and settlement patterns received general recognition. Suburbanization of residences, businesses, stores, and jobs, held in check by the depression and then the war, gathered irresistible momentum. The shakeout of the social classes, the erosion of the central city's economy, and the downward homogenization of the city's population seemed to be practically irreversible.

This process has been modeled by Jay Forrester in his *Urban Dynamics,* which, starting with empty land, describes a scenario of urban development whose logic leads from the presence of new industry, new housing, managers, professionals, and employed workers, to a situation characterized by mature and declining industry, a preponderance of underemployed and unemployed workers, and aged and blighted housing. The special virtue of Forrester's model is that it concentrates on the viability of the local economy as an autarky, and on its capacity to generate local jobs and local incomes sufficient to support the local people and their government. According to this model, the current predicament of the cities is the result of their own policies, especially those which are designed to ameliorate the condition of the poor but, instead, worsen it by increasing unemployment and dependency, encouraging the departure of the more productive sector of the local economy, and eventually segregating the poor from the growing and productive sector of the society. As Forrester sees the matter, these policies represent well-intentioned but misguided efforts by democratic politicians to meet the needs of the unfortunate. In part, this is surely right. But Forrester's mentor, former Mayor Collins of Boston, could have told him of other sorts of policies, enacted out of other motivations, whose burdens also speed the departure of businesses and persons to the suburbs. Welfare is neither the only nor the greatest of the costs that afflict the central city. Other costs and policies, deriving from less noble motives and serving less noble ends, have done far more to bring the city to its current predicament. Of these, none is more important than the growing demoralization of the city's employee unions and service bureaucracies.

AN EXCESS OF APPETITE?

In a classic article, William Baumol warned that cities whose expenditures concentrate in the services (police, education, health, and the like), where there is little or no expectation of increased productivity, face a staggering increase in labor costs. Municipal wages are set according to the rates for equivalent work in the private sector. But whereas wage increases in the private sector can at least partially reflect, and be partially offset by, productivity increases, there is no such justification for the increases which inevitably follow in the public sector. Even so, municipal employees consider their wage demands modest and reasonable. Shouldn't teachers be paid as much as truck drivers? Members of Victor Gotbaum's District Council 37 (American Federation of State, County & Municipal Employees), of whom 35 percent are Negroes and Puerto Ricans, do the dirty work of New York City—cleaning zoo cages, emptying bed pans, manning the sewers—for a median wage of $7500, which is well below the income required for a modest standard of decency for a family of four. Small wonder that *Newsweek* and Mayor Lindsay thought the union had a real issue. But given that the pension demands Lindsay acquiesced in would have burdened if not sunk his successor, it is no greater wonder that Governor Rockefeller and the state legislature were aghast.

The tragedy of these seemingly reasonable wage demands is that, in the face of little or no increase (and more than a suspicion of actual decline) in public-sector productivity, they can bankrupt the city. Indeed, they have already begun to do so. Over the last decade there has been a 54 percent inflation of state and local government costs (compared to 23 percent in the private sector), and a 72 percent increase in general government employee compensation (as large as that in the inflationary construction industry). As Lyle Fitch, former city administrator of New York, notes:

> When city budgets attempt to rise, as New York City's has, from $3.4 billion in 1964–1965 to $9.1 billion in 1971–1972, there is bound to be great strain, even if New York is the nation's richest city and imposes every form of tax yet devised by the municipal imagination. And when the increase of expenditures is associated with 45 percent to 80+ percent increases in the average wages of major employee groups, a 113 percent increase in pension requirements, and a lively suspicion of sinking productivity in many sectors, the fiscal mismatch takes on new perspectives.

In light of facts like these, the notion that it is a mismatch between local needs and local resources which has caused the cities' problems seems dubious indeed. As Fitch puts it, "*Mismatch* is hardly a suitable term for the relationship between a food supply which, even though substantial, is ultimately limited and a dinosaurian appetite which devours everything in sight and roars for more."

The situation of New York City, while extreme, is not atypical. The education function—often a city's most expensive—as a well-nigh unquestioned "merit good" has been allowed to go its merry way. In an article entitled "See, See the School. It Is Broke," David Rosenbaum of the *New York Times* point out that "it is in the largest cities where the problem is most severe and where solutions seem the hardest to come by. From Boston to Seattle, big city school officials are nearly unanimous in forecasting disaster unless additional sources of revenue are found. School expenditure in most cities has doubled or even tripled over the last decade—in Baltimore it went from $57 million in 1961 to $184 million this year; in New Orleans from $28.5 million to $73.9 million. These increases reflect many factors—inflation, increased demand—but mostly they are due to the rapidly rising salaries of teachers. In St. Louis, for example, the average teacher's salary rose from $7557 five years ago to $10,500 this year."

Expenditures like these would be more supportable if they were highly productive. But there is reason to doubt that they are. In the case of schools, for example, the educators' contention that educational quality (presumably an output) could be equated with teacher credentials, teacher salaries, classroom size, pupil-teacher ratio, and physical amenities was seriously called into question by the Coleman Report, which has been criticized but never refuted. Even more to the point is Ivar Berg's *Education and Jobs—The Great Training Robbery,* which offers considerable evidence for doubting that increased productivity is the efficient causal link in the oftnoted correlation between education and income. Rather he inclines to the view that education is a credential cop-out by which employers and personnel men hide their failure to relate job requirements meaningfully to personnel selection.

As Lyle Fitch and Henry Cohen have pointed out, our cities are suffering from a growing disjunction between the requirements of cost-efficient production of desirable outputs and the system of actual incentives to which municipal bureaucracies, politicians, and city employee unions are responsive. Thus, Cohen speaks of "the growth of bureaucratic and professional systems which have become impervious to review and change, with the result that the public sector, more than the private, becomes increasingly unresponsive to consumer demand. . . . " Fitch notes that "elected officials, particularly legislators, tend to be more interested in inputs (expressed in jobs, franchises, and contracts) than in outputs—delivery of goods and services. *Dominance of input interests leads naturally to rising government costs and a decline and deterioration of government outputs.*" This syndrome could be neglected in the nightwatchman city of laissez-faire because of the relatively small scale of the public sector. But in the city of large-scale municipal state capitalism—in New York City, for example, nearly one person out of three is on the public payroll—the fact that government services are more and more costly but of less and less value becomes desperately important, as does the failure of citizenship which it bespeaks.

THE CALAMITY OF PUBLIC SCHOOLING

The city's major problem is the underemployment and unemployment of its inhabitants, particularly its youth. While many jobs have left the city for the suburbs, and the largest number of new jobs are in the outer ring, the relation of the total number of jobs in the city to its declining population is not badly out of line. What *is* out of line are the educational requirements of the remaining good jobs and the educational qualifications of most of the inhabitants still in the city. Here is the real urban mismatch. And here Ivar Berg's disquieting book is ultimately hopeful, for it shows that the "mismatch" may be the result of inflated educational job requirements rather than of any authentic, practical incapacity to perform actual jobs. Could people in the city be prepared for and permitted to fill the jobs still in the city, much of the problem would be solved.

Municipal and educational leadership does not, however, address itself to the achievement of this happy result. Instead, it continues to promote an educational system which was originally designed for the medieval clergy, children of English gentry, and German scientists, and has since been vulgarized and extended throughout the American democracy. The one-room schoolhouse, supplemented by vocational training on the family or neighbor's farm, has been replaced by an education that conspicuously and snobbishly avoids contact with the world of work. Where the old education provided a smooth transition from juvenile status to meaningful adult roles, the new has kept the young immured in the cotton wool of an unrelated and unreal world of education. Lacking meaningful roles in the adult world, youth has sought solace and escape in a counterculture which denies the values youth has not been permitted to share. Meanwhile, where education retains its earlier form, as with the Amish, a 17-year-old high-school girl teaches at minimal cost what enormous sums fail to do elsewhere. Students who see in reading, writing, and arithmetic a meaningful preparation for adult roles to which they aspire, do learn. They do as well on standard tests as those in the best schools elsewhere.

The rediscovery of the importance of the world of work to give reality, control, and meaning to the world of education has been long in coming to the city. A serious and a sentimental objection to child labor, together with a union interest in protecting jobs, has played a part. A far larger part has been played by the dominance of a snobbish, anti-utilitarian, upper-class idea of education and by a democratic demand to generalize the conspicuous waste of upper-class education to the masses. Whatever value this "liberal" education may have had for the children of the middle class, it has been largely lost in its vulgarization. But along with the expansion of upper-class education to the masses there has come into being a new church and a new establishment, with all the sacral rituals and self-certification of the old. Its unproductive weight bids fair to press as heavily as did that of its medieval predecessor.

Education has become crucial for the central city for 2 reasons: First, because its credentials determine access to employment, and second, because it just might be made to provide students with real skills, which would in turn give the central city a valued and valuable labor force. Yet public education is achieving neither of these goals.

Christopher Jencks has expressed doubt that our educational system has ever earned high marks for achieving literacy. What it has done, he says, is to shape pupils up to the clock and to an acceptance of the situation and discipline of the classroom. In liberal and black militant circles, where docility is a dirty word, these are unfashionable accomplishments. Yet teachability and the capacity for disciplined behavior are prime requisites for employability and would be demanded by any employer, black or white. A school system which at great expense contrives to fail at achieving literacy in its pupils and sends them forth mindlessly rebellious and incapable of discipline is a parasitic cancer on the city.

MYOPIA ABOUT EDUCATION

It is not only militant blacks who think the actual practice of central city schools educates not for employability but for unemployability. United States Commissioner of Education Sidney P. Marland has remarked that many school systems prepare neither for the job nor for college.

To which some educators reply, "Only a philistine would claim that education should be other than for education's sake"—which amounts to saying that education should be for the educators rather than the pupils they process or the taxpayers who pick up the tab. An example of this kind of thinking occurred at a meeting in the office of the mayor of St. Louis, when a representative of the Missouri State Employment Service asked, "What do you do with kids who spit on the floor, fall asleep in the job interview, can't spell their own names or the name of the street on which they live, and can't find the place on a map where they are directed to seek work?" This question brought neither reply nor rebuttal from a representative of the St. Louis school system. Yet this system is given very high marks by the St. Louis *Post-Dispatch*.

The failure of the educational system to relate seriously and effectively to the employability of youth in the city is a disaster. The enormous and growing financial burden of public education could be cheerfully and hopefully borne if it were indeed a productive investment. But the disconnection of actual job requirements from the imposed educational requirements of employability has meant that the educational establishment has no incentive to train pupils to meet real job requirements. Education has thus turned out to be a counterproductive patent medicine, and its enormous expense has become a millstone round the city's neck.

Ivar Berg notes that the only institution that has seriously concerned itself with learning how to instruct city youth is the armed forces. The class-bound nature of the draft and the capable superstructure of the military have given the armed forces—at least the combat arms—a special interest in making the bottom of the manpower barrel employable for their purposes. Other institutions have been interested in making money out of the training process but not in the use of those they train. Berg may overstate the military's success, but he is right that there is at least a logic in the attempt of the armed forces, unable to rely on the credentials bag, to realize the potential of the available manpower to match the actual requirements of the jobs that need to be filled. Would that the city's political leaders could convince city school systems that realizing the potential of youth and matching that realized potential to available jobs is essential if the city is to be able to continue its support of the school system!

Among the most successful efforts to revitalize education have been the work-study programs undertaken in cooperation with industry by the more daring school administrators. In St. Louis some nine companies employ about 300 students. This is a pitifully small number in a city of 600,000 with a school population desperately in need of work motivation and educational motivation. Such as it is, the program seems a success. Southwestern Bell claims a retention rate of 82 percent, better than the rate among those it hires at the gate. Yet the participation of industry is infinitely less than it could or should be if, as its leaders claim, they wish the survival and prosperity of the city. Nor are the schools any more active in pressing to widen this bridgehead between themselves and the world of work. Many in the schools regard work-study as a threat to the "liberal" education that is their livelihood; industry finds it an enterprise that, despite its long-run promise, presents immediate problems insufficiently compensated for by immediate rewards; and political leaders, enamored of brick and mortar projects and their payoffs, suffer a similar myopia.

THE IRRATIONALITY OF URBAN POLICY

Of all the means of restoring the city, none seems more promising than achieving the satisfactory employment of its inhabitants, particularly its youth. In a city such as St. Louis, the condition of a few thousand black and white youths is a key factor in the troubles of the entire city. Their failure to find meaningful employment infects the schools with a sense of frustration and futility. The dirty, dead-end, intermittent jobs that are open to them offer a poor and unattractive alternative to crime, the hustle, drug addiction, and unemployment. They may well be a major cause of the increase in illegitimacy rates, the ADC rolls, and the incidence of the female-headed family with all its attendant problems. This marginal youth population, so well depicted in Elliot Liebow's *Tally's Corner*, acts as an almost Keynesian multiplier of social ill. Low and unstable incomes insufficient to maintain the housing in which such youths reside contribute to the spread of blight. Crime and blight lead to housing abandonment and the decay of the city.

Schools and security are the two reasons most frequently given for leaving the city. As for the former, a mistakenly liberal policy of homogenizing the city schools has led even working-class parents, black and white, to leave the city to assure for their children a safe and (they hope) productive education in the suburbs. They do so because of the efforts of a curious alliance of schoolmen, liberals, black militants, the media, and civil rights activists, who have in effect insisted that anyone seeking better education for his children must do so either outside the city or in private schools. Given the level of city taxes, only the well-to-do can afford the latter alternative.

Security is taken to be the business of the police. Like education it is consumed as a merit good with little concern for the cost-effectiveness of actual police activities. As Norval Morris has said, "Grossly too much money is going to police work when our system of justice can't process efficiently even the few persons the police arrest." Recently Morris reported that studies have shown that of every 100 crimes committed in the United States only about 50 are reported to authorities, leading to an average of 12 arrests, 6 convictions, and 2 persons sent to jail. Small wonder that Morris concludes that ours is an obviously ineffective law enforcement system. It is almost a pity that the New York police did not remain on strike long enough to demonstrate whether society could not manage with far fewer of them. Morris' figures suggest that their true value may be much smaller than we think.

The direct dollar cost of law enforcement is large, but not nearly so large as the cost of its failure to produce the product—security—which is its manifest function. The police and the criminal justice system seem much more concerned with the interests vested in the existing process than with the product or productivity of that process. To question the police and criminal justice system is much like questioning the efficacy of religion. In such matters faith is kept expediently apart from knowledge. The bulk of the street crime that causes many to flee the city is committed by youth. Most of these youths are known to the police, yet we have neither the wit nor the will to use this knowledge for crime prevention. Preventive medicine for crime is as far, perhaps farther, removed from the realm of practical public policy as is preventive medicine for the illness of the people of the city.

In this connection, too, an employment strategy such as that envisaged in the Administration's Manpower Bill of 1969 would seem to make the best of good sense. Wilbur Thompson has concluded that an investment in manpower is potentially the most powerful weapon in the city's arsenal to improve its condition. If the people of the city are broke, the city itself is likely to become bankrupt. It would seem that this would clearly follow, and therefore that running the city so as to employ fully and to upgrade the employment of its residents would be normal public policy. In fact, such is not the case. The city is not run rationally to concentrate its policies and resources on achieving the welfare of its inhabitants.

TWO KINDS OF POLITICS

The picture of Mayor Gibson facing the teachers' union (and all its union allies) over the well-picked bones of the city of Newark is an almost ideal type of the future that faces many older American cities. While not physically absent from Newark, the businessmen, after their brief moment of urban renewal and a flurry of ineffective corporate do-gooding, have abandoned responsibility for the city's future to the bureaucracies, the unions, and such leadership as the blacks and the remaining whites can muster. Thus Fitch remarks: "Newark . . . this year faces a deficit (in a budget which allowed for no service improvements) equal to nearly 60 percent of the yield of its property tax. Newark property tax rates, over 8 percent of full value and probably the highest in the nation, effectively subdue any impulse to construct or improve Newark real estate, and are a main factor in the high rate of landlord abandonment of housing units." The tax structure and its burdens, the quality of public services, the schools, and the quest for security increasingly motivate all who can to abandon a sinking ship. Only the image is wrong. The city is not a ship that will finally sink and have it over with. As David Burch suggests in his Committee for Economic Development pamphlet, the older city will inevitably remain, and it will have to find new specialties to justify its continued existence (such as it may be). It is now finding such specialties, and perhaps the most noteworthy of these is a role as an Indian reservation for the poor, the deviant, the unwanted, and for those who make a business or career of managing them for the rest of society.

Under such circumstances, two kinds of politics suggest themselves: One is the increasing acceptance of the model of an Indian reservation made up of inmates and keepers, economically dependent on transfer payments from the outside society made in consideration of custodial services rendered; the other is a politics of colonial emancipation, self-help, and the development of a viable local economy coequal with that of the outside society. The first pattern is the easy way, the drift course of events; in principle, if not in rhetoric, it is followed by such liberals as Mayor Lindsay of New York. The second policy is more difficult. It involves a head-on struggle with the bureaucracies and the forces that presently find it more profitable to milk the city through disinvestment, running down its plant, and wasteful public projects than to strive to make the city a profitable, going concern. The problem is compounded by our urban "Indians," who have accustomed themselves to a life of dependency, and by those who have chosen crime and drug addiction.

The magic remedy for those who knowingly or unknowingly accept the city's future fate as an Indian reservation is federal or other revenue sharing. The term "sharing" disguises the fact that this is a transfer payment from the outside society. Insofar as it is not an act of pure charity, it is for services rendered, because no export of goods is involved. In this situation, revenue sharing is a payment by the outside society to the city's bureaucracies and politicians to maintain a poor farm and a reservation. Part of this payment—as with the Bureau of Indian Affairs—goes for the subsistence and needs of the natives, another part to the keepers, and still another to those who can somehow make a profit in this business. While the purity of urban reservations is diluted by an admixture of still-functioning business structures and a resident productive population, the logic of their major use tends to drive out these incompatible other uses. Thus business and the productively employed, seeking escape from tax burdens, poor services, and crime, migrate or suburbanize. Even the keepers suburbanize. Black teachers and policemen follow white to the suburbs.

All too fatally, the organized interests of the city and of the underlying population become adapted to the folk culture of the reservation. The businesses leave or adapt. The keepers make keeping a business with no more concern for the inmates than is common among custodial employees. The politicians respond to the most highly organized and to those with cash; thus, despite rhetoric and spasmodic acts, the steady thrust of public policy is to serve the selfish interests of the public and private unions and of business. The underlying population becomes immersed in apathy, crime, drug addiction, and the all-pervasive hustle. There develops the adaptation that Lee Rainwater and Oscar Lewis call the culture of poverty. Others have called it, because of its disconnection from the dynamic outside economy, the slum of despair, as opposed to the older slum of hope where the inhabitants at least had their feet on a ladder leading upward. For still others, such as Edward Banfield, this is the unheavenly city, self-inflicted punishment or reward for those following an ethic of immediate gratification.

THE DILEMMA OF THE SHORT-TERM MAYOR

To transform the varied elements that have conspired to make the older city an urban reservation into a viable, humane cooperative for the improvement of its inhabitants' economic and social condition is a formidable if not impossible task. Forrester is clearly right that we have an historically created system that systematically produces physical blight, decay, and the concentration of an unemployed, crime-ridden population in the cities. This process goes on because individuals and institutions find it rewarding. Others who may object to it feel powerless to alter the seemingly fatal flow of events; like Wood's suburbs, they adapt to forces rather than adapt forces to their purposes. Part of the problem is cognitive, and part lies in the inadequacy of local political power to alter a system in being. Cities are caught in what game theorists call "the prisoner's dilemma": If everybody on the street paints and fixes up, everybody may gain; if you alone paint and fix up, you've wasted your money.

To alter a going system made up of powerful, entrenched bureaucracies and their allies in state and nation takes more political staying power than a local mayor, apt to be a transient bird of passage, can muster. A new mayor of Boston might be told by his Harvard advisors that remaking the school system to improve the skills of the city's youth would be a number-one priority for really upgrading the city. But a new mayor of Boston would have his eye on the governorship and would hope to make his move before events in the city caught up with him; he would therefore think carefully of the political costs and benefits before taking on the school bureaucracy and its allies. A black mayor of Gary might well conclude that his school system could go no way but up and employ a private firm with an accountability contract to upgrade the performance of his school system. In doing so he would incur the wrath of his teachers and of the state and perhaps federal education establishment, without any assurance that his measures would result in a publicly appreciated payoff in the time span his political survival required.

A mayor in a run-down city with a democratic government faces a Herculean task if he seeks both to change the city's priorities and to stand for reelection in two years. What has proved true almost universally of the newly emancipated colonies is all too likely to prove true of the older American cities: The rhetoric of promised improvement cannot be realized in an electoral time span. Neither can sustained, long-term economic development be achieved by a galloping succession of short-term mayors—yet such a succession is likely to be the case. The recipe for a longer tenure is Mayor Daley's machine. And this might be no bad thing if the constellation of interests, businesses, unions, perhaps the syndicate, and public employees were compatible with and supportive of a viable local economy. Whether this is indeed the case in Chicago, or whether Chicago is just another case of New York at an earlier stage is an open question. However this may be, where progress toward the Indian reservation is far advanced, the Daley solution seems implausible. For then the machine will be dedicated to preserving and profiting from the business of running the reservation.

SHIFTING THE TAB

The unwalled city as yet lacks the capacity for a politics of its own. With all the formal trappings of a democracy, its government, such as it is, is not directed to the purposeful improvement of the condition of its actual inhabitants. The structure of perceived interests that direct the key municipal actors leads them to undertake policies that bring about the city's decay. This is clearly the case with the employees' unions whose concern with pay and working conditions is disjoined from any concern with increased productivity. In questioning the inevitable character of Baumol's thesis about the divorce between municipal services and productivity, Fitch points out that "a recent study indicates that the cost of picking up refuse by New York City's highly mechanized sanitation department is three times the price quoted by private cartmen . . . down time on new city sanitation trucks is about 33 percent; the same as for the trucks they replaced; apparently garages cannot handle the minimal maintenance necessary to keep new equipment in operating condition." Fitch is certainly right that there is nothing inherent in most municipal services that renders their present technology beyond improvement. What he does show is that the present incentive structure makes it likely not only that there should be no improvement but even that present levels of efficiency should decline.

Faced with mounting costs of municipal services, other political actors and levels seem to prefer avoiding serious effort to force greater efficiency on employee unions. Thus Fitch points to another instance: "The Boston Metropolitan Transit Authority shows operating costs per passenger mile nearly twice those of other major transit systems, largely because of archaic labor practices, staffing patterns and work rules. Rather than seeking to improve matters by fairly obvious efficiency measures, the system has prevailed upon its congressional delegation to put pressures on the federal government for transit operating subsidies, which could soak up any conceivable amount of federal grant funds." The existing system of political incentives results in a politics of shifting the tab, failing to economize, and letting the future take care of itself. The unions are not the only ones who have no eye for the future. As Fitch again notes, "Some of the advocates of general revenue sharing, such as Governor Rockefeller and Mayor Lindsay, are apparently willing to pay fairly high premiums for federal income tax money as opposed to state income tax money, presumably because they do not have to bear the onus of higher federal income taxes."

AN URBAN N.E.P.?

One does not have to be a Skinnerian pigeon psychologist to recognize that the positive and aversive stimuli of our local and perhaps our state and national politics teach lessons and encourage behavior that is dysfunctional for the continued well-being of the city. The unwalled city can be safely exploited by those who can reside without. When not only businessmen and middle-class professionals, but even white and black teachers and cops can live in the suburbs, the most vocal and politically competent can solve their family problem of education and safety without solving that of the city at the same time. The divorce between the long-term interests of the city and the visible and compelling short-term interests of its key and controlling actors is *the* critical problem of the city. Those who now run the city lack any long-term identification with its future. The option of physical flight and disinvestment seems preferable to burning one's bridges and sticking with it. Many who have power over the city see themselves as powerless to do more than profit from its decline. Others have only the dimmest conception of the causes of the city's problems and cast about for moral slogans or gadget cures such as mass transit.

The city is without a government and a governing class committed to its future and possessed of a competent notion of the nature and causes of its ills. Given such understanding, there might be those left in the city with the possibility of political power who would find their true interests in the city's revived prosperity rather than in its continued decay. Unions with an almost Freudian death wish have destroyed newspapers and other businesses—such as the railroads—on whose prosperity their own depended. But other unions (such as the garment workers) have shown more enlightened self-interest than have their employers. Given the political potency of the public-employee unions, their conversion to an enlightened understanding of their own interest in the viability of the city's economy is of crucial importance.

James Q. Wilson, in a most perceptive essay, has pointed to the emerging trend of mayors playing to their media audiences rather than to their constituencies. This is of a piece with the incentives of our politics that make for urban decay. The constituency is the city's inhabitants. A politics that is more concerned with the audience is more concerned with civil rights posturing and sloganeering than with any real improvement in the condition of the city's inhabitants or with their organization to achieve long-term improvement. Such a politics will not seek to bring lower-class blacks and white ethnics into political working alignment to make the city a cooperative for their economic and social advance. The classical economists had in their theory of the market the model of an interacting system where the individual selfish interests of the actors would lead unintendedly to the common good. While the city was a limited affair, the classical market had enough reality to make it function. Now this seems no longer the case. Few citizens find their profit in businesses and actions that maintain and build the city. Most find their advantage in milking the city's stored-up capital, using such resources as still exist in collectively wasteful but individually profitable projects.

With the growth in the public sector the homeostatic principle of the classical market has broken down. The city moves toward the Indian reservation. But it could be in the rational long-term interest of those who now make their living in and from it to organize to preserve the city as a going concern, rather than to run it down. Whether such a conception of interests and possibilities can be given to those who have the power can only be determined in practice. Whether businesses can be found whose profits will accord with the building of the city rather than with its decay will determine the city's future. Perhaps we are not yet at a stage when the people of the city are prepared for an active politics of planned economic and social development. The city's best present hope—if hope is possible at all—may be a resort to something on the order of Lenin's New Economic Policy, in which self-help and self-interest might restore a functioning economy and avert the Indian reservation destiny.

part 7 POPULATION DISTRIBUTION

The last part of this volume is concerned with the geographic distribution of population. The trend in the United States has been one of increasing population concentration in large metropolitan areas. As Pickard noted in Chapter 1, projections to the year 2000 suggest that if present trends continue, the vast majority of Americans will soon be living in very large cities. Some experts have questioned whether such a concentration of population is desirable. They argue that people have been migrating to large cities because of the employment opportunities existing there, not because people desire to live in large places. If this latter view is correct, the trend toward population concentration may lower the welfare of the population and should be a target for public policy action.

The selections chosen for this part are concerned with the establishment of such a public policy. James Sundquist's article "Where Shall They Live?" helps to clarify the issues involved in population distribution. He asks if we, as a nation, desire increasing population concentration or if we want to adopt a public policy that provides incentives for a more dispersed population.

The other selections focus on different elements of the population distribution question. The Advisory Commission on Intergovernmental Relations in *Urban America and the Federal System* discusses the relative economic efficiency of different size cities in an effort to consider the feasibility of alternative policies. Niles Hansen argues that the government should encourage the growth of medium-size cities since he feels such a policy will aid the rural poor and meet people's preferences better than rural industrialization or increasing the population of our largest cities. The last selection is an example of the manner in which a program of population distribution could be implemented. This selection, from *Urban and Rural America,* illustrates the manner in which economic incentives could be changed so as to influence an employer to locate new activities in smaller cities and rural areas.

23
WHERE SHALL THEY LIVE?
James L. Sundquist

By the end of this century, 100 million people will be added to the population of the United States. That is as many people as now live in Great Britain and France combined.

Where shall they live?

If present trends continue—if they are allowed, that is, to continue—most of the 300 million Americans of the year 2000 will be concentrated on a very small proportion of the nation's land area. Projections of the Urban Land Institute place 60 percent of the country's population—or 187 million persons—in just 4 huge urban agglomerations. One continuous strip of cities, containing 68 million people, will extend 600 miles down the Atlantic seaboard from north of Boston to south of Washington, D.C. Another, with 61 million, will run from Utica, New York along the base of the Great Lakes as far as Green Bay, Wisconsin. Some 44 million persons will live on a Pacific strip between the San Francisco bay area and the Mexican border. A fourth agglomeration, with 14 million, will extend along the Florida east coast from Jacksonville to Miami and across the peninsula to Tampa and St. Petersburg.

Most of the remaining 40 percent of Americans will live in urban concentrations, too—and big ones. In this decade, the larger concentrations have been growing fastest; metropolitan areas over 150,000 grew faster than the national average of 9.8 percent between 1960

Reprinted from *Public Interest,* No. 18 (Winter 1970) by permission of the publisher. Copyright © National Affairs, Inc., 1970.

and 1965 while the smaller areas grew more slowly, as the following data show:

Size of Urban Area	1960–65 Growth Rate (Percent)
20,000– 50,000	7.6
50,000– 100,000	8.3
100,000– 150,000	8.4
150,000– 250,000	10.6
250,000– 500,000	9.8
500,000–1,000,000	11.8
Over 1,000,000	9.8
All metropolitan areas	10.1
Nonmetropolitan areas	3.9

SOURCE: Adapted by the Advisory Commission on Inter-governmental Relations from Rand McNally.

These trends, continued for the next 3 decades, would place 77 percent of the coming 300 million Americans on 11 percent of the land (excluding Alaska and Hawaii). Only 12 percent of the population would be outside urban areas of 100,000 or more population.

Is this the way we want to live?

Two questions are presented. The first pertains to regional balance. Is it desirable that population be massed in a few enormous "megalopolises" along the seacoasts and lakeshores? The second relates to rural-urban balance (or, more accurately, the balance between metropolitan and nonmetropolitan areas). Is it in the best interest of the country, and its people, to continue indefinitely the depopulation of rural and small-town America and the building of ever bigger metropolitan complexes, in whatever region? In short, the 300 million can be highly concentrated in a few "megalopolises," or they can be distributed more evenly as among regions and dispersed in a more nearly balanced way among large metropolitan areas, middle-sized cities, and thriving small towns and villages. Which do we want?

But there is an earlier, and even more fundamental, question. Is population distribution a matter upon which the United States should have a policy at all?

POPULATION POLICY OR LAISSEZ-FAIRE?

The projections of the enormous population concentrations that are in prospect have appeared in the popular press, but they are presented as Sunday supplement curiosities—as glimpses into the inevitable and ordained future—not as a subject for public debate and acceptance or rejection. Yet surely the subject is one worthy of debate. How each family lives is profoundly influenced, even controlled, by the size of the population cluster in which it is embedded. The degree to which population is massed determines the amenity and congeniality of the whole environment in which adults and children live and grow and work. It affects their personal efficiency, their sense of community, their feelings about the relationship between man and nature, their individual and collective outlooks on the world. The impact of size is most emphatic on the lives of the ghetto dwellers of the great cities, of course, but no one in a megalopolis is immune. The resident of Scarsdale or Winnetka is not wholly spared the stresses of big city life; the larger the metropolitan area, the greater the strains and irritations of commuting and the more inevitable that the environmental pollution that arises from population concentration will affect the most idyllic suburbs, too. In any case, the desirability of population concentration must be measured by its consequences for the majority of families who live at near-average or below-average levels, not upon the few who can insulate themselves in political and social enclaves.

So the question is, what kind of environment do we want to build? The nation, through its government, has established policies on matters of far less crucial import, yet the extent to which the country's population will be concentrated remains essentially laissez-faire. That would be all right, perhaps, if by *laissez-faire* one meant free choice by the individuals and the families that make up the population. But it is far from that. The movement of people from smaller to larger places is, to a large extent though no one knows the exact proportions, involuntary, forced migration. Young people going freely to the cities in search of adventure and opportunity make up part of the migrant flow, but only part; among the rest are millions of uprooted, displaced families who have little desire, and less preparation, for life in large cities and whose destination is often inevitably the city slums. These displaced families are simply forced into the migration stream by economic forces they cannot control.

The spatial distribution of population is determined, of course, by the distribution of jobs. With the exception of the limited numbers of the self-employed and the retired, people are not in reality free to live just anywhere. The vast majority are employees who must live where there are jobs, and the location of jobs is not their choice. The concentration of the country's population is the result of employer-created job patterns that the people have had to follow.

For the most part employers have not been free to create jobs just anywhere, either. They have been bound by considerations of economic efficiency—the location of raw materials and of markets, the transportation cost differentials of alternative locations, and so on. As a result, the basic pattern of population distribution has been designed by the play of economic forces, not by men acting rationally as environmental architects; events have been in the saddle once again.

It need not be. In the past, population distribution has been a subject of conscious national policy and it can be again. In the first hundred years of the nation, the government pursued a deliberate policy of dispersing population westward. Motivated in part by desire to confirm its title to the empty continent, the government subsidized turnpikes, railroads, and river navigation, herded Indians onto reservations, and opened public lands to settlement.

Once the continent was spanned, governmental programs continued to encourage a balanced regional development—reclamation, navigation, and electric power projects traditionally, and more recently the more sophisticated and broader efforts authorized in the Appalachian Regional Development Act and the "depressed areas" legislation of the 1960s. The government enacted rural development programs specifically aimed at rural-urban balance, administered for the most part by the Department of Agriculture.

But there is apparently no clear sense of national purpose like that which motivated the early policies for western development. The present regional and rural development programs essentially are the product of legislative log-rolling—the chance balancing of political forces analogous to economic laissez-faire. Urban programs need rural votes so urban areas support rural programs. The West, or the South, or the Appalachian states can muster enough political strength to enact limited programs. But they are offset—more than offset, probably—by other programs that encourage population concentration, like the postwar housing programs that fostered suburban growth around big cities but were inoperative in most smaller cities and rural areas. Congress responds to the pressures of its various constituent regions more or less in proportion to their relative political strength, which means that future congresses will be less and less likely to tilt the benefits of its programs toward nonmetropolitan areas, that are declining in relative political importance, unless it is guided by a conscious policy of population distribution.

Perhaps it is enough to repeat the well-worn observation that a lack of policy is itself a policy. If the nation chooses not to have a population distribution policy, then it is, in effect, accepting the agglomeration that is in prospect, in preference to any alternative spatial distribution patterns that might be brought about by decisive intervention to influence and control the forces that shape the future.

Is it possible to develop a better population distribution pattern than the one in prospect, if the country's scholars, philosophers, and politicians were to put their minds to it?

MAKING A POPULATION DISTRIBUTION POLICY

It is far easier to agree in the abstract on the logic of having a population policy than to agree upon the policy itself, which may be the most practical and telling argument for laissez-faire. But let us see what might be involved in such an exercise.

Two criteria are apparent. A population distribution pattern could be designed either according to what is considered good for people or according to what they want. (As we know from documents as early as the book of Genesis and as late as the Surgeon General's Report, those are not necessarily the same.) Unfortunately, in either case we must do our thinking without benefit of solid data because no one knows for sure either what is best for people or what they want. Nevertheless, there are many clues.

Even in the absence of quantified evidence, it seems reasonably clear that our largest urban concentrations have grown well beyond the point at which diseconomies of scale begin to show. The costs of moving people and things within large metropolitan areas are demonstrably greater than the costs of moving them in smaller population centers. Commuting distances are obviously longer, the time loss greater, the costs higher. The flight of industry from central cities to the suburbs is a reflection, in part, of the cost of transportation to and within congested areas. The cost of urban freeway construction varies directly with the population density of the areas affected, and subway systems are an enormous expense that only the larger metropolitan areas require. Such municipal functions as water supply and sewage and solid waste disposal are probably also subject to diseconomies of scale, for the simple reason that the water and the waste must be carried over longer distances. San Francisco, for example, had contemplated dispatching a 70-car train daily to carry its solid waste over 300 miles into the mountains on the Nevada-California border.

The diseconomies are ultimately measurable, at least in theory, in dollars and cents. Other disadvantages of scale are less measurable but no less real. Air pollution, for example, is a function of the dense concentration of automobiles. Similarly, water pollution is more amenable to control in areas where population is dispersed; there, given the will, the way is at least available.

One other factor that must be considered in any calculation of costs and benefits of urbanization is the social and economic cost of migration itself. To decide which new plant location is *really* most efficient, it is not enough to measure only the building and operating costs of the plant, although that has been the sole criterion of our laissez-faire philosophy. There are enormous costs, as well as appalling cruelties, in the forced displacement and migration of populations, whether it be Negroes from the South, mountaineers from Appalachia, or small businessmen from the declining regions of the Great Plains and the Midwest. (In the 1950s, more than half of America's counties suffered a *net loss* of population.) Families lose their homes and savings and equities and property values along with their most deeply cherished associations; communities lose their tax base for public services; community institutions wither. Some of the migrants are too ill-prepared, too sick, or too poor to adjust to city life successfully; many of them wind up on welfare, and they burden every kind of institution. Yet these costs and losses are not borne by the industry locating the plant, but by people and communities, thereby entering no one's cost-benefit equation, no one's computations of efficiency. If they did so enter, then calculations of simple efficiency would no doubt show that, as a general rule, it is far from economical from the standpoint of the *whole* society to create new economic opportunities where the people are rather than allow existing communities to die while building other whole communities from the ground up in the name of "economic efficiency."

Moving from the physical to the social environment, hard data on disadvantages of scale are even more difficult to come by. Yet we know that as population in general is concentrated, so is poverty (large ghettoes exist only in large urban concentrations) and crime, drug addiction, family breakdown and every other form of social pathology. It may be specious to argue that rural poverty is better than urban poverty when both are bad enough, yet the fact remains that the social evils associated with poverty tend to be mutually reinforcing when the poor are herded together in concentrated masses—as studies of public housing populations, for example, have clearly shown. Racial tension and rioting are not limited to big cities, to be sure, but in their most terrifying aspects they seem to be. Perhaps most important of all, the problem of unemployment and underemployment of the urban poor appears all but insoluble in the largest urban complexes, because transportation systems just cannot economically link the inner cities where the poor live with the scattered suburban sites where the new jobs are being created. In smaller places, by contrast, people can even walk to work.

For all these reasons, it is not hard to accept as a hypothesis, at least, that our largest metropolitan agglomerations are less governable, less livable and economically less sound than smaller urban centers. If this is the case, then it should not matter whether the people like their agglomerations; in the public interest, they should be dispersed. However, what little evidence is available suggests that people do *not* like to live in unlivable places; they are there, in substantial proportion, against their will. A Gallup poll in 1968 showed that 56 percent of Americans would choose a rural life, if they were free to choose, only 18 percent a city and 25 percent a suburb. Even a majority of the inhabitants of Paris—surely one of the most livable of large cities—were shown in a polling sample to prefer small town life. The polling methods may be suspect—the Parisians may have been comparing the city life they know to an idealized life in a romanticized rather than a real small town—but the results are indicative if not conclusive.

More important, from the standpoint of judging what people want, is the plain fact cited earlier that a high proportion of population migration is involuntary movement. Except for economic pressures, many, perhaps most, people would not move to the city in the first place. And they go home eagerly when the economic pressures shift. Each slump in the auto industry finds the Appalachians in Detroit heading back to the hills, and the first-generation Puerto Ricans in New York City characteristically look upon themselves as transients who will return home as soon as they are financially able to do so.

It should be possible, within a reasonable time, to fashion a quantitative methodology that would supply at least some hard data on these questions—both on the economic costs and benefits of population concentration and on the reaction of human beings to the life styles they find themselves compelled to assume in centers of population density. Let us suppose that these data agree in confirming what intuition seems to tell us: that our largest metropolitan agglomerations have grown too far beyond the human scale, that their further growth should be arrested, and that their population should, if possible, be lessened. What then? Other countries have become concerned about population concentration—Great Britain, for instance, has been worried for two decades about the drift of people to the densely settled south—without finding the means to check or reverse the concentration process. Is there any reason to think that the United States can do better?

GETTING THE PROBLEM ON THE NATIONAL AGENDA

The first problem is one of gaining attention and getting interest. Henry David has remarked that, to keep its sanity, a society must practice "selective inattention"—it simply cannot attack all of its problems all at once. Population distribution is one of the problems that, until very recently at least, had been marked for inattention.

Over the last decade, only one leading figure in public life has made it his mission to sound the alarm on the question of population distribution policy. That was the recent Secretary of Agriculture, Orville L. Freeman. For the whole of his 8 years in office, he led a personal crusade for what he initially called "rural areas development" and later came to call "rural-urban balance." Before a House Subcommittee in 1967, he said, "I say it is folly to stack up three-quarters of our people in the suffocating steel and concrete storage bins of the city, while a figurative handful of our fellow citizens rattle around in a great barn full of untapped resources and empty dreams." And then he got carried away: "The whiplash of economic necessity which today relentlessly drives desperate people into our huge cities must be lifted from the bleeding back of rural America."

Freeman's metaphors could be excused; no one listened to all his years of sober pleas and reasoned argument. True, President Johnson gave him moral support and himself made a speech or two on rural development and sent the Congress some minor measures, but the subject remained low on the president's priority list and even lower on the lists maintained by the Bureau of the Budget and other staff agencies that advise the president. As for the congressional committees on agriculture, who might have been expected to take some leadership, Freeman could not even get them to set up active subcommittees to consider rural development. Their concern for rural America extended to the price of agricultural commodities and the location of Department of Agriculture research stations, but not much further.

The nation's intellectual community, insofar as it was aware of the Freeman thesis, treated it with a disdain that blended into outright hostility. Teachers, writers, scholars, and editors for the most part live in cities; it is there that newspapers are published and television shows produced. The country's intelligentsia is wholly urban now; the voices that once sang of rural life, the Hamlin Garlands and Willa Cathers and Robert Frosts, are now stilled without replacement. One can stock a library with books on "the urban crisis," but try to fill a single shelf with works that deal in depth with the corresponding rural crisis!

A composite view of the urban intelligentsia toward rural America can be portrayed, with a touch of caricature, something like this: culturally, the cities have a monopoly, and have had since the Age of Pericles. Urban means urbane; rural means rustic. The theater, the concert hall, the museum are exclusively urban institutions; the countryside cannot produce the higher culture, and those who insist on living there are, by definition, both culturally unrefined and, what is worse, content to remain so. Economically, rural America is destined for decay; the economic forces that built the cities are too powerful to be reversed, even if it were desirable to do so. Freeman's "back to the farm" movement (which, for the record, is not what it was) is romantic nonsense that flies in the face of every economic reality. Sociologically, rural America is a backwater populated by misshapen characters out of Faulkner, given to choosing as their leaders men like George Wallace and Lester Maddox, and to hunting down civil rights workers and interring them on the banks of the Tallahoga River. Politically, it is time that rural America got its come-uppance; the farmers have been exploiting the cities far too long through outrageous programs that pay them enormous subsidies to cut production while the urban poor—and the rural poor as well—go hungry. Let the land grant colleges—the "cow colleges," that is—worry about the Podunks and the hicks and hayseeds who live there; we are an urban nation now.

This picture of the rural areas is not, unfortunately, wholly unrelated to reality. The fact is that the rural areas of the country *are* disadvantaged in many ways: they *are* culturally isolated (although their isolation has been drastically reduced by television and good roads); they *have* declined economically; their governmental and social institutions *are* often primitive and backward; racial exploitation *is* rife. But the cities are not all that superior. There is truth, too, in Freeman's counterportrait of big cities as places of "congestion and confusion, crime and chaos, polluted air and dirty water, overcrowded schools and jobless ghettos, racial unrest . . . and riots in the streets."

But there are signs, now, that the intellectual world may at last be rediscovering rural and small- town America and looking with fresh eyes upon the problem of rural-urban balance. Like so many other trends of current history, this one was set in motion in August 1965—in Watts. The analysts of that explosion, and those which followed, suddenly discovered that the problems they called urban had rural roots. "We're being overwhelmed," cried the urbanists. "Stop the migration. Get these people off our backs!" Joseph P. Lyford was among the first to see the rural-urban relationship. "Why," he asked in his study of a New York slum, *The Airtight Cage*, "do we treat the consequences and ignore the causes of massive and purposeless migration to the city? Why are we not developing new uses for those rural areas that are rapidly becoming depopulated? Why do we still instinctively deal with urban and rural America as if they were separate, conflicting interests when in fact neither interest can be served independently of the other?"

So the rural and the urban interest may have converged, finally, and it is out of such convergence that effective political coalitions are born and problems attain their place on the national agenda. The prospects for such a coalition are expressed most sharply in, of all places, the 1968 Republican platform. "Success with urban problems requires acceleration of rural development in order to stem the flow of people from the countryside to the city," reads the GOP's plank. The language is not without irony for the party of small-town America and the party that enacted the Homestead Act. Should development of rural America be accelerated because rural people are suffering economically and, as God-fearing Americans, deserve a better fate? No. Should it be accelerated because rural development is a worthy goal on its own merits? Not at all. The whole subject is treated under the heading, "Crisis in the Cities"; rural development should be accelerated because the problems of the big cities, where the Democrats live, must be solved.

The leadership for a rural development coalition, also ironically, will have to come from those very cities. Groups with names like the Urban Coalition, the Urban Institute, and the Urban League will have to assume the burden of worrying about rural America, because there is no rural coalition, no rural institute, no rural league. Nobody has ever organized to speak for rural and small town people in the nations's councils as the United States Conference of Mayors, say, and the Urban Coalition speak for city people. Farm groups exist, to be sure, but their interest is the economic interest of farmers as producers, and most rural Americans—whatever the definition of the word "rural"—are not farmers but small-town and small-city dwellers. And they are not organized at all.

When rural America is saved, it is clear, it will be for the wrong reasons and under the wrong leadership. But that is better than not being saved at all.

THE OUTLINES OF A PROGRAM

The first requirement of any program to cope with America's population distribution ills—and the greater ills that are in prospect—must be a research component. As I observed earlier, those who would cope with the question have hardly any data at all on the consequences of population concentration, on the diseconomies and disadvantages of scale. (What data exist are summarized in the excellent 1968 report of the Advisory Commission on Intergovernmental Relations, *Urban and Rural America: Policies for Future Growth*, from which the figures used earlier in this article were taken.) Criteria do not exist for deciding how many people in a metropolitan area are too many or, at the other extreme, how much dispersal is too much dispersal.

Nevertheless, the country cannot afford to wait until all the analyses have been completed and all the facts are in. Action normally must precede research; it takes the actuality or imminence of action to attract scholars, and the funds required for their support, to an issue. The objective must be to move toward an ideal population distribution pattern while at the same time perfecting its design. And that is possible; in driving to the Pacific, one need not have a map of the entire route to know that he begins by heading westward.

We can begin by defining one objective—to bring to a halt, as nearly as possible, all involuntary migration. The purpose of governmental policy, then, would be to permit people to live and work where they want to live and work; if they prefer to move to the big city, well and good, but if they want to remain where they are the objective should be to bring the jobs to them. That would serve the dual end of protecting the big cities against the unwanted influx of the displaced poor, and of taking from the shoulders of the poor themselves—and the involuntary migrants who may not be poor—the burden of paying through their own hardship and economic loss for the adjustments in employment patterns brought about by technological advance.

This proposal will be confronted at once by the objection that some rural areas are too remote, too backward to be salvageable in any circumstances—that no matter how much they are subsidized they are beyond the reach of economic opportunity. I hide behind the qualifying phrase; forced migration should be brought "as nearly as possible" to a halt, and where a rural community lies beyond the possibility of redevelopment (the Appalachian "head of the hollow" communities come to mind) then it is by definition impossible to help. However, the number of people living in such communities is far smaller than is usually believed, if one understands that the jobs to be provided need only be *near*, not *at*, the community concerned. Commutation is a fact of life in this automobile age in rural areas as well as on Long Island, and rural people commonly travel daily to jobs within a radius of 25 to 50 miles. Circles with 25 mile radii drawn around small cities that have a proven economic potential—proven by the fact that they are growing now— cover the vast majority of the country's rural population east of the high plains, and if the circles are extended to 50 mile radii they blanket almost the whole country but for a few sparsely settled sections of the western mountains and the plains.

In the administration of the Appalachian Regional Development Act and the Public Works and Economic Development Act, growth centers are designated, and investment is concentrated in those places to stimulate the growth not just of the centers themselves but of the hinterlands they serve. Usually every rural settlement in an area being assisted is within reasonable commutation distance of a growth center. The commutation radius can be greatly increased, of course, by the improvement of road transportation, which is part of the rationale behind the heavy emphasis in the Appalachian program upon the construction of "developmental highways."

A population distribution policy, then, would seek to encourage an accelerated rate of growth in the smaller natural economic centers of the country's less densely populated regions, as the alternative to further concentration of population in the larger metropolitan areas. To effectuate such a policy, the present approaches would have to be extended in both breadth and depth. First, they would need to be expanded beyond Appalachia and the other presently recognized redevelopment areas to cover all areas that are sources of out-migration. Second, they would need to be greatly improved in potency, so that they have a decisive impact upon the migration stream. Present federal programs are limited to public investment—roads, hospitals, vocational training schools, and so on—to strengthen the "infrastructure" of the nonmetropolitan areas, and loans and loan guarantees to encourage private investment. To these would have to be added the policy instrument of tax incentives that has proved so effective in stimulating and channeling investment both for war production and for peacetime economic growth. If an extra investment tax credit were available for defined types of new industry located in the places where the national population distribution policy called for it to be located, then jobs would be created where the people are rather than in places to which they have to migrate. Specific legislation to aid the development of new cities would also be helpful, although for the most part existing smaller cities should be the nuclei for urban growth. *Urban and Rural America: Policies for Future Growth* carefully catalogs a wide range of other possible program measures.

The rub will come, of course, when the Congress begins to write the language defining exactly the places eligible for benefits. While the objective of aiding sources of out-migration is simple enough in conception, the problem of drawing boundary lines is not. Specifically, growth centers that serve areas of out-migration would have to be included among the beneficiaries, even though the centers themselves were areas of in-migration. But only up to a certain point. A cutoff population figure would have to be established, at the point where a growth center is considered to have grown large enough, or at least to be able to attain its further growth under its own power. But given the old-fashioned booster psychology that still conditions the thinking of the leadership of even the largest cities, the Congress will find it difficult to designate any area, even the New York City area, as one that is destined—if national policy can bring it about—to stop growing. Real estate values still benefit from population increase, and wholesale and retail trade increase, no matter what the ancillary evils of population concentration. To most community influentials, bigger and bigger still mean greater and greater and richer and richer. A population distribution policy may therefore ultimately have to await a major shift in the national psychology.

When the country has to be jarred loose from a traditional outlook and shocked into a new one, the best means is often the institutional device that the United States has adopted from Great Britain—the royal commission. Such commissions have sometimes jarred us in the past; the Kerner commission, despite adverse circumstances, did so. Population distribution policy seems singularly appropriate as a subject for study by such a body. To its credit, the Senate passed a resolution in 1967 and again in 1969 to create a Commission on Balanced Economic Growth. It remains for the House of Representatives and the president to act.

24
URBAN AMERICA AND THE FEDERAL SYSTEM
Advisory Commission on Intergovernmental Relations

WHEN IS BIG, BAD?

Is there a point in the growth of urban areas where concentration ceases to be an advantage and becomes a serious handicap? Are there important diseconomies of urban scale?

Obviously it is "more expensive" to live in a city than a rural area; for one thing, people in cities pay cash for some goods and services that rural residents pay for partly in their own labor. But there are more goods and more services—more amenities—available in cities than in suburbs and small towns, and higher incomes too. An examination of whether, in fact, "diseconomies" occur after cities grow to a certain size must be very carefully handled. As mentioned earlier, an Advisory Commission study of this question indicated that for cities over 250,-000 population per capita expenditure for certain public services may tend to stabilize at a significantly higher level than for less populated places.

The question then shifts to possible diseconomies of metropolitan scale. As made clear earlier, most of the growth in coming decades will come not in the great central cities but in the suburbs and satellite cities around them. Residents in these parts of the metropolis feel that they may capture many of the advantages of urban life without its liabilities. But are there other liabilities which arise from the size of the modern "spread city"?

Big metropolitan areas seem to reach a stage of size "maturity" after

Reprinted with omissions from *Urban America and the Federal System,* 1969.

which they are no longer attractive to industrial location, and their population-growth rate levels off to considerably less than that of smaller metropolises. From this, we might conclude that the "free market" of locational competition can be counted upon to prevent the development of excessively large metropolitan areas. This would argue against any deliberate governmental effort to influence locational forces, for example, by trying to steer further urbanization mainly toward areas other than the largest ones. But such an optimistic laissez-faire view might be questioned on several grounds.

First, physical problems may reach crisis proportions well before diseconomies of scale deter further industrial concentration and thereby stop continued population growth. Air pollution—a "sickness of cities"—is an example. The earth as a whole has an enormous volume of air (a million and a half tons per person), with great capacity for containing pollutants. But most air pollution arises in urban centers, which commonly have more than ten times the weight of air-carried particles found elsewhere. Even with present population densities and fuel-using practices, according to the experts, cities "are coming uncomfortably close to using up all their available air,"[1] while a fourfold rise in the capacity of power-generating plants that burn fossil fuels is projected by the year 2000.

Second, some contend that huge size and complexity purchase private economic efficiency at too great a cost from the standpoint of human values and effective governmental and social institutions. As one writer has expressed this view:[2]

All of this (population concentration in huge urban centers) has raised some very serious questions not only about the impact upon the physical needs to be met but about the kind of society it implies. Is the multimillion population urban agglomeration likely to offer the kind of physical, social, and aesthetic environment which will stimulate a rise in the cultural level of the individual and awaken his latent talents for participation in social, political and intellectual activities? Will such agglomerations achieve societies of high quality and enduring vigor? Does this kind of development offer enough variety and choice for people of the next two generations?

Third, it can be argued that the strong thrust toward increasingly metropolitan growth would at least be dampened if government were more conscientious in charging the parties responsible for economic

[1] Roger Revelle, "Pollution and Cities," in *The Metropolitan Enigma*, James Q. Wilson, ed. (Washington, D.C.: Chamber of Commerce of the United States, 1967), p. 87, quoted in *Urban and Rural America: Policies for Future Growth* (Advisory Commission on Intergovernmental Relations, 1968), p. 57.

[2] Oliver C. Winston, "An Urbanization Pattern for U.S.," reprinted in *U.S., Congressional Record, 90th Cong., 1st Sess.,* October 10, 1967, p. S 14506–7, quoted in *Urban and Rural America, op. cit.,* p. 56.

costs that arise from concentrated urban development. It can hardly be doubted, for example, that some decisions about the location of particular industrial plants would be different if the owners had to provide for costly installations to minimize their pollution of the air, or to foot the entire bill for highway facilities to deal with traffic congestion they create.

Such considerations suggest that some of the minuses of large-scale urbanization receive inadequate attention in the myriad of decisions which produce the modern metropolis. This does not, however, offer any directly useful guide to optimum or maximum urban scale, and, as the Regional Plan Association has pointed out:[3]

> Many of the negative aspects of large city living are not inevitably linked to size but are, rather, socially, institutionally and politically determined. Their drawbacks can be alleviated or eliminated through the political process by a more equitable distribution of public investment, through pricing policies that make individuals more responsive to the consequences of their actions, through technological advance and through imaginative and rational planning and design.

METROPOLITAN HETEROGENEITY, MUNICIPAL HOMOGENEITY

The dominant central city of earlier decades was a heterogeneous one with people of different ethnic backgrounds, races, and incomes. With suburbanization, however, marked jurisdictional differentiation has occurred. The metropolis as a whole has wide socioeconomic variations but individual governmental jurisdictions within it reflect a far more homogeneous character. As mentioned earlier, the central city typically retains most of the nonwhites and the majority (63 percent) of the metropolitan poor. Even in the suburbs, however, there are sharp social and economic differences among political jurisdictions. It was pointed out that the view from "suburbia's cracked picture window" shows residents of the wealthy bedroom community differing markedly from the people in the industrial enclave and both differing from the people in the "poverty pocket" or other lower-income suburban neighborhood.

Race adds a special dimension to this picture of urban people. As recently as 1940, 77 percent of all American Negroes still lived in the South. Between 1940 and 1966, a net total of 3.7 million nonwhites joined in a great exodus to central cities of other regions. Of all American nonwhites, 65 percent now live in metropolitan central cities, while most of the remainder still live in the rural South.

About 17 percent of the residents of central cities were black as of

[3] The Regional Plan Association, *The Region's Growth, A Report of the Second Regional Plan* (New York: 1967), p. 22, quoted in *Urban and Rural America, op. cit.*, p. 57.

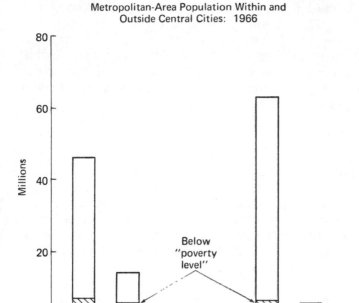

Metropolitan-Area Population Within and
Outside Central Cities: 1966

1960. Six years later the proportion had climbed three percentage points and if recent trends continue the 1985 figure will be nearly 31 percent. By contrast, only 5 percent of the urban fringe population was nonwhite in 1960 and this proportion slipped to 4 percent by 1966. According to present projections and barring any major breakthroughs on the urban housing front, the 1985 figure will come to about 6.1 percent.[4]

Different groups in our society bear the burden of poverty unequally. The most poverty-prone are nonwhites, members of families headed by a woman, members of large families, the aged, and families whose heads are unemployed or underemployed.

Contrary to a widespread impression, only 3 out of every 10 poor people live in the central cities. Nearly half the poor live in rural America, though very few (only 8 percent) of the poor are on farms. Of the estimated 51 percent of the American poor in metropolitan

[4] 1950 and 1960 data from U.S. Bureau of the Census, *Current Population Reports,* Series P-23, Nos. 24 (October 1967) and 26 (July 1968); 1985 estimates (using 1967 SMSA boundaries) from P. L. Hodge and P. M. Hauser, *The Challenge of America's Metropolitan Population Outlook 1960 to 1985* (New York: Praeger, 1968), p. 26.

areas, as of 1966, the majority lived in the central city (9.4 million out of 15.2 million, or 63 percent), partly because that is where the majority of nonwhites live. Almost half of the white poor in metropolitan areas live in the suburbs—demonstrating, incidentally, that suburbia shows more racial than economic prejudice.[5] These intrajurisdictional social disparities clearly accentuate the fiscal crisis of core cities with burgeoning budgets and eroding revenues.

BULLDOZERS, PROGRESS, AND PEOPLE PUSHED ASIDE

The process of urban development, in and out of cities, has meant displacement of large numbers of people, currently involving as many as 100,000 families and individuals annually, according to some estimates. This displacement on more than one occasion has been the match that touched off a riot.

Displacement actions by local governments include urban renewal, public housing construction, and condemnation of substandard structures under local housing codes. State governments also have caused widespread displacement in building state and interstate highways, and both levels have been assisted in these efforts by federal grant programs. Within metropolitan areas, the brunt of dislocation falls mainly upon the poor, the near poor, the lower-middle class, the nonwhite and the aged.

Physical change and development—whether under private or governmental auspices—obviously cannot avoid some impact upon those whose homes or businesses are in its path. But government with its unique power of eminent domain has a special obligation to soften the blow and fully underwrite burdens that result from its own developmental and housing-related activities. Yet, the record to date indicates that government has only begun to consider the human factor in its ever increasing land acquisition activities.

[5] Data in this section are drawn from various articles by Mollie Orshansky for the Social Security Administration, notably "Counting the Poor: Before and After Federal Income-Support Programs," in *Old Age Income Assurance* (U.S. Congress, Joint Economic Committee, December 1967), Part II, p. 197. The criterion of poverty which the Social Security Administration has developed is an income measurement which takes into account family size, number of children, and farm-nonfarm residence. It is annually adjusted to reflect price rises, but does not distinguish between rural nonfarm life and metropolitan life. Unquestionably, living costs are lower outside metropolitan areas, while incomes tend to be higher within. Thus the rural nonfarm poor are better off relative to their neighbors and compared to the metropolitan poor; but by what degree it is not possible to say.

THE RURAL REMAINDER—AND ITS PLANT

The shift from rural to metropolitan America has depopulated farms and drawn young people out of the small towns and the cutover, strip-mined, automated-farming, and mechanized mining areas of our country.

Many scattered small towns, with under-occupied housing, abandoned or half-used schools, empty stream-side factories and under-used utility facilities, present a black picture of wasted "fixed plant." The idea is sometimes expressed that some of these towns carry the seeds of expansion and, with assistance, could absorb some of the development that otherwise would occur elsewhere. Yet, in many cases, their governmental institutions, originally designed to handle the less difficult challenges of an earlier age of greater self-sufficiency, frequently are unable to provide the kind of public services needed today. Local government expenditures per person in many rural jurisdictions are disproportionately high for frequently inadequate levels of service. To complicate matters, the limited administrative machinery and scarcity of leadership often combine to hinder the planning and development necessary to overcome their handicaps.

With a static overall population growth since 1950, a declining farm sector and a generally less favorable position (as compared to metropolitan areas) regarding its educational and health facilities, housing, poverty, and income levels, rural America at this point in time faces a highly uncertain future—a future which in various major respects is closely linked to that of her urban brethren.

JOBS HERE—UNEMPLOYMENT THERE

If present trends continue, the rural population will continue to shift—though at a reduced rate given its reduced number—away from many rural areas and from small towns that are remote from metropolitan areas. Attractive job opportunities there will continue to be scarce, and the areas will experience further siphoning off of the young and able work force. The resulting greater concentration of older and unskilled workers among those remaining and the further decline in the capacity of many towns and hamlets to support basic public services will hasten the erosion of significant sectors of rural America. There are, of course, exceptions to this predominant picture. Some towns and independent small cities are experiencing a modest population growth and can anticipate a viable future existence, fed by their locational advantages for certain types of production or services. Moreover, numerous moderate-sized, nonmetropolitan cities no doubt have a real potential for sound development. But a drastic change in recent trends would be needed for such situations to be widely spread.

Within metropolitan areas the expansion of industry and commerce —especially those of the labor intensive type—along the suburban fringe seems likely to continue, thus widening the gap between the declining economy of the central city and the dynamic one of many of its suburban neighbors. What growth there has been in central cities has tended to offer employment opportunities in the professional managerial, technical, and highly skilled sectors—in short, jobs for suburbanites.

With the relative drop in central city job opportunities, the migrating poor, less educated, and nonwhite logically should shift to the suburbs. But the scarcity of older, low-cost suburban housing and the persistent barrier of discrimination in the case of blacks tend to sustain the white noose around the central cities. For some migrating poor-whites, small settlements along the metropolitan periphery also prove attractive.

Throughout this brief assessment of the broad contours of the metropolitan challenge runs the general theme of the paradoxical nature of recent urban development. In probing the many facets of this challenge, we encounter a series of major public policy questions stemming from paradoxes such as these:

(1) the emergence of an urban nation, but an economic and social decline in our nation's larger cities;

(2) the romantic, traditional notion of an America with limitless amounts of land, but an urban America of today with a scarcity of this much-needed factor of growth;

(3) the hymnal ideal of gleaming "alabaster cities," but the reality of blight, slums and slurbs;

(4) the venerable Jeffersonian tenet of the resolute and resourceful agrarian, but the here-and-now fact of rural decline;

(5) the cultural ideal of social heterogeneity but the jurisdictional fact of greater socioeconomic homogeneity;

(6) the presumption that government should be one of the guardians of our collective social consciousness, yet the reality of governmental harshness and injustice when it proceeds to acquire land; and

(7) the elemental American democratic precept of equal opportunity, but the evident geographic, transportational, and housing barriers facing many of the disadvantaged in rural and core-city America, severely restricting their freedom of choice.

25
A GROWTH CENTER STRATEGY FOR THE UNITED STATES
Niles M. Hansen

This paper proposes a national regional policy based on the development of employment opportunities in intermediate-sized cities, with the condition that a significant number of these opportunities be made available to residents of economically lagging areas. The strategy set forth is based on three propositions, which will be considered in turn. First, it is not generally feasible to base a national regional strategy on the industrialization of rural areas. Second, it is quite possible that our largest metropolitan areas are too big in terms of both economic efficiency and public preferences, so that their growth should be, if not checked, at least not encouraged. Third, with expanded manpower and human resource development programs, and with expanded comprehensive relocation assistance, it is possible to provide alternatives to rural poverty other than the metropolitan ghetto. At the end of the paper the Piedmont Crescent will be considered as the kind of intermediate area upon which a national growth-center strategy could be based.

ATTRACTING INDUSTRY TO RURAL AREAS

Insofar as any coherent regional policy exists in the United States it has been devised and implemented on the assumption that it is feasible to attract sufficient industry to lagging, and for the most part rural, regions

Reprinted by permission from *The Review of Regional Studies,* Fall 1970.

worse first
annual

of the country to give the people in these regions economic opportunities comparable to those enjoyed by other Americans. Thus, the hot-
house industrialization of rural areas has been advocated by, among
others, the Department of Agriculture,[1] the Department of Labor,[2] the
President's National Advisory Commission of Rural Poverty,[3] and the
writings of some scholars.[4] The author has dwelt at some length elsewhere on the appropriateness of these proposals, so only a few summary remarks are given here.[5]

The experience of other countries which have been trying for longer
than the United States to promote the growth of large lagging regions
indicates that such efforts have not been generally successful.[6] Moreover, although there is evidence from the United States and abroad of
greater equality in the geographical distribution of manufacturing, this
does not imply any concomitant decrease in regional income differences or any relatively greater attractiveness of small towns or rural
areas. Recent employment growth has been accounted for primarily by
expanding tertiary activities, which have been located primarily in metropolitan areas. Those industries that have tended to leave metropolitan areas have been characterized by relative stagnation or decline;
they often seek cheap labor in areas with a redundant agricultural labor
force. In contrast, rapidly expanding sectors favor metropolitan areas
because of their numerous external economies.[7]

CITY SIZE: ECONOMIC EFFICIENCY AND PUBLIC PREFERENCES

The continuing expansion of large metropolitan agglomerations is by
no means necessarily desirable. Questions of efficient city size are difficult to evaluate because of the impossibility of measuring adequately
the external economies and diseconomies of metropolitan growth from
a social point of view. Moreover, economists have almost completely
neglected the issue of personal locational preferences (though they
have given considerable attention to time preferences). There are a
number of students of metropolitan growth who maintain that there is
no evidence that any city is too big, in the sense that marginal costs
exceed marginal productivity.[8] On the other hand, there are those who
maintain that some cities have in all probability already become too
big.[9]

Such information as we have with respect to people's residential
preference patterns indicates that they prefer medium-sized cities.
Neutze's findings for Australia show that although firms and families
prefer centers with 2,000,000 or more people to small towns, "for
many, and quite possibly for most, the advantages of shorter journeys

to work, less traffic congestion, and the like make the medium-sized center more attractive."[10] By "medium-sized" Neutze means centers with populations of from 200,000 to one million.

French survey data also show that the social costs of urban congestion are considerable and that they are significantly felt by the populations involved. Most Frenchmen would prefer to remain where they presently reside or to live in a locality of more or less similar characteristics. In the Paris agglomeration, however, only a minority of the residents would really prefer to live in the Paris region. Seventy percent of the Paris residents favor a diminution of the population of the Paris region; similarly, in other areas of heavy urban concentration, such as Flanders, the Artois, and the Lyon region, there is also strong public support for a diminution of their populations.[11] From these and similar findings, Girard and Bastide conclude that "if the expressed aspirations could be satisfied, the movement away from the countryside, however vigorously condemned, would continue, but a regroupment would be made to the profit of medium and large provincial cities, and Paris would cease to grow. Thus . . . decentralization efforts conform to the wishes of the population."[12]

Such data as we have for location preferences in the United States show a similar pattern. Data collected by the author from a sample of Mexican-Americans in South Texas indicated that they preferred smaller cities to either large cities, on the one hand, or small towns or rural areas on the other. Similarly, a study of location preferences of graduating seniors in five eastern Kentucky counties showed that they would prefer living in Louisville or Lexington to either living in a big northern city or remaining in their home counties.[13] In more general terms, a Gallup poll survey released in May, 1968 showed that 56 percent of the American people would prefer living in rural areas or in small towns—*if jobs were available.* In comparison with a poll taken two years earlier, the proportion of persons expressing a preference for city or suburban living dropped by seven percentage points, whereas the proportion preferring a rural location rose by the same amount.[14] No reasons were given for this shift, but presumably increasing tensions of life in large urban centers were a factor. In any case, the number of persons actually moving to rural areas will bear little resemblance to the expressed preferences because the job availability condition will not be satisfied. On the other hand, if life in big metropolitan areas is so unaccommodating, why do they continue to grow? The author has examined this issue at some length in a previous study, and a summary of that discussion will be presented here.[15]

One of the major conclusions derivable from the assumptions of classical economic theory is that factor mobility will equalize returns to various classes of homogeneous inputs, other things being equal. Space, however, is not homogeneous. Agglomeration of economic activities results in a wide variety of external economies, so that purely market forces tend to concentrate economic activities in a few focal areas. These external economies include relative abundance of public overhead capital, proximity to buyers and sellers, the presence of numerous auxiliary business services (banking, brokerage, insurance), educational facilities, and a well-trained labor force. The attraction of investment to already concentrated areas tends to raise the marginal product of capital in these areas, thereby inducing immigration. Growth of a relatively skilled labor force, induced public overhead investment, and other induced activities further enhance the attractiveness of such areas for private investment. This cumulative process results in even greater concentration of economic activity and population. However, it also entails numerous social costs, including traffic congestion, inadequate parks and recreation facilities, slum neighborhoods, natural beauty marred by buildings and billboards, and air pollution. Unfortunately, there is nothing in the nature of things to halt this process, because the external diseconomies of congestion often are not internalized by private firms; or if they are internalized, they are not of such a magnitude as to offset the external economies of agglomeration. It is this disparity between social and private costs that causes jobs to be created in areas where the net social product is less than it would be in an alternative location (because the wage is higher in congested areas as a result of labor's increased productivity based on privately internalized economies; and because the wage may reflect a payment made to help overcome the external diseconomies borne by the individual). The latter phenomenon is most clearly seen in the supplements paid by oligopolistic firms to professional and managerial personnel to induce them to live in New York City.

It may be argued that individuals will increase their welfare by moving into concentrated areas so long as their marginal private gain in income outweighs their own internalized marginal diseconomies associated with congestion. However, this does not imply an increase in social welfare in a Paretian optimal sense, since such action, by increasing concentration, increases the diseconomies absorbed by previous residents. Some previously inframarginal residents might then prefer to leave the area. This would be the case where income loss from outmigration is less than the increase in marginal disutility resulting from increased congestion. On the other hand, social and economic rigidities, such as habituation to friends and surroundings and the costs of moving, will keep many of these people from moving; they will tend not to minimize their welfare loss unless increased disutility in the agglomeration is substantially greater than the private loss of relocating.

The failure of the free market to halt the growth of large metropolitan areas suggests that public policy measures might be employed to retard their growth and to prevent other cities from expanding to a point where they become overconcentrated. Taxation and credit policy and land-use controls could be used to limit private investment in congested metropolitan areas. However, the more feasible alternative from a political point of view would be to encourage private capital to locate in other areas; public overhead capital could also be used to induce private investment to locate outside of large metropolitan areas. Some of these tools have been used, of course, by our federal agencies concerned with regional development. The problem is that they have been applied for the most part to promote economic growth in rural areas and small towns, and thus they have been not only economically inefficient, but also largely ineffective. To be sure, there may be some sites in rural areas with promising industrial potential, but the most efficient use of public funds might be to encourage the growth of medium-sized cities, especially those which have given some real evidence of growth characteristics. In these places public funds may be integrated with actual or potential external economies to produce rapid growth with a minimum of external diseconomies of congestion. Some may object to this policy on the ground that rapidly growing places do not *need* any form of government subsidy. This is quite true in the narrower sense, but if the growth of intermediate-sized centers can be accelerated with government aid by more than growth can be accelerated in lagging regions, and if the accelerated growth of intermediate centers can be made conditional on the granting of newly created employment opportunities to a significant number of workers from lagging regions (either by means of migration or commuting), then clearly it is economically efficient for the government to attempt to accelerate employment growth in intermediate centers. (In cases where local unemployment rates are relatively high despite high growth rates,[16] a policy of growth acceleration would also be made conditional on the employment of the local jobless.) This policy would be in harmony with our limited knowledge of both public locational preferences and efficiency and city sizes.

Brian Berry's work on spatial organization and levels of welfare indicates that labor markets appear to need a minimum population of 250,000 to be viable parts of the urban system. Above this level cities appear to have the conditions necessary for self- sustained growth. On the other hand, few cities with fewer than 50,000 persons seem capable of influencing the welfare of their surrounding regions. On the basis of these findings, Berry draws a number of policy implications. First, the influence of small centers is too limited to justify public investment in them for regional development purposes. Second, an efficient development strategy might concentrate on cities just below the 250,000 population level. Public investment would provide the push required to get these cities over the threshold to self-generating growth. Third, those persons residing on or between the peripheries of metropolitan labor markets should be given adequate education and training, as well as relocation assistance, so that they can find employment in viable labor markets. However, care should be taken to discourage them from locating in big-city ghettos, where employment problems often are as difficult as those in rural areas.[17]

The 250,000 population threshold is also invoked by Wilbur Thompson, who points out that between 1950 and 1960, only seven out of 212 SMSA's lost population. If one of these, Jersey City, N.J., is regarded as part of the New York-Northeastern New Jersey SMSA rather than a separate entity, then there were no population declines in SMSA's with over 500,000 people, and only two declines in SMSA's with over 250,000 people (Johnstown and Wilkes-Barre-Hazleton, Pa.). He concludes that "if the growth of an urban area persists long enough to raise the area to some critical size (a quarter of a million population?), structural characteristics, such as industrial diversification, political power, huge fixed investments, a rich local market, and a steady supply of industrial leadership may almost ensure its continued growth and fully ensure against absolute decline—may, in fact, effect irreversible aggregate growth."[18]

Neutze's investigations employing Australian data indicate that most of the advantages of a city of 500,000 are probably also found in a city of 200,000, but that if a city gets much beyond the half-million level the external diseconomies probably begin to outweigh the concomitant economies. In any case, he suggests that many firms will maximize their profits in centers with populations between 200,000 and one million.[19] "Let us say," writes Neutze, "that 500,000 was the best size, or at least that most of the firms that could be diverted from locating in Sidney would prefer, as an alternative, a city of about 500,-000. The objective should be to push the new center as rapidly as possible through the early inefficient stages to get it close to 500,000 and to prevent it from growing past that size. More firms and families will suffer from further growth than will gain."[20] It should be pointed out that Neutze probably underestimates the attractive power of large agglomerations. More firms reap more gains from external economies in big cities than he admits—otherwise, so many of them would not continue to locate in metropolitan areas even after they pass, say, the one million mark.[21] Government planners may try to discourage firms from locating in large agglomerations, but this is different from saying that a firm will be at a disadvantage in locating there. It will not in many cases because it does not internalize many of the diseconomies. Thus, policy measures to induce firms to locate in intermediate areas will have to go beyond simply trying to persuade them that it is to their advantage to shun the large agglomeration.

Finally, if we consider only government services, it is clear that intermediate areas are more efficient than either small towns or large agglomerations. Werner Hirsch estimates that the greatest economies of scale accrue to a government serving from 50,000 to 100,000 people. His findings are similar to those of the Royal Commission on Local Government in Greater London, which reached the conclusion that the optimum size of a city would be a minimum of about 100,000 people, and a maximum of about 250,000.[22] These results imply that cities that have passed the 250,000 mark may encounter diseconomies of scale in the public sector, but these will probably be outweighed by external economies in the private sector. On the other hand, small towns and rural areas once again are shown to be at a distinct disadvantage.

A GROWTH CENTER POLICY

What should be the essential ingredients of a growth center policy designed to take pressure off big cities and to give migrants from lagging rural areas an alternative to the metropolitan ghetto? One approach would be to build entirely new towns. However, there are a number of reasons why this probably would not be satisfactory. Although new towns have received considerable publicity as well as a great deal of support from planners, they have been primarily a physical planning device. Too little attention has been given to developing an economic rationale for new towns. British experience has shown that location decisions for new towns have not been made so as to maximize their chances for industrial development, and insufficient attention has been given to developing their employment base. Moreover, most of the literature on new towns demonstrates that they are designed to appeal to people who already live in urban areas and are attached to them. They also seem to be repetitive and monotonous in terms of physical design, and to be generally dull relative to the more animated "downtowns."[23]

Reston, Virginia, one of the more highly touted experiments with a new town in this country, has proven to be a disappointment. It has had difficulty in attracting residents and it is, in any case, largely a dormitory community rather than an independent center with its own economy, as originally planned. Columbia, another new town near the nation's capital, may meet with greater success, but it is still far from being a center designed to divert migrants from large metropolitan areas. Columbia may prove to be a successful experiment in urban planning, but it is nevertheless part and parcel of the Eastern megalopolis. Indeed, most new town proposals are geared to relocating people within metropolitan areas, and their costs are such that they have little relevance to people in the income groups in which most rural to urban migrants fall.

A more realistic approach to the problem of rechanneling migration streams would be to build on existing external economies in growing cities in the 50,000 to 1,000,000 population range, and more particularly in growing cities in the 250,000 to 750,000 range. These values are of course not magic numbers but rather rough indicators of the lower and upper limits for intermediate growth centers. As has been shown, there is evidence for believing that self-sustained growth is more assured in a city with 250,000 people than in smaller places. On the other hand, there is increasing danger the increasing external diseconomies will make the marginal social product less than it would be in an alternative city after a city passes the 750,000 mark. However, growing cities that are smaller than 250,000 or larger then 750,000 should not automatically be excluded from consideration.

It has been specified that a growth center policy should build on cities that are already growing relatively rapidly. The simple reason for this is that such places are demonstrating their ability to create new jobs. There may be cities, and even rural areas, that have not been growing but which for one reason or another may have real job growth potential. Places at or near the intersections of interstate highways may fall into this category. Nevertheless, without preparing a detailed and costly study of every county, village, town and city that claims to have growth potential (in Appalachia alone the states have designated about 125 areas as having significant potential for growth),[24] there is really no practical way to select a system of growth centers other than to rely on the record of the past, particularly the recent past. Sites that may benefit from interstate highway intersections, resource discoveries, or large-scale federal projects need not be automatically excluded if they have heretofore been relatively stagnant, but their case should be very strong if they are to be regarded as objects of growth center policy; otherwise, the Pandora's box of Chamber of Commerce salesmen will be opened.

It is not enough that a growth center policy be built upon rapidly growing cities of intermediate size. Their growth must be related to the employment of persons from lagging regions with high unemployment or low incomes. A rapidly growing, intermediate-sized city located, say, in the Midwestern corn belt may have little relevance to residents of any of our large, lagging rural areas. Workers from Appalachia, the Ozarks, or even the Upper Great Lakes may be unlikely to be persuaded to move to this city, nor would Mexican-Americans, Indians, or Negroes. In this event the city would not qualify as a growth center. Such a policy implies that education and training programs in lagging areas be geared to employment opportunities in growth centers. Finally, while in many cases it may be possible for workers in lagging areas to commute to growth centers, often they will have to move, in which case programs of comprehensive relocation assistance should be provided.[25] Although growth centers would have to be selected partly on the basis of commuting and migration data, this does not imply reinforcement of existing migration patterns; too often this means movement from rural areas to big-city ghettos. However, migration studies can give insights into the population flows linking lagging rural areas to rapidly growing, intermediate-sized cities, flows which could be reinforced by a growth center policy. The Piedmont Crescent provides an instructive example in this regard.

EDA DEVELOPMENT CENTERS AND THE PIEDMONT CRESCENT

The Piedmont Crescent includes nine SMSA's: Charlotte, Durham, Greensboro-High Point, Raleigh, and Winston-Salem, in North Carolina; Greenville, in South Carolina; and Atlanta, Columbus, and Macon, in Georgia.[26] The western portions of these three states are included in the territory of the Appalachian Regional Commission, while the eastern portions are included in the territory of the Coastal Plains Commission.

The states of North Carolina, South Carolina and Georgia have fourteen urban places or sets of places that have been designated by the Economic Development Administration as Economic Development Centers (see the Appendix). The Public Works and Economic Development Act of 1965 limits such Centers to communities or localized areas with fewer than 250,000 persons where resources hopefully can be used most rapidly and effectively to create more jobs and higher incomes for the populations of their surrounding areas. Although these Centers need not be within depressed areas, they are supposed to promote economic growth and thereby alleviate economic distress in the redevelopment areas of the districts to which the Centers belong.

Despite rapid growth,[27] none of the Piedmont Crescent SMSA's has been designated as a Development Center, although each is either in

TABLE 1. Estimated migration[a] from Appalachia and the Coastal Plains to SMSA's in the Piedmont Crescent and to EDA Economic Development Centers in Georgia, South Carolina, and North Carolina, 1960–1965

	(1)[b] Population in 1960 (thousands)	(2) Migrants from Appalachia	(3) (2) ÷ (1)	(4) Migrants from Coastal Plains	(5) (4) ÷ (1)	(6) (2) + (4)	(7) (6) ÷ (1)
Atlanta	1017	24,000	23.6	19,500	19.2	43,500	42.8
Other SMSA's	1556	35,000	22.5	30,400	19.5	65,400	42.0
Other SMSA's, excluding Columbus and Macon	1157	32,600	28.2	26,500	22.9	59,100	51.1
EDA Development Centers	1075	10,900	10.1	18,700	17.4	29,600	27.5

[a] These estimates are based on one percent Social Security sample data.
[b] U.S. Bureau of the Census, *County and City Data Book*, 1967.

TABLE 2. Estimated[a] average income change for migrants from Appalachia and the Coastal Plains to SMSA's in the Piedmont Crescent and to EDA Economic Development Centers in Georgia, South Carolina, and North Carolina, 1960–1965

Sending Areas (1960)

Receiving Areas	Appalachia				Coastal Plains				Appalachia and Coastal Plains			
	(1) 1960 Income	(2) 1965 Income	(3) Change	(4) Percent Change	(5) 1960 Income	(6) 1965 Income	(7) Change	(8) Percent Change	(9) 1960 Income	(10) 1965 Income	(11) Change	(12) Percent Change
Atlanta	2180	4147	1967	93.0	2317	4188	1871	80.8	2241	4165	1924	85.9
Other SMSA's	2619	4114	1495	57.1	2252	3549	1297	57.6	2448	3851	1403	57.3
Other SMSA's, including Columbus and Macon	2664	4143	1479	55.5	2238	3581	1343	60.0	2473	3891	1418	57.3
EDA Development	2798	4512	1714	61.3	2050	3585	1535	74.9	2325	3926	1601	68.9

[a] These estimates are based on one percent Social Security sample data.

or bordering on Appalachia or the Coastal Plains. With the exception of Atlanta, 2 of the Piedmont Crescent SMSA's had 1960 populations of somewhat over 250,000 (Greenville, 255,806; and Charlotte, 316,-781). The rest varied between 111,000 and 246,000. Thus, most of the SMSA's in the Crescent would be able to qualify as Development Centers; with the exception of Atlanta, any of them would be able to qualify with only a relatively small change in the population limitation set by the relevant legislation. Evidence that they are in fact relatively efficient growth centers—in the sense of providing jobs for residents of lagging areas—is given in Table 1.

The migration estimates presented in the third row of Table 1 pertain to the polynucleated urban region extending from Raleigh to Greenville. This core area, the Piedmont Industrial Crescent,[28] is an intermediate urban area in the sense employed earlier in this paper. The total population of the SMSA's in this region is not much above that of the combined EDA Development Centers in the three states under discussion. However, the Industrial Crescent SMSA's are providing substantially more jobs to Appalachian and Coastal Plains residents. In relation to their own population, the Industrial Crescent SMSA's are providing 51.1 jobs per 1000 inhabitants, whereas the comparable value for the Development Centers is only 25.7. If the Georgia SMSA's of Columbus and Macon are included, the SMSA value is still a relatively high 42.0, which is approximately the same as that for Atlanta.

The average income estimates shown in Table 2 indicate that the greatest gains were made by migrants to Atlanta. In this case the increase was 86 percent, as compared with 69 percent for the Development Centers and 57 percent for the other SMSA's, irrespective of whether Columbus and Macon are included. These gains of course reflect increases over time as well as differences attributable to location; however, differences in percentage change values are reflections of locational differences. Excluding Atlanta, it should be noted that the 1965 values (column 10) are not very different for SMSA's and the Development Centers. The higher rate of increase for the migrants to Development Centers is primarily related to their lower incomes in 1960.

In general, then, an efficient growth center strategy would put greater emphasis on relating problems in the lagging areas under discussion to job opportunities in the Piedmont Crescent. While there does not appear to be any income advantage for migrants going from lagging regions to Piedmont Crescent SMSA's relative to those going to EDA Development Centers (unless Atlanta were to be included for policy purposes), there are many more jobs for migrants in the Crescent SMSA's.

IMPLEMENTING A GROWTH CENTER STRATEGY

What measures might be undertaken to implement a growth center strategy along lines discussed earlier in this paper? The composition of a development aid tool kit, such as that now used by the Economic Development Administration, should be changed, since the tools will be applied to areas which are already economically healthy and growing, rather than to areas which have relatively poor growth prospects. There should be more emphasis on measures that will appeal to growing industries and less emphasis on subsidies whose principal appeal is to small firms in slow-growing, low-wage industries. There should be more money devoted to equipping relatively sophisticated industrial sites and less to building water and sewer lines (which may be sorely needed in rural areas, but not a central concern of an agency whose purpose is to initiate self-sustained growth). The kinds of tools will have to be more varied and flexible than those presently applied in small towns and rural areas. The latter often need so many improvements in order to make them relatively attractive to firms, especially the bigger and more rapidly growing ones, that whatever a development agency can do within the constraints of its limited resources is not likely to change greatly the total "package" of factors that a firm considers when making a location decision. This is especially true to the extent that a "worse-first" policy is either explicitly or implicitly followed in granting federal assistance. On the other hand, the growth center that are being proposed here would have a large variety of external economies. This means in the first place that a given type of aid extended by an economic development agency would not be so visible as it would be in a lagging area. However, if used wisely, it could produce more employment opportunities in the growth center because it could be combined with these external economies. The development agency should seek out the bottlenecks that are hindering or preventing a firm from locating or expanding in the growth center and attempt to provide the assistance needed to overcome the resistance. The situation may call for a certain type of investment in amenities or in more directly productive infrastructure, or for a labor training subsidy, or for some combination of aid devices. Efforts also might be made to enlist the cooperation of prominent business leaders, as is now being done for job creation programs in the ghettos. In any case, it is essential that the aid be made conditional on the extension of job opportunities to persons from lagging regions (and in part to the unemployed and underemployed residents of the center).

The emphasis that is given here to the development of intermediate cities as the principal focus for a national regional policy is based not only on the job growth potential of these cities, but also on the fact that problems related to their growth are still amenable to solution. The massive renewal needs of our large metropolitan areas can still be avoided by careful planning in growth centers. "A city of 'optimal size,' " writes Benjamin Higgins, "must be big enough to be urbane in its range of activities and small enough to provide effective proximity to these activities for its residents, with the available techniques of city planning and transportation."[29] Unless the government knows what places are going to grow it can provide public facilities only after the demand has appeared. If there is planned growth of a relatively few centers, then they can be provided with an integrated and coherent system of public facilities in advance of the demand.

Finally, the selective nature of out-migration from lagging areas means that they tend to lose their most vital people—the best workers, the young, the better educated.[30] Moreover, there is evidence that when employment opportunities appear in a lagging area there is a return movement of workers. Since these returnees are frequently more highly skilled than the members of the local work force, the hard core unemployed of the area may find little relief for their problems.[31] Thus, out-migration may cause cumulative difficulties in a lagging region, and the benefits from an increase in local employment opportunities may help return migrants more than the local residents. Of course, the positive multiplier effects of any new activity will indirectly benefit the community as a whole, especially if leakages to other areas are minimal.

Whatever may be the consequences of out-migration from lagging areas, it is still clear that policies that merely try to check migration —even by attempting to subsidize the industrialization of rural areas—do little service to either the nation or the individuals concerned, at least from an opportunity cost viewpoint. The remigration problem in particular shows that the real problem of lagging regions is underinvestment in their human resources, rather than migration as such, which is a symptom rather than a cause. Hopefully, a national regional policy would aid areas with problems occasioned by out-migration to attain new equilibria with a minimum of friction. The nation may also deem it desirable to aid persons in these areas whose prospects for either local employment or for retraining and migration are not bright; older workers in particular would fall into this category. However, it must be recognized that we are talking here about welfare and not about economic development policy. In any case, the main thrust of public policy in lagging regions should still be in the direction of active manpower and human resource programs, including comprehensive job information and relocation assistance.

APPENDIX

Economic Development Centers: Georgia, South Carolina, and North Carolina

EDA District	Number of Counties	Economic Development Centers
Central Savannah River	13	Augusta-Swainsboro, Ga.
Coastal	6	Brunswick-Hinesville, Ga.
Coastal Plain	9	Valdosta-Tifton, Ga.
Georgia Mountains	14	Gainesville-Toccoa, Ga.
Heart of Georgia	9	Dublin, Ga.
Northeast	9	Athens, Ga.
Oconee	7	Milledgeville, Ga.
Slash Pine	9	Waycross, Ga.
Southwest	13	Albany-Bainbridge, Ga.
West Central	8	Americus, Ga.
Southeastern	10	Wilmington-Fayetteville, N.C.
Savannah	4	Aiken, S.C.
Pee Dee	6	Florence-Darlington, S.C.
Upper Savannah	6	Greenwood, S.C.

NOTE: This list includes all relevant centers designated through March, 1969.

REFERENCES

The research summarized in this paper was made possible by the financial support of the Office of Economic Research of the Economic Development Administration, Department of Commerce, under Project #OER-227-G-68-11. Additional support was received from the Manpower Administration, Department of Labor, under Project #81-19-68-17. The findings do not necessarily reflect the viewpoints of either agency. The author also would like to acknowledge the assistance of David Hirschberg and Dann Milne in data preparation.

1. *Communities of Tomorrow—Agriculture 2000* (Washington, D.C.: U.S. Government Printing Office, 1968).
2. *Manpower Report of the President, 1968* (Washington, D.C.: U.S. Government Printing Office, 1968), pp. 128-139.
3. *The People Left Behind* (Washington, D.C.: U.S. Government Printing Office, 1967).
4. See, for example, William H. Nicholls, *Southern Tradition and Regional Progress* (Chapel Hill: University of North Carolina Press, 1960), pp. 13-14; Dale E. Hathaway and Brian E. Perkins, "Occupational Mobility and Migration From Agriculture," in *Rural Poverty in the United States* (Washington, D.C.: U.S. Government Printing Office, 1968), pp. 185-237.
5. See, for example, "Regional Development and the Rural Poor," *Journal of Human Resources,* forthcoming; "Unbalanced Growth and Regional Development," *Western Economic Journal,* 4, No. 1 (Fall 1965), pp. 3-14; and *French Regional Planning* (Bloomington: Indiana University Press, 1968).

6. Hansen, "Regional Development and the Rural Poor," *op. cit.*
7. Victor Fuchs, *The Growing Importance of the Service Industries* (New York: National Bureau of Economic Research Occasional Paper No. 96, 1965); *Changes in the Location of Manufacturing in the United States Since 1929* (New Haven, Conn.: Yale University Press, 1962); and Erling Olsen, "Erhvervslivets Lokalisering," *Nationaløkonomisk Tidsskrift,* Nos. 1–2 (1965), pp. 18–30.
8. See, for example, William Alonso, "Urban and Regional Imbalances in Economic Development," *Economic Development and Cultural Change,* 17, No. 1 (October 1968), pp. 1–14; Hans Blumenfeld, "The Modern Metropolis," in *Cities* (New York: Knopf, 1965), pp. 48–49.
9. Edgar M. Hoover, "The Evolving Form and Organization of the Metropolis," in Harvey S. Perloff and Lowden Wingo, Jr., *Issues in Urban Economics* (Baltimore: The Johns Hopkins Press, 1968), p. 268; and "Some Old and New Issues in Regional Development," University of Pittsburgh Center for Regional Economic Studies Occasional Paper No. 5, 1967, p. 6. See also, Kevin Lynch, "The City as Environment," in *Cities, op. cit.,* pp. 192–201; Kingsley Davis, "The Urbanization of Human Population," *ibid.,* p. 23; and René Dubos, "Promises and Hazards of Man's Adaptability," in Henry Jarrett, ed., *Environmental Quality in a Growing Economy* (Baltimore: The Johns Hopkins Press, 1966), pp. 27–29, 38.
10. G. M. Neutze, *Economic Policy and the Size of Cities* (Clifton, N.J.: Kelley, 1967), pp. 109–110.
11. Hansen, *French Regional Planning, op. cit.,* pp. 34–37.
12. Alain Girard and Henri Bastide, "Les problèmes démographiques devant l'opinion," *Population,* 15 (April-May 1960), p. 287.
13. These findings are reported in detail in a forthcoming report prepared for the Department of Labor. See also Robert L. Wilson, "Livability of the City: Attitudes and Urban Development," in F. Stuart Chapin, Jr., and Shirley F. Weiss, eds., *Urban Growth Dynamics* (New York: Wiley, 1962), pp. 359–399; and John Gulick, Charles E. Bowerman, and Kurt W. Back, "Newcomer Enculturation in the City: Attitudes and Participation," *ibid.,* pp. 356–357.
14. Cited in a speech by Secretary of Agriculture Orville Freeman before the Conference on Rural-Oriented Industry, Washington, D.C., 13 May 1968.
15. See Hansen, *French Regional Planning, op. cit.,* Chapter 1.
16. High growth rates are by no means necessarily associated with low unemployment states. See George Iden, "Unemployment Classification of Major Labor Areas, 1950–1965," *Journal of Human Resources,* 2, No. 3 (Summer 1967), p. 391; and Gene Laber, "Unemployment Classification of Major Labor Areas, 1950–1965: A Comment," *Journal of Human Resources,* 3, No. 4 (Fall 1968), pp. 515–519.
17. Brian J. L. Berry, "A Summary—Spatial Organization and Levels of Welfare: Degree of Metropolitan Labor Market Participation as a Variable in Economic Development," *Research Review* (EDA) (July 1968), pp. 1–6.
18. Wilbur R. Thompson, *A Preface to Urban Economics* (Baltimore: The Johns Hopkins Press, 1965), p. 24.
19. Neutze, *op. cit.,* pp. 103, 109–118.

20. *Ibid.,* pp. 117–118.

21. Between 1962 and 1967 there was about a 16 percent increase in employment in the fifteen largest SMSA's for employees covered in *County Business Patterns.* See Bureau of the Census, *County Business Patterns, 1962,* U.S. Summary (Washington, D.C.: U.S. Government Printing Office, 1963), pp. 164–166; and *County Business Patterns, 1967,* U.S. Summary (Washington, D.C.: U.S. Government Printing Office, 1968), pp. 231–233.

22. Werner Z. Hirsch, "The Supply of Urban Public Services," in Perloff and Wingo, *op. cit.,* pp. 509–511.

23. Jonathan Lindley, "The Economic Environment and Urban Development," a paper presented to the Eighth Annual Conference, Center for Economic Projections, National Planning Association, 28 April 1967, p. 17.

24. Ralph R. Widner, "The First Three Years of the Appalachian Program: An Evaluation," *Appalachia,* 1, No. 11 (August 1968), p. 19.

25. The feasibility and efficiency of such programs have been demonstrated. See Audrey Freedman, "Labor Mobility Projects for the Unemployed," *Monthly Labor Review,* 91, No. 6 (June 1968), pp. 57–62; "Moving to Work," (Washington, D.C.: Labor Mobility Services Unit, U.S. Employment Service, 1968); Garth L. Mangum, "Moving Workers to Jobs," *Poverty and Human Resources Abstracts,* 3 (November-December 1968), pp. 12–18.

26. C. E. Bishop and F. A. Mangum, "The Crescent's Human Resources," in James G. Maddox, ed., *Growth Prospects of the Piedmont Crescent* (Raleigh, N.C.: Agricultural Policy Institute, North Carolina State University, 1968), p. 15.

27. Between 1950 and 1960, the population of the United States increased by 18 percent, while that in SMSA's grew by 27 percent. With the exception of Durham (10.2 percent), all of the Piedmont Crescent SMSA's grew faster than the overall national rate, and all but three grew faster than the rate for all SMSA's. U.S. Bureau of the Census, *City and County Data Book, 1967* (Washington, D.C.: U.S. Government Printing Office, 1967). The Bureau of the Census estimates that the population of the United States grew by 8.1 percent from 1960 to 1965, and that in SMSA's by 9.1 percent. During the same period the Piedmont Crescent SMSA's had the following estimated rates of growth: Atlanta 19.6, Columbus 19.3, Raleigh 15.4, Charlotte 14.7, Macon 11.7, Durham 9.8, Winston-Salem 9.5, Greensboro-High Point 8.1, and Greenville 3.8. U.S. Bureau of the Census, *Current Population Reports,* Series P-25, No. 415, "Projections of the Population of Metropolitan Areas: 1975" (Washington, D.C.: U.S. Government Printing Office, 1969), pp. 15–18.

28. F. Stuart Chapin, Jr., "Introduction," in F. Stuart Chapin, Jr., and Shirley F. Weiss, eds., *op. cit.,* pp. 1–21.

29. Benjamin Higgins, *Economic Development,* rev. ed. (New York: Norton, 1968), p. 468.

30. John Lansing and Eva Mueller, *The Geographic Mobility of Labor* (Ann Arbor: University of Michigan Survey Research Center, 1967); Hathaway and Perkins, *op. cit.*

31. John B. Parr, "Outmigration and the Depressed Area Problem," *Land Economics,* 42, No. 2 (May 1966), pp. 149–159.

26
URBAN AND RURAL AMERICA
Advisory Commission on Intergovernmental Relations

In the following two recommendations, the Commission suggests a number of measures that should be studied and considered as possible components of national, state, and local urban growth policies. Some of these measures are particularly suited for consideration at the national level, some may be proper for action at either the national or state level while others are appropriate only for state and local consideration. For instance, the federal government has the primary role in tax incentives for industrial location and policies influencing population mobility. Loan programs to influence location may be undertaken by both federal and state governments. Suggestions are included for federal and state roles in land acquisition and improvement for large-scale urban and new community development. These approaches include both institutional arrangements and financial support. Finally, the states are urged to consider measures to strengthen local government capability to deal with urban growth.

Possible approaches to implementing a national urban growth policy are included in Recommendation Four and approaches suggested for consideration by state governments are made in Recommendation Five. Recommendations of the Commission made in previous reports that are relevant to urban growth policy are summarized at appropriate points in the following discussion.

Reprinted with omissions from *Urban and Rural America*, 1968.

RECOMMENDATION FOUR. POSSIBLE COMPONENTS OF A NATIONAL POLICY DEALING WITH URBAN GROWTH

The Commission is of the opinion that national governmental policy has a role to play in influencing the location of people and industry and the resulting patterns of urban growth. Some of these ways are of proven capability; others are untried. The following should be considered as useful approaches to the implementation of a national policy regarding urban growth:

(1) Federal financial incentives, such as tax, loan, or direct payment arrangements for business and industrial location in certain areas;

(2) placement of federal procurement contracts and construction projects to foster urban growth in certain areas;

(3) federal policies and programs to influence the mobility of people, to neutralize factors producing continued excessive population concentrations, and to encourage alternative location choices; such policies and programs might include, among others, resettlement allowances, augmented on-the-job training allowances, interarea job placement and information on a computerized basis, and the elimination or reduction in the "migrational pull" of interstate variations in public assistance eligibility and benefit standards;

(4) strengthening the existing voluntary federal-state programs of family planning information for low-income persons;

(5) federal involvement and assistance under certain conditions (such as assurances of an adequate range of housing) for large-scale urban and new community development.

Influencing industrial location

Earlier in this report, the mechanisms of community economic growth were examined; it was noted that actual growth depends on a community's success in attracting additional spending within its confines which in turn leads to a multiplier effect. It was pointed out that this multiplier effect can be generated by any additions to spending, but that business investment decisions and governmental outlays constitute the two potentially—if not actually—most dynamic sources of new spending. Moreover, we also found that both of these categories of decisions significantly affect population movement and the location of economic growth.

Currently, neither business investment decisions nor governmental spending are weighed in terms of mutual consistency or their impact on the national urbanization process. The present pattern and projected future trends of urban development portend, as we have seen, growing urban congestion, intensified urban and rural poverty, and an economic mainstream with large backwash areas. To achieve a better geographic distribution of economic and population growth—to implement a national urbanization policy—the Commission in this section suggests several approaches to influencing industrial location that should be considered by the federal government. In the following section, several measures to influence population movement are presented.

In administering locational incentives, care must be taken to assure that they are used selectively to accomplish urban growth policy objectives. Such objectives would involve encouraging industrial location in and population movement to certain clearly identified areas. The following is an example of the kinds of communities and areas that might be so identified:

(1) *Labor surplus rural counties* generally are areas of underemployment, characterized by an older, underskilled, and undereducated population, resistant to moving. Absence of transportation and communication linkages as well as natural resources make economic growth unpromising. *These factors combine to suggest an area policy of job training for residents and assistance in relocating to job surplus areas other than major metropolitan centers.*

(2) *Labor surplus city neighborhoods* in large urban areas are characterized by considerable underemployment and unemployment, recent out-migration of "blue-collar" industry and difficulty of resident job seekers in traveling to blue-collar jobs in suburbs, but ample public investment in facilities vital to industry. *These factors suggest a policy of attracting new business and industry to such areas and of providing assistance in helping firms employ and train unskilled workers; and simultaneously, of launching a program of relocation assistance for residents to specific job surplus areas either in the suburbs or outside the metropolitan area.*

(3) *Small rural growth centers* generally are "urban places" located in essentially rural counties not part of any metropolitan area. They have experienced a steady population and job growth in recent years; serve as major trade, transportation, service, and social centers for their surrounding areas; and are relatively free of major socioeconomic problems. *These traits prompt a policy of attracting more business and industry, assisting industry to train more workers, and inducing both rural and urban people of low income to move in, through relocation assistance.*

(4) *Medium size cities with job opportunities* generally have substantial physical plant in place, steadily growing population and economic activity, socioeconomic problems still open to solution, and strong linkages to sizeable surrounding areas through good transportation and communication. *These factors indicate a policy of attracting low-income people from rural and large metropolitan centers through relocation assistance to fill the expanding job opportunities.*

(5) *Labor shortage suburbs* in large urban areas are major growth points, characterized by high level economic activity, and an expanding demand for many kinds of labor, including blue collar. *This suggests a policy of enabling low-income workers to live near suburban employment and assisting low-income in-migrants from other parts of the metropolitan area to relocate near suburban jobs.*

(6) *New communities* ideally are characterized by initiation and growth of communities of diversified population and economic activity. Policy indication: relocation

assistance for low-income in-migrants from labor surplus areas and, where a pro rata share of low-income housing is ensured, governmental assistance for the developer in acquiring and developing land.

Of the above types of communities, one warrants further comment at this point: "small rural growth centers"—towns and smaller cities, not in metropolitan areas, with "growth potential." Growth potential, in our opinion, would be indicated by the presence of certain favorable conditions identified in recent studies of the Economic Development Administration and Appalachian Regional Commission studies. These include:

(1) steady recent growth in population and economic activities;
(2) strong linkages to a sizeable surrounding area for which the community acts as a major trade, service, and social center;
(3) transportation and communication ties to the area; and
(4) availability of land for development, and other desirable topographic features.

While the presence of such features would be favorable indicators of growth potential, the small size of the communities suggests that such growth cannot be considered a sure thing. In other words, the likelihood of sustained balanced growth in a small community is much more fragile and problematic than in larger communities. For one thing, these communities must contend with the inexorable "pull" of large urban centers upon rural people. Outside (governmental) help then is probably needed to increase the chances of turning potential into actual growth.

Aggregate business investment in new plant and equipment now approximates $60 billion annually. While much of this replaces outmoded facilities and machinery, a vast amount represents the opportunities private enterprise sees in new products and new markets. The diversion of an incremental fraction of this amount by the use of fiscal incentives to small rural growth centers and to labor surplus neighborhoods in large metropolitan areas could well change the disturbing trends and future economic prospects for vast areas of the nation.

Through its own direct action and through purchases from the private sector, government has vast potential for influencing the locus of economic activity. An obvious example is the decision respecting the location of public facilities and associated public employment. Accordingly, whether or not government chooses to influence private business locations through the exercise of tax incentives or other fiscal devices, it can use its own authority to spend, purchase, and locate public buildings to encourage population shifts and economic growth in selected places.

Encouragement of economic growth is already a part of federal, state, and local governmental policies. For urbanization policy purposes, however, such measures need to be *deliberate* and *selective*. Their purpose—after all—is to channel private investment to those locations where economic growth will have its maximum impact on urbanization policy goals—where a policy will move a community to the "take-off point" from which it can reach new economic heights.

Governments, then, obviously have in their grasp a number of levers capable of influencing a shift in the location of economic activity. The series of possible actions described below show how use might be made of the vast fiscal resources of the federal government in furtherance of national and state urban growth policies. Possible state actions are set forth under Recommendation Five.

ENACTMENT OF LEGISLATION BY THE CONGRESS TO PROVIDE FEDERAL INCENTIVES FOR BUSINESS OR INDUSTRIAL LOCATION IN FURTHERANCE OF NATIONAL URBAN GROWTH POLICY

The national government can use its fiscal resources to influence the location of economic activity in order to achieve a more balanced distribution of population and economic growth. This would involve legislation to encourage business and industry to locate in small rural growth centers and in those neighborhoods of large urban areas chronically classified as sections of concentrated unemployment or underemployment by the Secretary of Labor. An incentive program for firms locating in areas targeted for population and economic growth might well include: (a) preferential tax treatment in the form of a federal income-tax credit—a subtraction from computed tax liability—granted by the Secretary of the Treasury upon certification of the Secretary of the Commerce; (b) preferential financing arrangements in the form of below market rate loans granted by the Secretary of Commerce; or (c) location cost offsets in the form of direct payments by the Secretary of Commerce based on capital outlay or operating cost differentials between the costs that would be incurred by a firm locating at the targeted site and at a more economically advantageous site elsewhere, but in no case should the payment exceed a specified dollar amount.

If measures such as these are adopted, the dollar amount of any tax credits or preferential financing arrangements, estimated by the Secretary of the Treasury, should be included each year for informational purposes in the President's budget. Also, the enabling legislation should bear an expiration date of a few (for example, 5–7) years in the future so that the Congress and the Executive Branch might assess costs and benefits of the subsidy approach.

The facts and trends disclosed in this report indicate that more jobs will be needed in small rural centers with growth potential if they are to attract the jobless from both rural and urban areas, and in large central cities to help reduce underemployment and unemployment. The federal government should consider seriously the merits of direct, positive action with regard to the greatest single determinant of future population distribution in the United States—namely, the geographic location of new business and industrial enterprises. Jobs could be created in rural growth centers and central city neighborhoods if business and industry were given an incentive (in the form of a federal income-tax credit) to locate there. This would be of great assistance in (1) setting in motion a braking force on future population concentrations, and (2) coping with existing urban problems.

Rural growth centers outside metropolitan areas provide a near-at-hand destination for poor out-migrant jobseekers from rural poverty areas who would otherwise head for big urban centers, thereby aggravating an existing labor surplus situation. Proximity is also likely to enable these communities to attract those rural jobless who are reluctant to leave their home community—those constituting the hard-core rural poor. Finally, such small places may also attract out-migrants from the central cities in search of jobs. The factors which could assist the federal administrator distinguish small communities that have "growth potential" from those that do not, have previously been suggested.

The foregoing alternatives, as they relate to rural areas, are parallel to legislation pending in Congress—S. 2134, the proposed Rural Job Corporation Development Act of 1967. This bill would provide a series of tax incentives to encourage private investment "with the aim of utilizing more fully and effectively the human and natural resources of rural America, slowing the migration from the rural areas, which is principally the result of a lack of economic opportunity, and reducing the population pressures on our metropolitan areas." Incentives include increased tax credit against investment in plant and machinery, accelerated depreciation schedules for such investment, extra deductions for wages paid to low-income persons, and assistance in worker training.

In addition to upgrading the economy of rural America to reduce the urban pull, steps can be taken to alleviate the immediate problem of unemployment in central cities. The latter, after all, is caused in part by the long-sustained in-migration of rural poor. Positive federal action could attract business and industry to central city neighborhoods of labor surplus.

The unemployed in these neighborhoods consist mostly of semiskilled and unskilled workers. Their joblessness is the product of a number of social and economic forces including:

(1) the flight of industry to the suburbs, caused by such economic factors as a general shift to production techniques which require extensive land and single-story production lines;

(2) in-city traffic and parking congestion;

(3) development of circumferential highways or beltways bringing markets and supply sources closer to suburban locations; and

(4) the lack of adequate mass transit between central city and suburbs, making home-to-job travel costs prohibitive for the city blue collar worker; while at the same time economic or racial barriers bar him from moving his residence near a suburban job.

In time, it is hoped, that some of these barriers will be lowered or removed with improved mass transportation, the provision areawide of housing for low- and moderate-income families, and the diminution of racial discrimination in the suburbs. Efforts also will have to be made to retrain and relocate some of the city's jobless. Meanwhile, however, attempts might well be made to bring jobs into large central cities. This means bringing into their neighborhoods business and industries which can offer blue collar opportunities needed by the semiskilled and unskilled workers constituting the labor surplus.

Existing federal programs in urban communities emphasize individual services and rehabilitation; they are not directed toward influencing private industrial and business location decisions to locate plants near available people in city neighborhoods. The Economic Development Administration is prevented, by a restrictive statutory definition of redevelopment areas, from entering most urban communities. The Department of Labor has programs to provide training for employees, but does little to stimulate creation of new jobs. The Office of Economic Opportunity *had* a tangential responsibility for helping create urban jobs through its funding of Small Business Administration Development Centers, but this program has been terminated. A federal incentive program for industry and business locating in central city labor surplus neighborhoods would be an important step toward filling this gap in federal program for stimulating job creation in central city neighborhoods. It also would serve to increase a city's tax base, thus allowing provision of more and better public services.

Governmental incentive techniques to influence business and industrial location may take the form of preferential treatment, preferential loans, or direct payments. Each technique has its advantages and disadvantages relative to the others and each must be considered in the light of how well it effects a net social benefit. For example, should incentives be offered to all firms making a location decision in a designated area? The market orientation of many retail and personal service businesses suggests that a locational incentive to these firms may not be very useful in providing additional social benefit. Should incentives be designed to increase, up to a limit, depending upon the amount of capital investment or should they vary with the labor force characteristics of the firm? The net social benefit of a business location decision is more likely to be greater if the firm is labor intensive rather than capital equipment oriented. Finally, should incentives be made available to firms locating with short-term leases in an approved area? Some provision probably should be made for the firm's length of stay in a designated area.

Tax incentives.   A federal income-tax credit might be a percentage of various bases: (1) investment in plant and equipment; (2) amount of payroll; and (3) value added to produce. Each method has its virtues. The first would tend to encourage investment in the nonlabor factors of production, thus emphasizing automation and technological improvement. The second would emphasize the use of labor and thus would more immediately further the objectives of an urbanization policy seeking to attract people by jobs. But it might tend to discourage technological improvements. The value-added base—relating the amount of the tax credit to the amount of value added by the business or industry's own activities—would steer a course between the other two. Under any of these three approaches, the Secretary of the Treasury would be required to grant the tax credit upon certification of eligibility by the Secretary of Commerce.

The tax credit approach has several virtues when compared to the alternative subsidy arrangements. Business could count on the tax credit more than it could on the availability of low-interest loans or direct subsidy payments. Tax policy changes are less likely to occur than changes in policy respecting the other forms of subsidy, depending as the latter do on the overall Federal financial condition.

Tax credits interfere least with business decisions. Although the tax credit would be conditioned on a specific business location decision that accords with general policies adopted by Congress, it would not subject business to the detailed scrutiny normally associated with Congressional appropriations or Federal lending activity. Tax credits have greater appeal to business simply because they permit greater flexibility in managerial decisions.

Because tax credit incentives would represent a cost to all taxpayers not benefitting directly from them, they should not and need not be of indefinite duration. Within a few years after tax credits are initiated they will either have had an impact on urbanization or have proved ineffectual. By incorporating a termination date in the legislation, review of the program after a trial period would be assured. This would also forestall, without further legislation, any continuing draw down on federal resources in the absence of a showing to the satisfaction of the Congress that tax credits were achieving their desired objective.

The tax incentive would represent federal benefits to its recipients, just as a direct grant or subsidy. To make this clear, the Secretary of the Treasury should estimate the amount of the credit used annually and state it as an expenditure in the budget. This would identify the credit properly, and would permit the Bureau of the Budget and Congress to scrutinize it in relation to the tangible benefits obtained in terms of the geographic dispersion of industry and of jobs added in labor surplus areas.

The tax incentive approach is not without its critics. They point out that tax incentives are erratic in operation because the amount of the benefit to any individual depends upon number of unrelated circumstances connected with his own tax computation: whether he has any tax liability at all, what his effective rate is, and so forth.

Another criticism leveled at the tax incentive approach is that it may involve "tax people" in decisions which they have no special competence to make. If the federal government wants to reward people for making certain business location decisions, the administration of these incentives ought to be handled by personnel familiar with location problems.

Where two Federal agencies are involved in determining what firms are entitled to tax benefits, a complex administrative process may result, with the self-administering feature of the program, and the functional specialization of governmental agencies (for example, tax administration) lost. Subsidy payments might just as easily be made under the supervision of trained personnel and on a more timely basis than that associated with annual tax filing deadlines, according to these critics.

With a tax incentive, it is usually impossible to distinguish between results that relate to the incentive and results that would have occurred without it. This means that some part, frequently a large part, of the government's revenue loss may go as a windfall to those who were prepared to take such action without regard to the incentives.

Critics also note that because the tax writing legislative committees will have difficulty in evaluating data relating to whether or not particular location decisions were made in response to the tax incentive. Congress might find it expedient, even after enacting temporary tax incentive provisions, to extend the incentive more or less automatically. This, the critics contend, is a likely outcome, because the governmental costs covered by tax incentives are less obvious to the public than direct expenditures.

Critics further belabor the tax incentive approach because it must rely exclusively on the profit motive which requires that business concerns focus on increasing the productivity of the trained worker rather than on the need of the unskilled and unemployed. Moreover, they argue, it is of uncertain value to promote new and independent firms which lack the opportunity to write off their losses in a risky location against profits earned at well-established sites.

Below-market-rate loans. Loanable funds may be in short supply or the risks normally associated with a business venture may result in relatively high interest rates and therefore effectively deter business and industrial firms from locating in areas where economic growth would be desirable. The federal government should reduce the financial obstacles for business and industrial location in small rural growth centers and in areas of chronic labor surplus to facilitate job creation in areas specifically identified for future economic growth, pursuant to a national urbanization policy. To accomplish this objective, the Secretary of Commerce could be empowered to offer lower-than-market-rate loans to influence geographic location.

Below-market-rate loans for business ventures have been used in a variety of Federal programs: to assist small businesses unable to obtain needed financing elsewhere on reasonable terms; to help victims of flood or natural disasters; to help veterans buy a business or otherwise enable them to undertake or expand a legitimate business venture; and to assist various kinds of private and public organizations in supplying electrical services to rural areas (rural electrification).

The Public Works and Economic Development Act of 1965 authorizes the Secretary of Commerce to make loans to aid in financing any project within a redevelopment area for the purchase or development of land and facilities (including machinery and equipment) for industrial or commercial usage if financial assistance is not reasonably available from private lenders or from other federal agencies. EDA made 63 project loans in 1967 in 26 States and Puerto Rico. They amounted to $50.6 million out of total project costs of $88.7 million.

Incentives for business and industrial location in the form of below-market interest rate loans have several advantages. While some business firms can obtain a substantial pool of funds from a variety of sources such as bank loans, company equity, or local development companies this accumulation may nevertheless fall short of meeting the minimum needs for developing a new site or enlarging an existing operation. By making additional funds available at favorable interest rates the federal government can fill the margin between resources and fund requirements needed to allow an otherwise sound business venture to proceed.

The Federal loan approach has substantial business appeal because it makes additional funds available without threatening the equity or control of the entrepreneur. Yet the soundness and security of the public's investment can be adequately protected by the federal agency administering the loan.

Opposition to this approach could be expected from those who question the use of federal credit for private gain regardless of the basic merits of fostering a better population distribution in the country or of alleviating the immediate problem of unemployment in central cities. Others would contend that this approach would result in unfair competition to competing business and industry also seeking to expand but not in areas designated for favorable federal loans. A more pertinent criticism is that the loan technique may make the size of the benefit dependent upon the amount of capital invested rather than upon the volume of payrolls.

The below-market interest rate loans would represent a Federal subsidy to their recipients akin to a direct grant. It would be appropriate therefore that the Secretary of the Treasury estimate and report the dollar cost of such federal loans for budgetary purposes in order to give Congress and the Executive Branch an opportunity to evaluate the cost effectiveness of this incentive designed to broaden the locational choice for industry and to create new jobs in chronic labor surplus areas. To give the public iron clad assurance that it will not be asked to bear in perpetuity the cost of an unsuccessful program, authorizing legislation for low-interest federal loans should contain a termination date beyond which the program would automatically cease in the absence of affirmative Congressional action to continue it.

Direct payments. The most straightforward method of encouraging the wider geographic dispersal of business and the creation of new jobs in urban centers of chronic labor surplus is to make direct subsidy payments to entrepreneurs who locate in the designated areas. The economic development purposes to be served may be of such transcendant importance that his approach would be warranted.

To establish an effective direct subsidy program that would channel job creating economic activity to specific sites, a payment that would offset either higher capital outlay or operating costs could be made. A direct subsidy based on cost differentials would put areas of desired economic growth on a par with other areas as far as direct business costs are concerned; the payment should not, however, loom large enough to enable subsidy areas to capture all economic development. This could be assured by putting a dollar limit on the amount of the direct subsidy payment.

The direct subsidy approach has much to recommend it from both a business and governmental viewpoint. Without minimizing the difficulties of administration—many of which are encountered whenever government seeks to promote its objectives by offering incentives—the cost to the public of a direct subsidy payment program can be determined more readily and with greater precision than can tax incentives or below-market-rate loan incentives. Direct subsidy payments require detailed planning by the business applicant, but this prerequisite increases the prospect that the subsidy will fulfill its purpose. For the businessman, the subsidy approach represents a "no strings" financial contribution to the firm to be used as management sees best fit.

The very openness of this approach may constitute its principal weakness. Both the businessman and the administrator of the subsidy could expect criticism from those who are prone to second guess their decisions.

In opposition to the use of any special incentives to influence industrial location, it can be argued that, regardless of the importance of national policies designed to direct economic growth and job creation to areas of urgent need, no program to provide Federal incentives for business and industrial location is warranted. Sound economic development, so the argument runs, rests on the natural selection process that weeds out the marginal undertaking and nurtures the productive enterprise.

Many of the costs entailed in providing public incentives for private effort are intangible. The same may be said of the alleged benefits. As a practical matter, the task of evaluating the costs of and benefits from incentive programs exceeds the validity of measurements at hand. It also can be argued that an incentive program might tend to become open-ended with far-reaching consequences. Regardless of the limited objectives an incentive program might be designed to achieve, proponents of the approach would constantly argue that the objectives could be accomplished more quickly and more universally by expanding the size and scope of the incentives. By becoming less selective, the incentives would lose their intended effect. As Benjamin Franklin once observed: "A benefit to all becomes a benefit to none."

By continuing to rely solely on the profit motive to determine where and whether business and industry will locate, critics believe that the public will be assured of protection from bootless adventures in the field of economic planning. The federal government's resources would be husbanded for legitimate public purposes, rather than squandered on a Federal incentive program designed to have business act in a fashion that it would often act anyway from its own self-interest and in the absence of any incentive.

Critics also contend that every program of public incentives for private effort has severe drawbacks. They feel that tax incentives, for example, are by and large Congressionally licensed raids on the Treasury. No one is able to say for sure how much they cost or what return the public is getting on its investment. These critics note that many tax students argue that history has demonstrated that once a tax gimmick gets into the Internal Revenue Code it figuratively takes the legislative equivalent of a nuclear blast to get it out. Moreover, tax incentives assign a higher priority, in effect, to economic activity freed of liability than to any other activities or programs, including national defense, that are supported by annual appropriations.

Finally, the critics warn that low-interest loans from the government to private business are a sinister type of incentive. They represent a dual-type of unfair competition—unfair to businesses financed in conventional ways and unfair to banks and the investment community whose major source of income is arranging to finance business ventures. Direct subsidies to private firms, so the argument runs, are completely alien to the American enterprise system except for activities essential to the national defense.

All of these arguments, of course, warrant careful consideration in the formulation of federal incentives to influence the location of new business and industrial establishments as one of the possible components of a national urban growth policy.

INDEX

73 74 75 76   9 8 7 6 5 4 3 2 1